Martin Ba[...]

A FOOL AND
HIS MONEY

**High finance,
low living –
understanding
financial markets
and those who
work in them**

19: iV: 95

*For Peter, and for Allyson –
Love Hugs + Kisses,
Brother Baker (S.J.)*

ORION

Copyright © 1995 Martin Baker

The right of Martin Baker to be identified as the
author of this work has been asserted by him in
accordance with the Copyright, Designs and
Patents Act 1988.

First published in Great Britain in 1995 by Orion
An imprint of Orion Books Ltd
Orion House, 5 Upper St Martin's Lane, London
WC2H 9EA

A CIP catalogue record for this book is available
from the British Library

ISBN 1 85797 688 6

Filmset by Selwood Systems, Midsomer Norton
Printed in Great Britain by Butler & Tanner Ltd,
Frome and London

For Kate

Sua quemque fraus, suum facinus, suum scelus, sua audacia de sanitate ac mente deturbat

It is a man's own sin, his own guilt, his own effrontery which unseats his mind from its sanity.

– Cicero, *In Pisonem*

Or maybe ...

> Ho hum, the tune is dumb,
> The words don't mean a thing.
> Isn't this a silly song
> For anyone to sing?

The yodelling song, *Snow White and the Seven Dwarfs,* Walt Disney

Contents

Preface   xi

Chapter I – The Market   1

Q. What Is a Market Anyway? A. A Group of Smart, Highly Paid People With a Common Economic Purpose and the Collective Intelligence of a Baby Trout.

Chapter II – Foreign Exchange   12

What really happens inside the locked vaults of the foreign exchanges. Ideological conflict. Control and regulation – psychology v. police work.
Why drugs and German sports cars are essential to facilitate the free exchange of international capital.

Chapter III – Bankers, Brokers, Advisers, Intermediaries: People Who Sell   34

People Who Sell. The polyvalency of the word 'sell' i) Meaning number one – noticing that the market lemming decked out in Vuarnet shades and a new pair of Reeboks is taking thirty million of his little chums for a clifftop jog. ii) Meaning number two – wielding the carrot-flavoured stick iii) Meaning number three – persuading people to buy, and the attendant problems, such as a) image b) hypocrisy, snobbery, myopic self-contradiction. The hierarchy of money – i) Salespeople ii) Grocery store-type advisers iii) Tied agents – or pushy bastards iv) Independent advisers v) Brokers – private client vi) Institutional brokers vii) Private bankers

Chapter IV – Banks – Ivory Towers in Transition   72

In search of an identity. Banks and self-transformative emptiness – why saying 'bank' is like hitting people with peas. History as an irrelevant factor in the content of banking practice, but a vital part of banking form (alias the bullshit that you pay for). The non-institutional nature of banking offices. One immutable banking tradition – gratuitous sex. Why central bankers aren't bankers at all. Retail bankers – storekeepers in cheap suits. Custodian bankers – so boring, other bankers think they're dull. Investment and 'merchant' bankers. Insider deals. How to find a chainsaw when insider dealers claim to be trees in a rain forest. Why insider trading really is a crime. Non-bank bankers. Rock star or mutant snail? – The ultimate banking question. Bankers as cultural imperialists – how Tom Wolfe got it right without really knowing why.

Chapter V – And the Word Was Made Flesh: Mutual Fund Managers, Pension Fund Managers and Trustees and Their Investment Consultants. With a Nod to Venture Capital Funds III

The most important difference between a divine, universally present non-corporeal being who is the fundament of creation, and a fund manager. The vast majority of the world's population dismissed in 381 words. Mutual fund statistics as a one-way ticket to Toy Town. Are fund managers good at what they do? Indices and their magical effect – managers become foetal balls of wailing pinstripe. Four pieces of rhetoric (including Specious Nonsense in a Ballgown, Mark II) and two pieces of action. Public comprehension of financial management – somebody else's air crash. Pension fund managers and the promotion of child slavery. The next link in the chain – investment consultants. Venture capitalists' strange physiques – three eyes and no balls.

Chapter VI – Hedge, Swap, Derivative Fund Managers – The Left Hand of God 143

The multi-billion-dollar video game. Level one – who are these people? And why should we care? Level two – the wall. Level three – technical torture. Level four – blind man's buff. Level five – beat the market, Part I. Level six – the hall of mirrors. Level seven – the genius factor.

Chapter VII – Ethical Investment – Render Unto Caesar That Which Is John Stuart Mill's 168

The death (almost) of greed, the origins of the ethical investment industry, some issues for 'ethical' consideration – (i) does our disapproval of the provider of a product taint the product? (ii) whose morality? Moving moral goalposts and the profit motive (iii) emerging markets and ethical investment – better turkey than murky. But does it work as an investment? And as an exercise in ethical purity? (i) It's fine if you don't care about the intentions of the people providing the product (even though the fund itself discriminates against investee companies on exactly this basis) (ii) The problem of inter-connectedness (iii) The primacy of the profit motive – the absurdity of imputing moral significance to a market's moving up or down. Ethical investing as pure evil – the perfect example of self-regarding harm.

Chapter VIII – Credit and Charge Cards – A Plastic Passion 189

The credit card that flies below personal radar. Plastic as part of daily life and a way of escaping from Sting in a rain forest. How Japanese fund managers invest in Minnesotan farmers. Sustaining the passion – (i) corporate cards and the modern marriage – obey, love and honour major credit cards. A tangent – plastic and other forms of holiday money compared. Why you should make sure that you do leave home without a traveller's cheque. Sustaining the passion – (ii) affinity marketing as a facilitator of shallow ostentation, or the promotion of self-deluding dick-headedness. Affinity cards as financial tranquilliser.

Chapter IX – Lawyers – The Best Money Lawyers Can Buy 202

Tough career choice I of the late twentieth century – abattoir superintendent or litigation lawyer? Tough choice II (clients only need apply) – death or bankruptcy? Lawyers as Mafia-indoctrinated nuns. A homily – lavatorial hierarchy as snobbery in its purest form. The dawn of client awareness and the jackal v. commercial chambermaid theory of legal practice. Legal 'creativity'. Lawyers as spittoons. Why Roman lawyers are best.

Chapter X – Financial Journalists: Et in Arcania Ego (especially Ego) 216

Ulysses revisited – why what financial journalists' offer the world is every bit as useful as myrrh-scented traffic lights in rural Calabria. Factual reporting and the Hall of Mirrors. Objectivity – alias truth as a fashion accessory. Things designed to impair journalistic objectivity – freebies and public relations people. Professional ethics and expenses – the night I was chairman of British Steel. What you get – our best shot. When it goes wrong – the conch-shell theory of insider trading. Good reporting – and curiosity.

Chapter XI – Living With the Lunatic 234

The market as adopted idiot child. What to do – Financial advice, Part I (including a tour d'horizon of choice financial lunacies from the seventeenth century through to the present). Financial advice, Part II – How to exploit the inadequacy of number as a relational metaphor, explained two ways. (i) Method number one – briefly, with jokes. Oral sex made boring, or indexation made interesting, the choice is yours. (ii) Method number two – at length, without jokes. Absurdism, the lunatic, and what it all really means (maybe). Regulation and control. The Market – Our final choice.

Acknowledgments

This is more of a list than an essay, since, despite the best efforts of many of the people mentioned below, I appear to have saved my tendency to gush for the main text. Nevertheless, these brief thank-yous are heartfelt. The order is more or less chronological.

Aline Sullivan and Bill Mitchell, thanks. Especially Bill, whose encouragement and advice helped me work up the early chapters into something really tasteless. Bill, I want to have your children. Now. Really.

Wet sloppy kisses to Kate Brown, for her consistent refusal to laugh at my best jokes or otherwise be in any way impressed by my occasional attempts to play the author. Also for her extremely good judgment and fine analytical skills. And her patience.

My wise men were superb. Thanks to: Professor Jonathan Story of INSEAD and latterly Oxford University; Hamish McRae of *The Independent*; prize-winning hack, bestselling author and colleague at the *International Herald Tribune*, Alan Friedman; Jon Gage, financial and economics demi-god at the same paper, and Martin Bowen, elderly footballer and partner at that fine and prestigious City law firm S. J. Berwin & Co (and yes, that was a plug). They were all diligent, kind and tolerant, despite being extremely busy.

Jonathan Lloyd is the world's best literary agent. And that's official. Jane Wood at Orion is a hymn to compassionate intelligence in human form, and – this is the bit where we get chillingly serious – Anthony Cheetham has a brilliant literary and business mind, which led him to commission this book. Thanks.

Finally, a nod to those without whom this venture would not have been possible. Colin Dinwoodie (the man in the background), Harry Scott, Erich Halberstadt, Irving Ropner, and the boys from the 'Ukrainian stetl', Leo Cooperman and Jason Polecat. They alone know the vital roles they played.

Love, hugs and kisses to you all, and your mummies.

Martin Baker
Paris, February 1995

Preface

Why smoking is good for you, and skiing can seriously damage your health (maybe).

The rosy-fingered dawn of a new millennium is almost upon us. With it will come a plethora of crank punditry – doom-laden prognoses for mankind and planet Earth, and largely inaccurate histories of the mess we have made of things over the last thousand years. This text is, at best, only marginally different. You have been warned.

But it does at least aspire to accuracy. It also, more or less, refuses to be downhearted. As they say in the bars of Dublin, the situation may be desperate – but at least it's not serious.

Except that it is. And seriousness, together with its ugly sister, obviousness, are the foes of this book – along with the arch-enemy, their third sibling, who shall for the moment remain nameless.

So be wary. In the name of history, a lot of sanctimonious, self-serious, blindingly banal nonsense awaits us. Those commentators who limit their Olympian perspectives to the last hundred years will probably tell us that the twentieth century has been a sinister era. It has created mysterious, profound, unfathomable dangers while simultaneously promoting the seven-second attention span, the sound-bite conversationalist, and a general cultural consciousness of breathtaking shallowness and triviality.

Well, this is probably true. But this combination of horrifying danger and the inability to contemplate it for longer than it takes a goldfish to swim the length of its tank are the best conditions possible for having a really good time.

Somewhere out there in a central ex-Soviet republic, a desperate army officer is looking to feed his starving family by selling a mobile thermonuclear device to someone – anyone – with a few thousand in small-denomination dollar bills. Maybe less, if the deal can be sweetened with a Big Mac and a large order of fries. An age of super-terrorism, of diffuse, uncontrollable, terrifying threats, is surely upon us.

So living, as we do, closer to the edge of the precipice than ever before, one thing at least is clear. Now is the best time there has ever been, throughout the brief and miserable history of the human race, to hang out and chow down. Spread the picnic blanket on the ground, gulp down the Prozac and the oak-matured Aussie white, look into the abyss and start humming 'There'll always be an England' – or the tune from whatever part of today's ethnically cleansed world you're from. Tomorrow, don't forget, we probably die.

Now all of this provides good reason to be cheerful. But there is another legacy of the twentieth century that is even more terrible, and consequently hilarity-provoking. It is a disease that has spread across the world over the past two decades in the most astonishing way. It is the third sister to seriousness and obviousness, uglier than either of them. It is the disease of certainty.

The carrier of the disease – the black rat that brings the plague – is an idea that has crossed the world many times over in the past twenty years. It is the notion that the market is perfect, or at least perfectible, and somehow brings with it certainty – a kind of promotional free gift, like a plastic toy in a cornflakes packet.

In a social context, the horror of certainty, the I-am-right-you-are-wrong culture, has engendered a terrible stifling of debate. It has also created in me a dread of people a) who live life on a level where being right or wrong is simply a question of fact, not of argument, and b) who are convinced that their facts are right. Having social intercourse with people like this is about as much fun as taking a course in do-it-yourself disembowelment. Unfortunately, at the dimming of this particular century and millennium, these people appear to be growing in number.

Which is perhaps why I find myself arguing some strange propositions. For example, you can at least contend that smoking isn't so bad for you after all (the nicotine is beneficial, it's just the trace elements in the tobacco and the carbon monoxide that are harmful). In some respects, given that nicotine facilitates concentration and soothes the nerves, smoking is good for you. Of course, I argue my position from the impregnable ground of ignorance, being a filter-tip virgin. Tobacco has many fine qualities to recommend it – it's expensive, addictive, its consumption irritates other people, etc – but, inexcusably enough, I just don't do it on the grounds that it's boring. It has to be. It's the drug my *mother* takes.

But the fact that I have never smoked a cigarette (translated into late twentieth-century demotic – *not my drug of choice*) is, apparently, excusable. What really upsets people is displaying the temerity to criticize the slavishly followed fashion for skiing. It doesn't take long before it becomes a real pleasure to suggest that in so many ways skiing is bad for you – the expense, the broken limbs, the pathetic conversations about *snow* (you know the white, cold stuff that's clearly a stimulating topic of debate). Worst of all, it turns otherwise acceptable human beings into proselytizing automata, monsters who insist that you must, just must ski, because you would love it. They have the certainty disease in a particularly scabrous form.

Who cares if these people are right or not? Show me a person with that level of conviction, and I'll show you a person I could happily nail to a tree. What's nice is not being sure, being able to say that smoking is good for you and skiing can seriously damage your health (maybe).

But my topic is not certainty in general, merely in its financial manifestations – the belief that the market is always right.

In pursuit of market certainty the world has gone into a kind of privatization mania over the past few years. Billions and billions of dollars' worth of industry have been sold off into the private sector or seduced out of the private sector to replace public funding. It's difficult to generalize (or at least generalize accurately), but I'll try. In general, this has occurred without a great deal of thought about whether the whole process is always – as it rather often is – a good thing.

What a market really offers us is discussed in Chapter I. For now, suffice it to say that those who appeal to the market to bring automatic validity to their arguments are usually about as open-minded as those who dare to presume that their political opinions are 'correct'.

Whatever the reader may make of it, this book knows what it wants to be, a haven of doubt in a world of spurious financial certainty. Amongst all the worshippers of Mammon, it seeks to be the agnostic's bible.

Because, you see, Mammon doesn't really bear very close scrutiny.

From a distance he is the effulgent icon of money, pure capitalism and the cult of the market. He is god of the month. Closer up, we can smell that second-hand chicken jalfrezi and yesterday night's strong Belgian beer. We can wonder about the cleanliness of his Hom undershorts, and we can decide that we won't be having the cheesecake after all.

The idea of exploding the icon of Mammon was born of tears. And, as is almost always the case, the tears were shot through with self-pity.

At the time, I thought I was weeping for John McCarthy. He seemed, on that great day of his release, worth crying for – a nice boy genuinely deserving of our sympathy.

Not for one nanosecond would anyone want to swap places with McCarthy. Almost suffocated in masking tape every time he was transported between cells, having to spend many hours with Brian Keenan (whose best-selling account of his time as a hostage succeeds, against heroically impossible odds, in being both alienating and dull). No. McCarthy's life was clearly hell in the late '80s and early '90s.

Yet that internal voice persisted: 'All right, the unlucky bastard was handcuffed to a radiator for five years. What about you? You've been chained to the markets, enslaved in a kind of cult that makes Moonie-ism look like an extended lunch with William Burroughs. What are you going to do about it?'

So here it is. An inside view of the markets and the attitudes that go with it, drawn from the clear air just outside the temple of finance. It's important here to differentiate between the markets and the people who work in them.

As a journalist, it's very difficult to do an even vaguely competent reporting job if you despise the people you're dealing with. And the great majority of those who work in finance are not despicable in the least. Individually, they are often intelligent, knowledgeable and eager to engage in debate. Compare these qualities with those demonstrated by people in the arts (like, say, publishing or the theatre) where the slightest challenge to the prevailing orthodoxies of judgment and taste is often treated as a personal slight. No. If you're looking for genuine rottenness and personal worthlessness (and corruption too, come to that) you're probably wasting your time seeking out a bond dealer. A much more likely prospective whore would be, say, an alcoholic literary agent or a failing fringe theatre producer.

Having said that, certain people in the financial markets and ancillary areas have been mentioned more than once – and not in the most laudatory terms possible. To them, I hold up my hand and say 'sorry'. They are victims of their own celebrity, and illustrate the general themes of this book.

I have tried to cover the key areas of finance as it affects the lives of the affluent (and, yes, book-buying) public. In each market – banking, funds, credit, broking – a different kind of mania prevails, a different culture flourishes. Lawyers have been included as the enablers, the foot soldiers of capitalism. And financial journalists, who have done so much to promote the more dangerous market myths, do not escape.

Finally, the concept of the market itself, black rat or otherwise, should get a small vote of thanks. This book's thesis is that the unquestioning adoption of the market as arbiter of what is right is a mistake. In fact, it is like abandoning the notion of independent thought and joining a cult, which is a rather stupid thing to do.

It is, I recognize, because of public interest in financial markets that this book is in print, and that you, dear reader, have bought your copy. For which my thanks, and the sincere hope that, though parted from your money, you will not consider the purchase unduly foolish.

CHAPTER I

The Market

Q. What Is a Market Anyway?

A. A Group of Smart, Highly Paid People With a Common Economic Purpose and the Collective Intelligence of a Baby Trout.

The Market – money, power, wealth, sex, unlimited supplies of chocolate. For the children of the '80s and '90s, orphaned in so many ways, The Market has been a kind of parent. Sometimes the wicked stepmother, sometimes the fairy godmother, occasionally the dastardly Uncle Jasper of Victorian melodrama. The *fons et origo* of all things, good and bad, it's always there, clothed in its sexy, off-the-shoulder epithets: twenty-four-hours-a-day, global, liquid, The Market is most definitely good in bed.

And not only is it a good, dirty lay, it sleeps around. Even across liberal, left-of-centre dinner tables The Market is recognized as a philosophical touchstone, one that provides a core of certainty. If The Market likes a service, a product, a movie, a persona, then it has a definable, unarguable value. Whatever the aesthetic and educational merits of Barney the Dinosaur or Mr Blobby (respectively US- and UK-oriented phenomena of roughly equal beauty and powers of ratiocination), there's one thing about which you'll get no argument: The Market likes them.

This is more than a purely semantic, epistemological difference. It is the difference between popularity and value, and the latter word carries a rich payload of ethical and moral connotations. Even people who hate Barney the Dinosaur, who suddenly find themselves longing for the intellectual heights of Disney's *Jungle Book* as their children watch Barney drag the common denominator of human communication ever lower – even *they* accept that The Market likes Barney. And that means that Barney and Mr Blobby – who was, incidentally, briefly touted by the UK media as a candidate for the British premiership – have Value. That value translates into real

I

money (nowadays this means money that does not evaporate through inflation as soon as you open your sweaty palm, thanks, again, to The Market). In a world afflicted by confusion The Market brings the magical cipher of certainty. The fact that it is the narrow, mathematical certainty of a number is a positive blessing. Suddenly even the most unfathomable conundrums have some tiny kernel of meaning, albeit weird and one-dimensional. 'What is the Meaning of Life?' asked the British humorist Douglas Adams. '42,' he answered himself. How right he was. Except that the correct answer is now 35, Life having been in something of a bear phase recently.

Or is certainty the disease, not the cure? All this conviction is a frightening thing. Think of Orwell's *1984*. Imagine if he had taken the market economics road to totalitarian, blinkered thought. For Big Brother read The Market, for the Minister of Truth read Reagan or Thatcher. The only thing that remains the same is Winston, poor old allegorical humanity, struggling away against total knowledge and power, and a tight, apparently impregnable logic. Welcome to the world after 1984, an age that has produced an entity known, in all seriousness, as the Perfect Market Theory. Yes, PMT – or, when you consider the inherent idiocy of the idea, perhaps that should be PMS, for Paradigmatic Market Silliness. In any event, The Market is taken so seriously that acronyms like this are flashed around investment houses – not noted for their respect for women's emancipation – without even a trace of a schoolboy snigger. PMT/S is just shorthand for the perfect market. The reductive condenser of certainties is itself purely distilled into three syllables. Perfect. Sorry – P.

All of which makes it even more enjoyable when the wheels come off. Like, for example, the time that the Tokyo stockmarket dropped more than $5 billion in two minutes because a retired UK pop star had a heart attack. The unfortunate man in question was named Lonnie Donegan. Donny who?

Let me explain: Mr Donegan's claim to a place in the marmoreal halls of fame rests on a smash hit song called 'My Old Man's a Dustman'. Well, it was a smash hit in Britain, at least. This was the very early '60s, before the Beatles conquered the universe. The song, being about a 'dustman', elsewhere known as a refuse collector, did not travel well. This was particularly so since part of its charm derived from its feel-good celebration of working-class culture, something which set off a peculiar reaction among the British, who impose upon themselves a nauseating little class system which only they could have invented (and which, writing as an expatriate Brit mercifully liberated from its worst excesses, we so richly deserve). By the late '80s Mr Donegan's star was no longer the brightest in the firmament, and had not been so for a full quarter of a century. Yet people remembered the song for its coarse good humour, and Mr Donegan had become something of a cultural icon of British insularity. To know who Lonnie Donegan was betokened a certain John Bull pride. People could speak with a sheepish pleasure of a British phenomenon that foreigners would never know or understand. All countries have their own totems of parochialism; these are celebrity versions of idiot sons that you want to keep indoors. Americans might think of the unmitigated ghastliness of Lawrence Welk, or Wink Martindale (except that the truly horrible 'Deck of Cards' sold internationally). The French have Johnny Halliday, and he – and this really is an outstanding achievement – is even *more* embarrassing. In short, no-one outside the UK knew who Lonnie Donegan was, and everyone was happy that way.

So he has a heart attack, and naturally enough, given his place in British culture, it's a news story. It is as if Britain's favourite garden gnome has been stolen. Mr Donegan falls ill in the early hours of the morning, and the wire editors, again naturally enough, put the story as the lead, if only because nothing else is happening. But the British news wires are read internationally, and when the story is posted as the early lead the Japanese market is still open and goes totally berserk. Why?

Ask a Japanese person to say 'Lonnie Donegan'. Then ask him to say 'Ronald Reagan'. *That's* why.

Add the phonetic confusion to the facts that the story is fronting the news wires, no-one has heard of Lonnie Donegan, and the man who will step into Reagan's shoes is Vice-President George Bush and you have a classic fear-based recipe for market mayhem.

On the strength of a supposedly dead Reagan and incompetent Bush shares plummeted. It was as if Tokyo stocks were having a cardiac arrest. For a few, panic-stricken minutes shares plummeted. Eventually they picked up, presumably thanks to some elderly Japanese teddy boy who fished out a mildewed copy of *New Musical Express* and gave the Japanese incarnation of the perfect market the information it needed to discount the news, which was, of course, utterly irrelevant to its prices.

There are two happy footnotes to this incident. One, Mr Donegan survived. Two, Dan Quayle wasn't Vice-President. Now that *would* have justified a crash.

But this is just a particularly rich diadem in a glittering treasure chest of market nonsenses. In his splendid book *Rumeurs – Le plus vieux media du Monde* Jean-Noel Kapferer offers a brief *tour d'horizon* of some of the wilder surges in market prices occasioned by rumour. Between 1968 and 1974, for example, the price of sugar had multiplied by a factor of more than forty. Rumour had it that the Philippines were suspending exports, that the Japanese and the Americans were in the market, buying massively and hoarding for profit. The frenzied rise in the commodity's price peaked in 1974, when the Polish government embargoed the export of 120,000 tonnes of sugar. 'Rationality gave way to scrupulously nurtured dreams and imagination,' Kapferer tells us. Eventually there was a change in *sentiment* – a strange word, but the only one that really describes this collective animus – and The Market chose not to believe rumours that tended to boost the price of sugar, which in October 1975 was one sixth of its 1974 peak.

Kapferer leads us calmly through other scenes of intense financial disorder and distress. In 1986, for example, the dollar skyrocketed on news of a military invasion of South Korea by the North. Within the hour it had fallen, badly burned, back to earth. The 'invasion' reported by Reuters news agency was in fact four deserting Chinese soldiers who had commandeered a plane.

As Kapferer rightly insists, not all rumour is false. He deems it a parallel, informal information system – effectively, the first pirate radio. But the truth or otherwise of a rumour is vital for The Market, which is attempting to find the correct price on the known information.

Yet The Market, this cipher of certainty, is peculiarly susceptible to rumour. The relatively small number of people that make a market means that rumours travel incredibly quickly. And all the people in the market are, supposedly, experts in their fields – who's going to disbelieve them? Why would they lie? Then again, there's the time pressure of the modern trading environment. Everything has to be assimilated and subjected to financial analysis in seconds. So there's no time for considered rational response, especially given that not reacting to a rumour is as dangerous as reacting. The Market is all about movement and flow. Stand still, trade on yesterday's information, and you're dead. Or at least, you're out of a job.

So already we are beginning to pick holes in the PMT/S. Devotees would argue that the PMT/S describes a perfectible entity, something that may never have the perfect prices but is always moving toward them. They would point out that the market 'corrected' itself quickly, that rumour is a perfectly valid part of the known or believed information that goes into asset pricing. They might even add that existence of the PMT/S is therefore, in the temporal sense, illusory, that the PMT/S works outside the constraints of linear time.

To which you might reasonably respond: 'Yeah, yeah. One cardio-vascular twitch too many and bye-bye to five big ones. What the fuck is The Market anyway?'

Good question. One to which the direct, literal answers are few, and mostly unsatisfactory, while the stock of euphemism appears to be inexhaustible.

Let's start with the euphemisms and the images, and move to such things I dare to call 'facts' later.

The more intelligent comparisons are complex, some of them engagingly so: The Market moves like a lunatic head-butting the buttons in a lift; it's like being handcuffed to a blind man who knows where to go but not how to get there, and he's going to take you with him; The Market is a pensive sprinter – it spends ninety per cent of its time thinking where it will go, and ten per cent of its time getting there. The Market is black, grey, bull, bear, trading sideways, choppy, rollercoaster. And here is a key paradox for the late twentieth century's siren of certainty – it moves in unpredictable ways. It is radically unpredictable, in fact. So much so, that merely to say The Market is difficult to call is a major understatement on a par with, say, suggesting that Catherine the Great was just a mildly eccentric woman with a certain fondness for horses.

Let's start the search for some factual underpinning to all this with something that is relatively basic and unarguable. What's absolutely clear is that markets are about money. And there are only five things you can do with money – buy it, sell it, borrow it or lend it. Or, if you have enough of it to improvise an armchair sculpture, you can always sit on it.

There are no exceptions to this rule. Every foreign exchange straddle, every deep-discounted bond transaction, every derivative programme trade using fractal mathematics can be quickly analysed down to the concepts of buy, lend, borrow, or sell (the armchair is irrelevant, unless cash is involved).

This reasoning may sound as primitive as medieval physics with its basic, flawed concepts of earth, air, fire and water as the constituent elements of the universe. There is however a crucial difference – when Newton and later Einstein produced their descriptive theories of the universe (essentially metaphors applied to describe the physical) they weren't trying to sell anything to anybody. The notion, for example, of the observer having a direct impact on the quality of the data observed doesn't have to have a common resonance, doesn't have to find wide acceptance, for it to be valid. Theories about The Market, however, *do* need majority acceptance. This is their one-dimensional beauty. There is no other validation of a theory, a security, a company or anything else required once you have made some money. Unless you get greedy and hang on, that is. As Baron Rothschild was fond of saying, when asked how he made his fortune from the markets of the early nineteenth century, 'I sold too soon'.

OK, so The Market is about money chasing more money. But what makes that money change direction? What is the animus of the Smart Money (another lovely obfuscation of the late twentieth century)? In other words, what, apart from rumours about the health of obscure singers, makes The Market move?

Profit. There are thousands of arcane theoretical indicators – the long bond yield divided by thirty-day interbank rates, a share's price divided by the income it generates, etc, etc – and they produce pretty lines that often have an important bearing on explaining what is happening. But the reason people participate in a market (and, with certain very limited exceptions, we are still talking about people as opposed to computers here) is to make money. They buy something with the ultimate goal of selling later at a profit. And the urge to take profit means that the temptation to sell as soon as we can make a turn becomes ever more difficult to resist. 'In the long run we are all dead,' wrote John Maynard Keynes.

So we have an absolutely true answer, phrased in absolutely relative terms, because to make profit you need a buyer to sell on to. Compare these two sets of questions and answers. The first set is stolen from a (probably apocryphal) Oxford scholarship examination:

Q. Is this a question? A. If this is an answer, that is a question.

Q. Should I buy this? A. If I can sell it later, for more, I should buy.

I will definitely buy if I know you will definitely buy it later (or before, if I am 'shorting' The Market, but the principle is the same). This idea is commonly referred to as relative value – I hold something you may want to buy at a higher price, either because you'll need it later or because you have specific needs. Note that word 'relative' creeping in again. The absolute truth of The Market is that there is no absolute truth. Everything I do depends on the approval of the financial majority, the ethereal stamp of approval which is market value. However overpriced the asset I've bought may be if judged by criteria like common sense, good taste, etc, my purchase has value – is validated – if I can find someone out there who will buy from me at a higher price. This theory of relative value has a street name, or rather a screen name. It is known as the Bigger Fool theory.

Probably the most famous example of the Bigger Fool theory is provided by Joseph P. Kennedy, pre-war head of the Kennedy clan, and father of JFK. He had the family millions invested in the stockmarket, like everyone else who was making a lot of money in the US in the late '20s.

Come 1929 Mr Kennedy has made a very great deal of money, and, again like many, many others, he is concerned. Common sense tells him that stock prices just cannot continue to climb the way they have been doing (although eminent Wall Street investment houses are going to great lengths to promulgate the idea that this is not just possible, but probable). Eventually Mr Kennedy has had enough, and cashes in the family millions and puts them on secure deposit and into the best-grade government securities. Three weeks later the market crashes.

Mr Kennedy acted on the Bigger Fool theory. He realized that there could be no-one, but no-one, left to buy stock when he found himself on the receiving end of a hot tip from his shoeshine boy. It became clear to him that all those mean, rich little old ladies from Connecticut had been fully invested months before. Who was propping up the ignorant, but well-advised (well-advised in a very technical sense) and rich? Why, the less rich, less intensively advised small businessmen. And now they too were fully invested, their money was being propped up by that of people like the Kennedy shoeshine boy, who was now proffering investment advice as he buffed and spat and waxed. Who was going to be fool enough to buy from him?

Not Joseph P. Kennedy. He saved the family heritage, and was therefore able to sustain the Kennedy family's influence and power in the US and, through his ambassadorship to the Court of St James, the UK. In view of the misfortunes the Kennedy family has suffered as a consequence of that influence, some might say that selling up when he did maybe wasn't the right decision. In market terms, however, there is no doubt. Asssesed on the basis of profit or loss, one or zero, score one.

So much for the investment parable. But there is more solid evidence to back the notion that the market can only sustain itself for as long as the supply of fools is plentiful. Let's take the US market as an example. American investors are probably the most sophisticated in the world. All right, the cabdriver's analysis of the prospects for his Microsoft warrant play is probably about as sophisticated and thoughtful as his views on race, immigration and instant cures for changing the sexual proclivities (and if they don't like it, castrate 'em) of every rock star other than Bruce Springsteen. But the fact is that as he brings you into Manhattan (which isn't really America, yes, yes) and plays his suicidal game of tag with a car that is more like a turbo-charged oil rig than a regular automobile, the cabdriver frequently diverts you from your imminent demise with tales of the market. And, even allowing for the mendacity which is the universal hallmark of people who drive cabs, he probably really does own shares. Believe me, at street level, that is financial sophistication. Try talking to a London or Parisian cabdriver about the stockmarket if you like short conversations.

So what about the American market? Well, it's now a proud boast that one household in two owns mutual funds. Mutual funds, trumpet organizations like the Investment Company Institute (ICI) in Washington, DC, are the best way for smaller investors to enter the markets. Investors pool their money in one investment vehicle that invests in lots of (usually) shares. They therefore diversify and spread risk, and another bonus is that you get a professional to invest your money for you. And the ICI is correct. But what is the sceptic's definition of a smaller investor? Right. A bigger fool.

The bigger fool figures are not encouraging. If we take two measures of the small investor's participation in the market we get a depressing answer each time. Let's try this first in the jargon of the markets, then in English. So, the liquidity ratios of mutual funds are a leading negative indicator for the markets. That means once the money fund managers have taken to invest on behalf of their clients is invested (when the ratio of spare cash to invested cash is low) the market typically falls some time later. The explanation is that all the small investors' money is in the market – and we know what happens next. It's the same story with simple numbers of investors. Although the number of investors is a function of the number of people in society, it's known that there's an invisible ceiling out there. When everyone's in on the good thing, it becomes a bad thing. If one household in two has a stake in a fund, how long does the market have to go before it runs out of households willing or able to buy a slice? On a zero-one score, small investors score zero.

This simple binary statement unites The Market in all its manifestations. From frenzied open outcry in the murk and sweat of the Bombay stock exchange, to the flickering, 4 a.m. cool of the Tokyo dollar-rate-trader's bedroom screen, to the retired dentist calling his broker in Council Bluffs, Iowa, everyone is trying to guess whether The Market's next move will be a zero or a one.

So here we have a few clues as to why the descriptions of The Market are so colourful – lunatics in elevators, etc. We are talking about billions and billions, sums of huge importance to the world economy. People understand that this is a significant way of raising capital, a key component in sustaining the capitalist mechanism that enables individual liberty to flourish and encourages financial creativity. They know that this is simultaneously the lifeblood of developed economies, the way forward for developing countries, and a key path to self-fulfilment for the individuals whose collective efforts propel those economies forward to greater world prosperity. And what do you have at the root of it all, as the driving force of the market mechanism? A giant moron picking eggs out of a hat and smashing them on his forehead. The good eggs are ones, the bad zeroes. And he just keeps going. He has an infinite supply of eggs.

Hardly surprising that the metaphors have a quality of suppressed hysteria. Market analysis is like a huge parlour game, the boring kind that families who behave like escapees from Norman Rockwell prints like to play at Christmas. The game is pleasant enough – all players are paid for their opinions and so get sweeties whether they are right or wrong. All they have to do is guess whether the giant moron will pick a good or bad egg out of the hat next.

Imagine the horror of having to do this for a living. We are way beyond Dante's depiction of the innermost circles of hell (which, of course, do not involve just physical pain, but also exquisitely tedious mental torture). This makes watching Barney the Dinosaur look like an intensive course in stochastic low-dimensional delta-range-analysis asset-pricing theory.

Or maybe it doesn't. But anyway, imagine the sheer horror of watching Barney and realizing that it actually *matters* what Barney does next. Money is to be made – millions, billions – from predicting which side of his coat the village idiot will dribble on next. And to find what powers this perfect binary machine, market watchers have to find all kinds of reasons as to why the next egg will be good or bad.

There are some who would deny that The Market has such a thing as a psychology, even one as primitive as that of our giant moron. They argue that it is specious invention to attribute a collective conscience to The Market. They are preachers of (you guessed it) the PMT/S, which allows only that members of the marketplace make rational decisions about pricing assets on the basis of rationally relevant information. If there is any apparent coherence of thought and deed, they claim that this stems entirely from the mechanisms of the market by which rationally relevant factors are applied toward the end of finding the perfect price for an asset.

The rational response to which is 'Bollocks!'. Not only does the pricing behaviour of The Market indicate that The Market has a mind, but it is perfectly natural and logical for markets to have collective psyches, since they themselves are creatures of the mind. A corollary to this is that market indexes are in fact a kind of numerical metaphor, one that tries to measure (and so describe) the financial world in a similar way to that in which theoretical physics tries to measure and describe the physical universe.

And if you want more of that kind of dense, impenetrable, quasi-scientific language, there's a whole section of the last chapter of this book devoted to explaining why it's natural for a market to have psychological barriers, where there's a whole lot more – if, as I say, you can stomach all that intellectual underpinning.

So what are market participants, in fact, doing? It's clear that they're actually second-guessing a hypothetical biggest fool, the financial vanishing point after which no security can ever be sold to any shoeshine boy or any cretin at all. All that econometric analysis, all those beta theorists, top-down generalists and bottom-up specialists have to discount their data and their methods at least to this extent: they have to wonder what it will do, this thing sitting on its throne of absolute cognitive zero, this moronic Ultimate Fool, this binary machine, this thing with all the native wit of a baby trout (estimated intelligence quotient – 6). They have to empathize, to cast their minds into the tiny, shadowed mental recess that belongs to the cognitive vanishing point. They must wonder what it will make of all their theories. Will it buy, or not?

Which is why my personal favourite description of the markets is a group of smart, highly paid people with a common economic purpose and the collective intelligence of a baby trout.

CHAPTER II

Foreign Exchange

> Heart of stone,
> Mind of steel.
> On the phone,
> Do the deal.
>
> — *Foreign exchange dealers' mantra*

What really happens inside the locked vaults of the foreign exchanges. Ideological conflict. Control and regulation – psychology v. police work. Why drugs and German sports cars are essential to facilitate the free exchange of international capital.

What really happens inside the locked vaults of the foreign exchanges

Spend time in a foreign exchange dealing room and you learn a lot of things you knew already. Money is power, money is sex – but sex isn't power. If it were, there would be a lot more women leading the teams instead of concentrating on what's known as Giving Good Phone. What you see – if you're allowed into the locked vault – is the trained killers of capitalism in action. The good ones are lethal in every situation. In unarmed combat – deals on the telephone (watch out for the women, especially) are as close to the personal touch as the foreign exchange markets ever come – these traders are masters of dissimulation, wearing a mantle of counterfeit calm. In high-tech, impersonal screen trade they move as fast as any glue-crazed nine-year-old video junkie when the cursor flashes. Half-man, half-machine, the paradigmatic foreign exchange dealer is a high-tech samurai, the chocolate Robocop of capitalism who makes twice his annual salary in bonus every time he eats himself.

Well, that's the theory anyway. It's actually a little more boring than a continuous round of cocaine-filled ashtrays, blow jobs in car parks and souped-up German sports cars.

12

But then again, not much more boring. Remember, money is sex, and, at the very least, four times the gross domestic product of the United States sluices its way through the treasuries of the major players every month. That means the entire annual output of the world's most powerful economic force (still, just, ahead of Japan) – the total sum of an entire year's sweated labour by 250 million people – passes across the ledgers of these traders every week. That means some $900 billion per day. That means, as a direct and inevitable consequence, that everybody sitting in front of a screen is wearing the girdle of irresistibility, sometimes with Thierry La Croix earrings thrown in for good measure.

When people say that foreign exchange dealing is its own little world, they are wrong. It's not just a planet, it's a vast and expanding universe of money. Just as physicists can't really say how many parsecs (and don't ask what they are) the universe measures across, so economists and financial academics can only guess at how much debt and liability is hurtling around the world, twenty-four hours a day. This is a completely unregulated market. All you need to participate is the respect and confidence of the other players. Which means you need vast quantities of money, and a track record that shows you can pay it out as well as take it in. The foreign exchanges are a huge, uncharted, untamable, unknowable universe. They constitute a uniquely pure form of capitalism, the like of which I have only experienced in Communist Russia, where the inadequacies of central planning had turned everybody into experts in barter and the squeeze plays of capitalism's heart of darkness, the black market.

But, perversely enough, the real nature of foreign exchange transactions is far removed from the squalor of the black market. And it is less purely speculative than many suppose. In many respects it resembles the insurance market – an ancient and revered form of making gigantic quantities of money (Or rather it was. The insurance market is still old, of course, but it has become somehow less glamorous and not quite so well loved since the Lloyd's of London losses of the late 1980s and early 1990s.)

Anyway, before we proceed, let's look at a typical deal, a basic transaction which constitutes a tiny fragment of the foreign exchange market mosaic.

Imagine that a French company wants to buy American goods. Delivery in six months' time, price $100 million. Payment due in dollars. For the French that's, say, 600 million francs. Given that there's free exchange of capital the French want to buy their dollars now so they can do their accounting in francs. Their bank buys the dollars for them, possibly using a futures contract. The idea is simple, that the parties agree to buy and sell currencies in a few months' time at a price agreed today. In a few months things may well have changed, but that's the price of certainty. If the French company acts now it can be sure of what will be going through its books, it can plan ahead, etc.

But then the company's bank, having made a little commission for the transaction, has an exchange rate risk on the dollar. It has $100 million worth of a position, in fact. So it sets off $95 million of the risk, and buys back the francs, or maybe another currency that its traders happen to like. And the bank that takes the $95 million onto its books will no doubt set off some of that risk. And so it goes on, almost down to the level of small change. In that sense, foreign exchange trade is somewhat like the insurance companies or bookmakers who take on a big risk and lay it off in the market.

So a single trade-related transaction can generate hundreds of times its own volume in foreign exchange. That's a very strong reason why the universe of money is so big. And it also explains, in part, why the markets have this terrible reputation for being seed beds of pure, speculative greed.

The other main reason for this reputation is that there is a lot of pure, speculative greed about. After all, what's the definition of a speculative play as opposed to laying off a risk? If you have free trade and capital exchange it's very, very difficult to differentiate. And if you're standing on the sidelines seeing all that money flying around it's very easy to be awed by the power and the size of it all.

In fact, given the untrammelled nature of the forces at play, and the sums involved, it's difficult not to start gawping and drooling like some rustic peasant at the Lord Mayor's Banquet. Read most of the press coverage of the exchanges every time there's a major market move, and you'll see what I mean.

So let's get back to the people and the cultural driving forces of the foreign exchange markets. From there, it might be possible to sort out a little better just what is really happening.

To reiterate. Money is power, money is sex, but sex isn't power.

When it comes to a contest between sex and power, power wins every time. The foreign exchange dealers are warrior-kings, omnipotent in their self-created environment, floating around in a universe of money with the ability to do whatever they want, provided it's financial.

There are only two limiting factors. The first is the technical capacity of their little space shuttles (quite big, if your sealed vault happens to have the capital resources of CitiBank, Société Générale or Daiwa behind it). You need to have the financial firepower to do the really big deals, and to take aggressive positions. No single player could ever hope to turn the market through financial muscle alone (ask a central banker, any central banker, about trying to lead the market in a direction it doesn't want to go – it's very expensive and *never* successful). What is possible is to take a position and hope that your determined pressing of the conch shell to the lips will make others hear and persuade them to follow.

Until relatively recently, foreign exchange deals were all about small-scale opportunism. Dealers saw a little hole in the market, and then exploited it. They might see a tiny discrepancy between interest rates in one currency and bond yields in another that could be exploited by linking the two through a clever trade. Remember the movie *Dark Star*? This was director John Carpenter's first stroke of genius: it was a story of astronauts in deep space, sealed up tightly in their little ship, with a mission to get out there and destroy unstable planets. Well, that's pretty much the story of a regular foreign exchange deal. You see the opportunity, an imbalance in currency and rates, and call up the laser power of the bank, or more likely nowadays a 'boutique' (of these, more later), and zap the profit opportunity.

Profit, of course, is the second constraint. Foreign exchange players owned by banks, insurance companies or big corporations can do what they want, so long as they produce income for the parent company. That's not too obvious to be worth saying because of its nature as an unqualified statement. At dealer level, we are not talking about the profit motive here, we are talking about the *only* motive.

End of press statement on behalf of the Sanity Party. If I were attending the press conference right now I'd be scrabbling for the microphone to get my questions in: 'Yes. Martin Baker, Envy Correspondent, *The Materialist Times*. Can I just ask you ...?'

Well, there are a lot of things requiring verification. For example, how come no-one knows how big the market is? Are there really no statistics? Is no-one in charge? And isn't it just fashionable to knock the foreign exchanges, and call them predatory, speculative, the jackals of capitalism, etc? Isn't that just another sad media cliché?

As to market size, I call in evidence 'Four Good Arabs'.

Before we get to them, let's look at the circumstantial evidence. If anyone does know, that person is keeping it a very tight secret. And anyway, the size of the market *is* unknowable. First of all because of its present structure. Anyone can play with the big boys, if the big boys like to be played with. There is no Securities and Exchange Commission, no Bank of England, no regulatory archangel. The foreign exchange market is an accountant's nightmare. Banks are among the longest established players in the field, and they typically have the most onerous duties of financial reporting. Try finding exactly what money any bank has made from foreign exchange dealing in any year, and – short of taking the financial director to lunch and the more obvious means of espionage – you will find yourself in the realm of pure speculation. The Bank for International Settlements in Basle tries to estimate turnover (I used BIS's extremely conservative figures earlier). But there is undoubtedly a vast area of the unknowable out there.

This is the Four Good Arabs factor.

What follows is a true story. Only the names of the fashion houses have been changed, to prevent them from becoming too popular.

It was around the time of the French elections in early 1993. The foreign exchanges had been having a great deal of fun with the European currencies. By 'fun' for the dealers, I mean, of course, other people's consternation and panic. The foreign exchange market had achieved a very, very dim state of awareness (being the absolute height of consciousness for any market) that if everyone hunted in packs it was possible to break out of the *Dark Star* syndrome of trading on isolated opportunities. If a large number of traders joined their firepower together, it seemed they could take out bigger targets – not just planets, but whole financial galaxies – despite the best efforts of the central banks, whether 'independent' or not, and the governments whose currencies they were trading. Or do I mean toying with? Imagine a shoal of baby piranha and a wounded hippopotamus. At the first sign of weakness (sometimes without even *that* as justification) the market discovered that using its collective strength it could strip a currency to its carcass in a couple of sessions.

For example, at the back end of 1992 the foreign exchange market forced the Swedes, who were trying to keep their krona in alignment with the German mark, to raise their overnight interest rate to the ludicrous level of 500 per cent. That's the kind of evil, predatory rate ascribed to moneylenders in Victorian novels, and currently only available from your friendly local gangster. Unfortunately for the Swedish government, the expedient of breaking the legs of a vast international market was not available. So it fell back on another means of punishment.

The rate rise was a way of hurting anybody caught selling krona they didn't have. (Shorting is a classic trick in a falling market – you sell me 10 million at 5 for delivery next week. When the market falls to 4 the next day you buy your 10 million, and when I take delivery I still have to pay 5. Net result: You make 1. By pretending you had the krona you accentuate its fall, because you are artificially inflating the supply of the currency. And the law of supply and demand is immutable.) The Swedish government effectively instigated a penal rate for any bank unable to balance its books at the end of the trading day. In other words, you could still short the krona, but woe betide you if you hadn't bought some in by the end of the session.

Anyway, penal measures notwithstanding, The Market wanted to sell the krona, and no government was going to stand in its way. The Swedes were forced to give up their attempt to shadow the German mark, which was for them a pre-cursor to being admitted to the European Union.

The Swedes were not alone. The Spanish and the Irish had to 'realign' against the German mark (actually the Exchange Rate Mechanism, but in practice, that meant keeping a certain value against the German currency). You didn't need a degree in rocket science to translate 'realign' as 'devalue'. A sensible enough measure, but treated as a national humiliation by the financial press, which showed its maturity and good judgment by treating the whole affair as a huge piece of public willy-measuring. And this is post-feminist, recidivist macho willy-measuring: it's not what you do with your currency that counts, it's really how big it is that matters.

The Italians and the British were roundly humiliated. Not having opted for the diplomatic euphemism of realignment, they had left the system altogether. Or rather, the foreign exchange market had systematically helped itself to the foreign exchange reserves of the Italian and British central banks to such an extent that eventually the governments retreated with all the grace and dignity of thoroughly whipped puppies.

One of the men who came to prominence in this time was a fund manager, George Soros. There is much to be said about men like Mr Soros, to whom the markets pay disproportionate attention. That comes later. Suffice it to say that it became known that Mr Soros' large fund, the Quantum Fund, had invested heavily, and spectacularly correctly, in a falling British pound. The fund made some $1.5 billion from the sharp decline of sterling. He became known – quite wrongly – as the man who broke sterling.

Why quite wrongly? Because he helped move it out of the ERM, but to attribute the currency's fall to Mr Soros would be like saying that the moon moved round the earth because of the gravitational force of a big, noticeable, heavy building, say the Empire State. Mr Soros has become a 'guru', and as such has a symbolic force far greater than his actual mass in the market (just as the Empire State, with its King Kong connotations, has more symbolic presence than the far bigger twin towers of the World Trade Center).

So I'm having lunch with Dagmar – blonde, beautiful, a dealer, Lacroix earrings, the works. She's Danish, and she's moved to Paris, she says, because she likes the steak (Why does this statement have my chromosomes kicking each other to death?). We talk, as one tries not to when sitting opposite a woman like Dagmar, of the foreign exchanges. And she drops a little bombshell into the conversation: she and her three partners, who work out of a 150-square-metre apartment, have more money under management than Mr Soros. It's just that Mr Soros is more visible, better known. Maybe he enjoys the publicity. Who are we to say?

But, but? I am doing my imitation of a lobotomized goldfish. How can this be? Admittedly, she is known in the markets. Their little boutique (for such it is, gentle readers) is also known. *How can this be?* Easy, she replies. All you need is Four Good Arabs. They give you billions, but require discretion above all else. Profit without publicity.

As I was saying, the actual size of the foreign exchanges is unknowable. Bye-bye, BIS. So here's a tip – if in doubt about the size of the market, guess on the large side. Oh yes, and then add a zero.

When you get bored of ruminating on how many pints of water there may be in the ocean, here's another nursery game: devise a way the foreign exchanges can be regulated. Given the nature of the market, it might seem like trying to regulate a jug of spilt milk, but in fact there is an almost-serious solution to the problem.

The starting point is to remember that there is a difference between regulation and control. So long as the international financial climate broadly favours free exchange of capital it's completely otiose to attempt to control the value at which that exchange takes place (although those who know the markets can repeat to themselves a little mantra – Gold standard, Bretton Woods, ERM – that shows people do keep trying). But if you can't dictate content, you can stipulate as to form: while you can't hope to stop the chimps at the tea party spilling their milk, putting bananas in each other's noses, and masturbating in front of the children, you can at least make sure they're well-dressed while they're doing it.

Which brings us to the compliance officer. The compliance officer is a colleague of the dealer, and is route number one to putting the spirits back in Pandora's box. Compliance officers were invented in the days when the idea of self-regulation was in vogue. This was a gloss on the 'pure' capitalist theory, that value and the seriousness of the players in the market mean that shoddy practices are soon discovered and never tolerated. The idea was to have people on the payroll called completely bogus names like 'internal policemen'.

When you look at the substance of compliance officers' jobs, things don't get any easier. They are there, basically, to monitor their colleagues' working methods for potential conflicts of interest, to ensure that they comply with codes of business practice probity, and to rat on them if they don't. Unsurprisingly, compliance officers are despised, ignored, and, perhaps less obviously, referred to in some financial houses as 'Helens' – after the deaf and blind American girl Helen Keller. Deafness and blindness (and preferably, in the view of many foreign exchange dealers, deadness) being ideal job quali-fications for would-be compliance officers. And anyway, 'Helen' is a lot easier to say than 'internal policeman'.

On the whole, compliance officers have little to do with the foreign exchanges. Their presence is tolerated – just – in other, less profitable, areas of finance. They are the distant cousins whose attendance at the family wedding merely indicates the extreme wealth of the family that allows such remote and obscure creatures to come and warm their hands at the hearth, and put their non-profit-making names on the payroll. All the adjectives that command respect in the financial world have a cast of undiluted machismo and up-front little-boy combativeness – thrusting, aggressive, dynamic, etc. Put them before the words 'compliance officer' and you have an oxymoron for modern times that ranks with Salman Rushdie's Open House, safe sex, Russian dentistry, stable relationship, etc, etc.

Of course, we're taking the hardest case here. It's hardly surprising that the Helens don't come out well when you look at their ability to clamp down on these great behemoths of profit. It's like accusing the European Union of being weak, bureaucratic, sloppily organized and poorly managed by overpaid people, many of whom have very fat arses, because of the EU's inability to act decisively over the travelling roadshow of butchery in what used to be Yugoslavia. Of course it can't act decisively. Military action is the hardest edge of the toughest part of common policy, foreign policy, for an entity like the EU. It is of course a bureaucratic mess (though by no means a bad idea), but that's because it can't do simple things well. Killing a lot of people causes problems for politicians, who need to be assured, as in the Gulf War, that they are getting value for money. Among other things.

So don't hold your breath waiting for compliance officers to make sure that the free exchange of international capital is conducted with dignity, probity, and – as they say in financial circles – transparency. Whatever that means. The Helens have been around for years, and they've had no role to play in any of the financial scandals of recent times. Correction, they have had a role to play, that of the Invisible Man.

There is some internal regulation of foreign exchange dealing, however. This is usually undertaken by the head of a team, who's invariably an experienced old hand at the game. But the foreign exchanges have their own peculiar climate of premature aging, like the higher slopes of the Andes, and attaining the age of thirty is considered to confer the status of ancient sage. To be thirty-five and yet still able to work without the use of a walking frame is an unvarnished miracle. A minor miracle, but still a wonder in the eyes of the over-confident, frequently under-educated, young people who actually do the trades. There is something terribly corrosive about being so close to such a vast torrent of money. Unless you wear lead-lined gonad protectors and live on ginseng and goats' urine cocktails you turn into Methuselah before you even get the chance to go grey. Such is the theory of financial commentators, whose judgment may, admittedly, have become somewhat addled by years of making up jokes about interest rates.

Anyway, the regulation conducted by these mature team leaders tends to consist of stopping the more obvious excesses of the team. This frequently means trying to persuade traders that dealing on their own account with the bank's money is, basically, theft. The reasoning goes that while theft has its merits as a form of extreme opportunism in a modern enterprise culture, this peculiarly individualistic kind of entrepreneurism is not to be encouraged. But it's not to be too actively discouraged, either. Try to stop a trader making money for himself when he's raking in millions for the bank, and you will find yourself without a foreign exchange team. All the team needs, remember, is a Good Arab or four, and suddenly that team is operating as a boutique and making a lot more of the money it trades for itself.

To underscore the point that the conflict between profit and 'internal discipline' is no conflict at all, let's look at a little incident of bad publicity for the exchanges in late 1992.

Internal discipline is mostly conducted along, shall we say, Augustinian lines. Saint Augustine – 'God, make me good, but not yet' – would have made an excellent trader, and an even better head of foreign exchange. You can imagine his beatific countenance as he gently disciplined the London-based trader who made the massive mistake of responding truthfully to a press question about a particularly wonderful day's trade. As a consequence of the dealer's remark, his employer was subjected to the horrified rage and contempt of a spectacularly ill-informed press. Questions were asked about the conduct of foreign exchange trade in the British parliament. Concern was expressed by many important people who clearly didn't know anything about the markets at all. Politicians talked darkly of reform.

The remark was admittedly a little indiscreet, and perhaps called for an examination of the regulatory issue. The trader spoke as sterling was being driven out of the ERM (its over-priced trading position against the German mark). The journalist asked how much the trader personally had made that day. The response was that by positioning himself to make money from a falling pound he had made (for his employer) some $15 million. This was the news peg on which the pundits hung their theses that the foreign exchange market was ranging itself against any attempt whatever to harness or control it. There was no doubt about it. Something had to be done.

And what was the result? You guessed first time: nothing. Zip. *Nada*. A festival of zilch, a hymn to inaction. As the Brits like to say, bugger all. No reform of the markets, the dealer didn't lose his job. In fact, he was headhunted shortly afterwards, despite his employer's promises of extravagant, please-stay bonuses. All this after the guy has indiscreetly disclosed what was proprietary information.

So the relationship between the institutions and their employees is just about as cordial as that between Duncan and Macbeth ('The raven himself is hoarse that croaks the fatal entry of two million Hong Kong dollars in my personal account...'). But it is the sweet milk of concord, compared to the way the governments see the market.

There's no doubt that the foreign exchanges are strong magic. They can turn teenagers into bloated goats, enslaved to the market and a string of expensive habits in a matter of months. They invariably turn politicians and government officials (especially if they are European) into the intellectual equivalent of a rubber glove full of custard – utterly messy, definitively useless.

Take the case of Denis Healey in the late '70s. Before (and since) he became Chancellor of the Exchequer, the man demonstrated a good mind and excellent, gladiatorial debating skills. He is a decorated soldier, which means he's not just got balls, but he's lucky. Yet in 1976 he berates the foreign exchange markets for selling sterling against the dollar. He tells the markets that the appropriate rate for sterling is two dollars. The consensus view in The Market at the time is that this is probably overpricing sterling a little, but the pound's rate, which is way below two dollars, still keeps on plunging. It's a market trend, everyone's enjoying the trip. The giant is having fun smashing little zeroes over his forehead and seeing which way the yolk dribbles. The Market is not going to be bullied by a politician. Shortly afterwards, Healey is so softened up by economic crises at home he can't decide whether to go to an International Monetary Fund meeting to beg for money to prop up the tottering British economy. He thinks he'll go, but then changes his mind in a sudden and public way – at the airport. The plane, full of financial journalists waiting to go to the same conference, is delayed for half an hour while Healey dithers. The journalists gleefully write the story.

Now that's sending the market a clear image of a man who knows how to make decisions. And then re-make them, again and again. Is he in charge of the UK economy? The answer is a resounding maybe.

But if I were awarding Oscars for gibbering, hysterical impotence, Michel Sapin, the ex-finance minister of France, would feature extensively on my shortlist. It is late winter, 1992 and Sapin – whose name, incidentally, translates as 'Christmas tree' – does not react well to the foreign exchange market's having a little tilt at the French franc. He argues, absolutely correctly, that the economic fundamentals (interest rates, growth of the economy, inflation) in no way justify selling the franc against the German mark. The German economy is doing worse than the French and looks set to continue doing so. Right. But what use is logic?

Nomination for Singularly Inapt Use of Reason: Michel Sapin. The foreign exchanges have seen that they have a perfect system in this ERM mechanism. They can sell a currency knowing that the country's central bank (and, in theory, the other countries' central banks too) will buy for as long as they can. That closes off half of the equation and gives them an artificial trading advantage.

Then there's the Nomination for Single Most Stupid Comment: Michel Sapin, for his dictum that in the French Revolution they knew how to deal with *agioteurs* (speculators) by cutting their heads off. Right.

Nomination for Most Embarrassing Performance: Michel Sapin, for most of his public utterances in late January and early February 1993.

Nomination for Most Paranoid and Ill-informed Xenophobia: Michel Sapin (and others), for promulgating the notion that there was an 'Anglo-Saxon' conspiracy to drive the franc out of the ERM.

The last one is the most serious, since some Frenchmen actually believed it. My response to conspiracy theorists is: get a life. Purchase yourself an existence. If you can't afford to buy one, rent one. The people who put those ideas round may inhabit planet Earth, but they definitely don't live on it.

There are two things to say, both of which are obvious on so gargantuan a scale they test the margins of worthwhile iteration.

1) As with most supposed conspiracy theories, disappointingly enough no-one's sufficiently organized to be in charge.

2) The foreign exchanges don't give a shit about the nationality of the baby they're taking the candy from. They'll take kronor, lire, punts, pounds, pesetas and francs (which they did on their ERM duck shoot, roughly in that order, and in very large quantities). All they want is money, and if successive central banks were prepared to donate the contents of their coffers to the dealers' Christmas bonuses (that is not meant to be a Sapin reference), then so be it. End of story.

Almost. There is at least one incident that may have afforded some 'evidence' for paranoid theories of conspiracies by the 'Anglo-Saxons' (in France this means anyone – black, white, yellow, or that delicate hue of grey-pink which identifies 'white' British people – basically, anyone who is not French). There is also a high-level systemic conflict between different capitalist ideologies, which helps to explain why the Brits and especially the Americans come closer to regulating the markets. But, as we shall see, this is a conflict of ideas, not nationalities.

The story that may have helped fuel the conspiracy theories emanates from one of the London dealing rooms of a French bank. We start from the uncontroversial premise that all French banks are essentially controlled by the French government and, to a greater or lesser extent, are used as instruments of French industrial and economic policy. So when the markets are taking their pleasure at the expense of the French government, they are emptying the treasuries of its banks. At this particular bank, the head of the foreign exchange team is a bright young man of thirty-two (i.e. a gnarled old veteran on the foreign exchange timescale) dutifully carrying out orders and buying when the rest of the world is screaming 'Sell, sell, sell!'. In addition to the straightforward duty to do as he is told, his orders come from an alumnus of the same *grande école* – than which there are few greater bonds in France.

So he takes up arms against a sea of sell orders and obediently gives away several millions to the gleeful markets. Meanwhile, the rest of his team, composed of Brits, Americans, Danes, Spaniards,

Chinese and a Hungarian, are trading not just the bank's pre-programmed loss strategy, but their clients' accounts. They are carrying out their orders all right, but protecting the corporate treasurers and the fund managers (an increasingly important category of client for these dealers). What they are doing, in fact, is what their instincts tell them to – they are trading the trend. Selling the franc and making lots of money for their clients.

And then the fateful moment arrives. The announcement comes through that the ERM is kaput. Technically, the convergence bands had been widened to allow a thirty per cent swing. But to pretend that this was not abandoning all notions of keeping the currencies aligned is ludicrous. It is as if a householder invents a burglar-proof house by taking all the doors and windows out and inviting passers-by to come help themselves to whatever they want. It has a certain logic to it – that which is freely given cannot be taken – but as a security device, it sucks.

So cometh the hour, cometh a terse little statement saying that a coach and horses have been driven through the ERM. The head of the foreign exchange team stares moodily into the screen that flashes up the message. He punches a few buttons. And then he turns to see his team standing on their chairs, arms aloft at forty-five degrees to the horizontal. They are singing a lusty version of 'Deutschland, Deutschland, über alles'. After all, it was the failure of the German central bank and government to lend their full support to the franc that had provided such an excellent day's trade for the rest of the team and their clients.

So you can see how such a tasteless joke can be misinterpreted. Even fifty-plus years after the end of the Second World War, Nazi-style salutes are not funny (especially since they lead people to believe that the fight was against Germany, as opposed to fascism). But those salutes did provide a succinct commentary on events in the market that day.

Ideological conflict

The only palpable justification for arguing that a real conflict is taking place on the foreign exchanges is ideological.

The issues are well summarized in a paper entitled *The battle of the*

Systems – Control of Enterprises and the Global Economy, by Professor Ingo Walter of New York University and INSEAD, a leading European business school in Fontainebleau, just outside Paris.

'How does the organization of the financial system, notably the role of banks, influence critical dimensions of domestic and international economic performance through the process of corporate control? That is, how does the institutional design of the financial system influence the character of the capital allocation process, national economic performance, and international economic and financial relationships?'

As you can see, Professor Walter is not afraid of the Big Picture. He postulates a world where the Japanese, German, French and Anglo-American models of capitalism are struggling for global dominance of developed and emerging capitalist economies.

Walter argues that the German model of capitalism sees a coincidence of interest among German finance, industry and government. As a result, 'the need to separate capital markets from credit markets has never been perceived as a prerequisite to the maintenance of financial stability.'

The French model is similar to the German, but less of a partnership, argues Walter. He alludes to the *dirigiste* tradition of a centrally managed French economy and observes that 'the power of the government remains much greater than in either the German or Anglo-American models, both formally through regulation and state ownership and informally through the network of *grandes écoles* alumni.'

This system is so powerful and so rigid, that it handicaps French banks in trying to deal in the market. It is, to a large extent, true that a graduate of one of the French prestige schools is set for life. Top jobs are guaranteed not on the basis of performance at the office, but on the marks attained at school. Once you're a *normalien*, you're a *normalien* – an Alpha who cannot change status any more than one of the inhabitants of Aldous Huxley's *Brave New World.*

The thinking that a *normalien* – typically a gifted mathematician – must be great trader is so ingrained that even a sustained track record of losing money will not dissuade senior French management that the guy they hired just isn't equipped with those weird skills that dealers need. This is especially the case if the boss happened to go to the same school as the dud trader.

There is one semi-legendary turkey trading in Frankfurt at the moment. He has lost millions for his French bank (i.e. state) employers. Overconfident during the big bond bull market of 1993, he nosedived spectacularly in 1994. To such an extent, in fact, that his colleagues have added a cruel little suffix to his initials. They refer to him not as NP, but NPV – negative present value. And yet, despite daily displays of naivety and incompetence, he has a senior position and his superiors have decided that he is one of the best traders in the bank. Because, as a product of his *grande école*, he *has* to be.

The Anglo-American model of capitalism, on the other hand, is all about market forces as opposed to societal control. According to Walter it 'substitutes the discipline of an informed marketplace in debt and equity instruments for centralized control of capital allocation and pricing. It requires full and fair disclosure of all material information about the financial affairs of companies to work effectively, and an impartial system of corporate governance that favours the discipline of free competition, and not close linkages among firms and between firms and banks. Government sets the broad rules – competition policy, trade policy, banking and securities regulation, etc – and thereafter outcomes in both the real and financial sectors are left mainly to the markets.'

If we use this systemic model to analyse what happens on the foreign exchanges, we see a huge ideological conflict between free trade and government control. When the French franc was ripped out of the ERM, the real struggle was between the irresistible forces of the market and the *soi-disant* immovable objects of government regulation. And, as we saw, it was no contest, a massive win for the markets against both German and French models of control. The major difference between the French and the Germans was that it suited some within the German government to have the French undermined by the forces of the market. After the events of summer 1993, there is no doubt which is the core currency for Europe. Nor is there any doubt as to who calls the shots.

Control and regulation – psychology v. police work

It is perhaps because they are part of a system they understand that American government officials have shown a masterful restraint compared to the Europeans. From the mid '70s to the mid '80s they mostly had to talk down a soaring dollar. Then the dollar began to slide in 1985. This was an event that caused near-panic in some dealing rooms, as many of the traders were so young they could claim, with some justification, that they didn't know how to sell the American currency. Both rise and fall were handled with deep-discounted understatement by the US authorities. Successive US governments have had the good sense to let officials from the Treasury talk (sparingly) about the situation – although President Clinton appears to have spoiled that record somewhat by making the unusual error for a politician of speaking honestly. He tells the markets he wants a strong yen, to help with the trade deficit against Japan. The markets, bizarrely enough, sell the dollar, weakening it. And then they decide that they are going to go against the US government's wishes after all, and start to drive the dollar up.

The man who has spoken most consistently to the markets is Alan Greenspan, who has held lots of important financial positions, and is today's God in Residence at the Fed. More importantly, he consistently gave every appearance of knowing what he was talking about. As a consequence, his words took on value in the market. They became a factor in the price equation. All the more so because Greenspan did not bluster or panic. His words, well chosen (and often extremely disingenuous), carried weight. Ex-Fed chairman Paul Volker, Greenspan's predecessor, was probably the best at playing this game. The markets treated him as the financial equivalent of Charlton Heston – not quite God, but as close as you're likely to come. A terse word from Volker was worth a good few points on one side of a currency rate or the other.

Thus, while the US government has been barely more successful in 'controlling' the foreign exchanges than any other, it has been cleverer. And it has not tossed its central bank's reserves into the oncoming tide in the hope of reversing it. The Fed appears to understand that the markets cannot be controlled, but they can, occasionally, be manipulated. The Fed prefers psychology to police work, and has consistently managed to play this central paradoxical chord in the foreign exchange market: it has shown that the best way to intervene is not to intervene at all. Save your words, save your money. What the markets will accept is not a policeman, internal or otherwise, but a psychiatrist, an entity that understands them.

Note, incidentally, the lack of bullshit conspiracy theories about Japanese economic imperialism. The US government appears to understand that the kind of rubbish the French establishment was screaming about conspiracy theories is counter-productive. In the markets, it means your words are treated with contempt, you are discounted as a buffoon, and you are not even thanked when the markets confiscate your central bank's currency reserves.

Central banks, by the way, frequently perform a regulatory function in ensuring that entities licensed as banks don't overstep their limits – in other words, the small ones without billions of assets in reserves can't sustain very aggressive, speculative positions. But that's all for the end of the day. And a day is a very long time indeed in the foreign exchange markets. Ask one of those thousand-year-old heads of department.

Why drugs and German sports cars are essential to facilitate the free exchange of international capital

There are two more issues worth examining. One is personal: who are these foreign exchange people, really? What are they like, that they should generate so much paradox, such a wealth of imagery? The other is practical: who needs them, anyway?

If you were writing the recruitment brochure for a foreign exchange dealer you might, for once, be justified in saying, as recruitment brochures invariably do: 'It takes a special kind of person to work in today's foreign exchanges [insert any other profession here]...' But this time you'd be right. It takes a quick brain, one able to do arithmetical calculation speedily and accurately. It takes a nerveless self-confidence, a weird admixture of boldness and an acute sense of danger. That quality is most often found in people who don't know they possess it, or, if they do, have the good sense not to think about it too hard. Typically, they are young, and pretty much not disappointed by life. Their backgrounds vary enormously. Some have a tertiary education, some even beyond (though MBAs and masters' degrees are relatively few – the 'properly' educated tend to take more conservative career options). Others operate entirely on street cunning. Most are men, but there are plenty of women, maybe a fifth of the whole foreign exchange universe. It is a classless world – even in Britain – all that is required is the warrior-king factor that I alluded to earlier.

The warrior-kings are masters of the binary call. They synthesize all the information on the screens, on the television and radio news, all the paper spewed out by the wires. They look at the market trends, the chart shapes, the hemlines of dresses (a renowned indicator of market direction), and then they just see how they feel and trust themselves to be right, to call zero or one, and to be right most of the time. All this in an instant, several hundred times a day, thousands of times a week. You see why this universe is an accelerating time machine, chewing up its inhabitants.

And they are the best at it. In *The Right Stuff*, Tom Wolfe compared astronauts to the champions who fought individual battles on behalf of whole armies. They would do battle on your behalf because they were the best you had, and as a consequence everyone loved them for it. Well, foreign exchange dealers are the Hectors and Achilles' of today. They are the people you would put in the pit to trade with your life. If there's a nuclear disaster in India they make the call on the dollar instantly and someone on the team trades the Thai baht seconds later (when it's realized that with the prevailing winds, Thailand takes the fallout). If there's a war in the Gulf, if the balance of power changes in Iran or Russia, if the trains go on strike, if the weather's nasty. It all affects market sentiment, it all affects the zero-one call.

Sometimes, it's just pure hunch about market mood. There's a story of a Canadian-US dollar rate trader who went in to work one day and saw that his stars and stripes tie pin was on upside down. So he sold US dollars and went long on the Canadian currency, buying big in the futures and the bond market. He timed it just right. He made his name. He got himself an annual bonus roughly equivalent to the yearly output of a heavily industrialized African city of 40,000 people.

Ever had a 'How much would you have to be paid to ...?' kind of conversation? You know, the kind of thing that schoolchildren, college students and broken-down old hacks sometimes have in particularly inert moments of idleness? It starts off with how much you would have to be paid to escort for the evening/kiss/fuck the ugliest boy/girl in the building. The bidding starts at $10 million, and comes down Dutch-auction style to $1 million in seconds. And then the level of seriousness with which this profoundly metaphysical issue is addressed nosedives, until someone says they would give Satan a blow job for $5. To which the response is: 'Oh really? I'd pay to suck Satan's dick ...'

Putting a price on events in the outside world is just as fanciful, just as metaphysical. The inadequacy of money is well known. Any ambulance-chasing lawyer will tell you the current value of losing a limb in a car crash. There's a league table of the price of suffering (damages vary according to personal circumstance, but the price in the book is what you start from, as though your left leg was a second-hand Ford). Why do we find that kind of ascription of monetary value so absurd? Because of the inadequacy of money, and ultimately numbers, to describe the outside world. Numbers are a form of relational metaphor that are good for measuring, but not describing things. But there's a whole essay to be written on that thesis, and its investment ramifications (see Chapter XI).

The point to be made here is that foreign exchange dealers are brilliant at guessing what value the market will put on the most bizarre events. Instant synthesis, and out comes a number.

It's a mindset some people find very hard to escape from. I have a friend who works in the currency markets (actually, he's a bond trader, but he'll do). He didn't want to work in the markets, he wanted a real job, but now he sells bonds. And like most people he has looked great when the market has been surging up. His strategy for most of one year was to leave an open position, go to lunch with his jacket on his chair, come back four hours later, close his position out (in the market you don't just sell, or even close your position, you close it *out*), and go home a hero. Needless to say, he's good fun to talk to, but there are certain things about his manner that lay people, that is to say ordinary people with psyches uncontaminated by finance, find a little out of the usual. Apart from a strikingly competitive nature, it's noticeable that if you say something that he thinks is factually incorrect, he'll wave his palms at you and shout 'Yours!' to indicate he's not buying that proposition. The markets. They are a way of life, a language composed entirely of zeroes and ones – just like the information you hear as music on a compact disc, just like the images you see on computer screens.

Given that this consciousness has overtaken them, the question

'Are we having a good time?', that philosophically complex notion of the pursuit of happiness, becomes of primary importance for foreign exchange dealers. It becomes the most important one, against which any number of zeroes count for, well, nothing. Like everything else, happiness becomes a commodity that is translatable into numbers. Thus the dealer with a $1 million bonus is precisely half as happy as the dealer with a $2 million bonus. What is the difference between $50 million and $100 million? For most people, this is a speculative question. Give them either sum and they would find themselves catapulted into the perfect obscurity that only true wealth can bring. For a dealer the answer is instant, and important – $50 million. That's a lot of Ones.

The commodity-like nature of happiness has physical mani-festations, as opposed to the dangerous amalgam of mathematical purity and base greed that computing your net worth must bring. For example, am I having a good time if my nose is trashed with cocaine? Forget all that crap about its being a mistake to confuse pleasure with gratification of the senses, the answer is 'yes'. Am I having a good time if I am driving around in an expression of western cultural supremacy, a symbol of the hegemony of money and the internationalism of post-war capitalist society (roughly trans-lated as a bloody big German sports car)? Yes, yes, yes.

And what about those blow jobs in the car parks? Man is unusual among primates in that he copulates in private (as for fellatio, well, go see a zoologist if you want to know what the monkeys do). This makes it difficult to argue for a sexual act's being a status symbol, a concretized One in the pursuit of happiness. However, it conforms to the precepts of frenzied materialism in this respect – the consensus view of blow jobs is that it is better to receive than to give. Although a colleague recounts meeting a female fund manager who, despite his determined attempts to talk dollar-yen trades, informed him that the administering of the said oral and lingual caresses to the erect male member was 'a top quartile activity'. Like I said, The Market – it's a language, a whole life.

The prevailing narco-SL soft-top image of foreign exchange dealers has not helped their popularity. This is where the extension of Wolfe's astronaut/champion analogy falls down badly. We are never going to see a John Glenn-style ticker-tape parade for a dollar-yen trader. Although the image of the wildly enthused throng leaning from Madison Avenue windows shouting 'Seventy yards of yen! Go, go, go!' has a certain appeal, if only that of extreme improbability (a yard of yen, incidentally, is market slang for a billion yen).

You really aren't going to get very far if you try to explain to people in the real world that dealers suffer from burn-out, that they are often very insecure, that their lives have been completely invaded by a one-dimensional mathematical world, that they are victims too (ah, the magic word – the static politics of victimhood). Try explaining that cocaine and sports cars are in fact essential comforters that keep the dealers mollified ('happy' in their own terms), that these things stop the foreign exchanges fracturing completely into thousands of tiny, ultra-powerful, predatory boutiques, that coke and cars are absolutely necessary to facilitate free international currency exchange. Try explaining all that and you will most likely get a robust counter-argument to the effect that these are strange victims indeed, they who have German sports cars, and expensive, instant-good-time drugs, and huge salaries (sorry, compensation packages with big salaries and mind-rottingly large bonuses). Or again, try explaining all that and you might just get a well-merited punch on the nose.

A different tack would be to suggest that, despite every appearance to the contrary, we actually need the foreign exchanges – if only because they do such a good job of making politicians look foolish.

But there is a more serious point. If you concede that the free international exchange of capital is a good, or at least pretty much unavoidable thing (it clearly is if you believe at all in free trade), you've automatically got to have the foreign exchanges. If you have foreign exchanges, you've got to have dealers (still – despite the ever-encroaching computer-traded programme). And that leaves a price to be paid. Drugs, cars and the boisterous behaviour of the traders aside, because of its very nature the market is extremely difficult to regulate. Moreover, it's nearly impossible to draw the line between speculation and covering risk. Given the very public lack of com-prehension of the way these markets work displayed by lawyers and politicians, I, for one, object to the idea that foreign exchange dealers, ugly as they are, should have their heads cut off.

CHAPTER III

Bankers, Brokers, Advisers, Intermediaries: People Who Sell

People Who Sell. The polyvalency of the word 'sell' i) Meaning number one – noticing that the market lemming decked out in Vuarnet shades and a new pair of Reeboks is taking thirty million of his little chums for a clifftop jog. ii) Meaning number two – wielding the carrot-flavoured stick iii) Meaning number three – persuading people to buy, and the attendant problems, such as a) image b) hypocrisy, snobbery, myopic self-contradiction. The hierarchy of money – i) Salespeople ii) Grocery store-type advisers iii) Tied agents – or pushy bastards iv) Independent advisers v) Brokers – private client vi) Institutional brokers vii) Private bankers

People Who Sell

People Who Sell are the cocktail party hostesses of the capitalist system. They mediate a confusing, arcane world, a world where the individual has to make difficult, technically complex choices about investments, savings, insurance (car, accident and personal), mortgages, healthcare, and all the other necessary nastiness of modern bourgeois existence. People Who Sell take you by the hand and lead you up to something that you thought was just a mass of fine print so confusing that the very thought of reading all that dense, continuous prose makes you want to cry. But the People Who Sell explain that this thing called a twenty-five-year convertible term assurance is actually a product, and that the two of you ought really to hit it off. Stand close and you look great together. In fact, you should go out on a date, maybe even try a little indiscreet necking in the hallway.

Or something like that. What salespeople say often has the logical flow and internal rational strength of a cream cake – but this is a *necessary* irrational cream cake. Without that chatshow-host psychobabble where are you? Staring uncomfortably into the middle distance, wondering whether you brushed your teeth that morning with instant gravy powder, that's where. There's no doubt about it, People Who

Sell take away that uneasy feeling that you're missing out on something through your own lack of sophistication. They deserve to wear those sexy little black numbers called broker's or adviser's commission. Without them, you probably aren't going to buy your much-needed twenty-year permanent health plan with six-month time delay on medical certification of incapacitating illness, are you? People Who Sell are the catalysts of commerce for everyone from individuals of the humblest means through to the Sultan of Brunei. They provide the spark that enables individuals and companies to organize themselves and to do deals. Through the collective force of thousands of individual wills they harness the power that animates whole economies. They are the engine oil, the lubricants of capitalism, and yet, much of the time, they are not even lubricious.

OK, the drugs have worn off now. Suddenly it's clear that this issue of selling needs to be approached from a more conventional angle.

So: people who sell are generally treated, even among their own kind, with a mixture of fear, hatred and contempt. Think of selling as sex – something even Freud failed to do, which is quite an achievement when you think that he managed to equate the hand movements in a rubber (no pun intended) of bridge to masturbation. But sex *per se* is not the most, er, penetrative tool of analysis. It generates a bewildering variety of responses between partners, depending on such variables as gender, species, and brand of battery-operated appliance.

Right. So let's specify what kind of sex we're talking about, and then find a line of analysis.

Selling is sex of the ancient, Model T Ford variety – sex between a man and a woman. She is buying, in the missionary position, lying back and thinking of revolving credit facilities. Meanwhile he, our seller, is grinding away as hard as he can with his sad little partially defrosted grey prawn of a proposition, hoping to work it up into something worthwhile.

Now subject this scenario to radical feminist analysis. Give it the Andrea Dworkin treatment. Suggest that this apparently consensual act is really rape, albeit of the kind where the rapist buys a bottle of wine. Suddenly this boring, arid little coupling is an act of domination, an assertion of will and strength and supremacy. The seller is raping the buyer, forcing – perhaps subtly – the buyer to submit. And it is the act itself that the seller cares about, his own selfish, commission-engorged member predominates, the thrill of the sale becomes all. There is no after-sales service. The seller moves on to the next dastardly deed, and the poor buyer is left behind, hoping against hope that it was a good deal after all, and that maybe the seller will come back and say so. The buyer is a warm human being who likes to cuddle, who has needs; she wants constant reassurance, she wants to be told that if the sale was great for the seller, the buyer's bottom line moved.

But clearly this line of analysis isn't going to get us very far either, unless you already know what conclusions you want to come to. In which case, all salespeople are rapists. Case proven.

Unfortunately, however, the facts don't fit the nice, tight little theory. Why? Because the real world is bigger, messier, but actually not quite as nasty as that line of analysis.

Let's take the most heavily traded single stockmarket in the world as an example. The New York Stock Exchange (NYSE) is big. It is the largest of three national stockmarkets in the US, the others being Nasdaq, a computerized system, and the American Stock Exchange (AMEX). The NYSE used to be more than twice as big as the other two markets put together, but it has not grown as fast as they have in the early years of the '90s. So that in 1990 the NYSE accounted for some seventy-three per cent of the turnover, but as share trading has expanded the NYSE weighed in at something less than fifty per cent of total trades at the end of 1993. That's still a lot of money, mind you. Roughly seventy per cent of US gross domestic product – around $4 trillion, if you are astronomer enough to have a feeling for that kind of figure. Put it this way, the NYSE turns over in a year an unimaginably vast amount of money. OK, so it's no more than the foreign exchanges will do in three busy days, but it's still enormous. Enormously demotic, in fact. Households – that is, individual investors – account for fifty per cent of the market. In 1992, nearly 600 corporations came to the market to offer their shares and raise finance for the first time, expanding the universe of traded shares by more than $39 billion (yet another Very Big Figure, best explained, no doubt, by the number of Froot Loops it would take to embroider an edible suspension bridge to the Moon, or some other intangible idiocy). According to figures from the National Association of Securities Dealers, a kind of financial salespeople's trade association, more than 51 billion shares changed hands on the NYSE in 1992.

So who are the people who do all this buying and selling to service the requirements of the households of America, strengthen the capital base of corporations, and, of course, whet a little speculative appetite? The answer is obvious: everybody. You don't get exclusive clubs that big. There are about 500 firms of stockbrokers operating on the NYSE alone. Each of these has scores of employees called commission brokers, who will buy and sell on behalf of clients, or on behalf of their employer (or, if they are playing a dangerous game, on behalf of themselves). There are other kinds of people involved in the trade, who rejoice in job titles such as odd-lot dealers, floor brokers, registered traders etc. But the commission broker is by far the most common. There is also a computerized system called Superdot 250, which links investment firms all over the US. The people involved in this are numbered in the tens of thousands. Are they, all of them, every man and woman, metaphorical rapists just selling for the sake of the sale, screwing their clients for the fun of it? Is it all one vast, capitalist crime, one that the buyers don't complain about because of guilt, shame, and society's preference for believing the word of the oppressive seller? Well, if it is, that's a lot of metaphorical wine. Not to mention a tankerload of life-hating attitude.

But if the notion of benignity is probably not wholly alien to selling, why is it that the concept of salespeople as cocktail party hostesses should be so wrong? Or, as economists like to say, fundamentally flawed? There are two reasons.

The polyvalency of the word 'sell'
(i) Meaning number one – noticing that the market lemming decked out in Vuarnet shades and a new pair of Reeboks is taking thirty million of his little chums for a clifftop jog

The first is probably where a financial textbook would have started in the first place – the polyvalency of the word sell. To sell often really means to trade, or again it can mean to execute a sales transaction. These uses of the word are distinct from one another,

37

and each is different again from the sense in which people who sell are salespeople, and give life to that process of which we've all been part, yet which somehow makes us feel a little bit itchy.

Let's start with offside case number one, the executing of a sales transaction. There used to be a set of people who did nothing but execute buy and sell orders. Their era was the Bad Old Days before fixed commissions on share dealing in the US and the UK were scrapped. From the individual investor's point of view, buying shares in the British market is still pretty much rooted in the I-Pay-Through-The-Nose-Old-Days era, since virtually none of the savings have been passed on to the consumer.

Now what is it exactly that these people (broker-dealers in the US, market makers in the UK) do, exactly? Well they make markets (for once the British appellation is clear). That means they buy and sell large blocks of shares in, say, IBM. They hold these shares in their own name, and buy and sell for their own profit. In other words, if IBM is priced at $56 they (henceforth 'the executioners', if only to save much towing of the jargonistic pantechnicon truck around the verbal parking lot) will offer shares to would-be buyers at $57, and will sell it at $55. The difference between those prices is the executioners' spread, or profit. In the market for a share like IBM, which is one of the twenty biggest companies quoted on the US exchanges, there are hundreds and hundreds of firms making a market in the shares. That means there's plenty of competition for business, so the spread on these shares tends to be narrow. This makes obvious sense from the investor's point of view – if you have $10,000 to invest you want as many shares as possible for your money, after all. And a dollar on the spread means you would get two to three IBM shares fewer for your money. Naturally, you go for the best execution price in the market. The obverse side of this particular coin is that when a small company is traded, the market can be what is known as 'thin'. This means there are few executioners holding stock or offering prices on it, and so, to ensure they make money on deals in this stock, the executioners will often take a big fat spread that cuts into investors' profits and accentuates their losses.

Executioners are the first point of contact for that mysterious thing which is The Market. It is they who process the orders, who see the first cloud of dust from the stampeding herd of bison – or is it that they're the first ones to notice that the market lemming decked out in Vuarnet shades and a new pair of Reeboks is taking thirty million of his little chums for a clifftop jog? Anyway, they're as close to the raw power of The Market as you can get. They *are* The Market, they make The Market in a very real sense. They have one imperative – not to run out of shares to trade. It's their job always to be one step ahead of the market's demands – which can be a very difficult task.

It hurts to admit it, but executioners are necessary to the efficient functioning of The Market. Imagine the hassle of having to consult the shareholders' register of some company you wanted to invest in, then ring up the shareholder and offer a price. Once you had a tentative bargain you'd probably have to ring up three or four more times to make sure that you weren't ripping yourself off – that you were getting the market price. Conclusion – executioners are middle men, but they make things easier. They may even be worth the money.

They are certainly, by the way, the best and the worst sources for market information. Ask an executioner why a certain stock rose sharply during a session and the response will come back: 'More buyers than sellers'. So banal, so profoundly true. Life, as Chekhov said, is a carrot.

So selling as execution of a sale necessarily involves people who sell, but people who sell who are *necessary* are a little too clean and uninteresting to contribute worthwhile clues as to what it might be, this great mystery of the sale.

ii) Meaning number two – wielding the carrot-flavoured stick

Selling as a piece of trading is a different thing again. When a seller makes a play in the market this is a positive piece of financial strategy. Take, for example, the case of an investment bank that buys shares in a company its corporate analysts have identified as a takeover target. If a takeover actually occurs we can see the awesome power of the seller in the capitalist marketplace.

The process of identifying a takeover target usually occurs because the share price of a company is low. Let's stay with Chekhov and take the case of a company that makes carrot-flavoured sticks. The share price might be low because nobody is buying carrot-flavoured sticks any more. Maybe the public wants a simple product – a vegetarian meal or a good thrashing (this is not to say that consumers of vegetarian meals deserve a good thrashing, pleasing though such a notion may often be). Or it might be that the management of the company is incompetent, so incompetent, in fact, that the financial press has noticed. And – thrice crows the cock of ineptitude – the management is so dumb it hasn't even bribed the media with trinkets and free trips, and dark, clarinet-playing public relations ladies with soft voices and assassins' eyes.

So then the company gets written about and reported on, and the bid comes in. It will be from one of the company's commercial competitors if the market in vegetable armaments is better than the company's performance might suggest. Or it might be from a land company or a plain old asset stripper. Asset strippers, incidentally, always deny they are asset strippers. A good example would not be hard to find among the ranks of multinational corporations. The classic trick is to deny asset-stripper status, but use give-away phrases like 'finding efficiencies' in the companies taken over. Anyway, a cynical asset stripper will acquire a company, make promises about continuing employment and assert its respect for the great blue-collar tradition of vegan violence in whatever miserable area the company has its manufacturing base, get its feet comfortably under the managerial table, and then set about finding efficiencies. This usually involves sacking half the people on the payroll. The acquired company then quickly becomes the sum of its parts on disparate markets – stick factory sold for scrap or to a competitor, carrot-growing land sold to an agrarian conglomerate. The old story.

And the role of the investment bank in all this? Seller. Concerned for the welfare of the company, taking a keen interest in the industrial base of a country that is justly proud of its ability to produce things you suck on while they cause pain, the investment bank will sell to whomsoever will do the right thing by the employees, the company and the country. Of course, if the investment bank is, say, American, and the company is in, say, Greece ... Well, the banker may just have to take a broader view than that of absurd nationalism. There will be a perceived need to help in shaping the world economy, to stimulate companies to produce things people actually want, etc, etc. The broader view is, however, frequently somewhat obscured by the vast short-term concern that looms in the foreground, namely profit. If money talks, the seller, from its position of power in the take-over battle, listens to the loudest voice.

Hardly the tyranny of the weak, is it? Especially when you consider what it is that often spurs investment banks to take a position (all right, the bank simply buys shares, but taking a position is the correct, slinkily powerful, market-wise kind of thing to say in these situations). The bank will often buy when it has just advised the company, perhaps as to the weakness of its position in a weak market, perhaps to offer help in raising extra money from the stock market. And if the bank then lets it be known, perhaps through leaks to the financial press, that the company is badly run, has an uninteresting, run-down product range – well it's almost a guarantee that the bank will make money on its investment, isn't it? Again, if an investment bank is spreading rumours there's little the management of the company can do to stop it in a market that thrives on the whisper. Which explains why just the two layers of managerial incompetence suffice to get a company taken over and make investment banks rich. It also explains why very few financial journalists are to be found in expensive restaurants with dusky press officers finding flimsy excuses to dive under the table to practise their clarinet-playing techniques.

You could argue that selling in this instance is really buying the idea. But that – Heaven forfend – would just be playing with words. No, there is a substantive difference here: the bank isn't just selling, it is trading. It is getting best value for having bought.

So trading is selling or buying, but selling isn't trading. Selling is a broader concept than trading. The word 'sell' can be used in the context of a bank trading a company's shares, in which case we know who is bending over for whose benefit.

iii) Meaning number three – persuading people to buy

So perhaps People Who Sell are really rather ordinary after all – neither knife-wielding (nor even wine-buying) rapists, nor social butterflies. Yet there remains something about selling things that sticks in the collective craw. Bear in mind that the selling we are dealing with here is neither trading nor the execution of sales. It is this mysterious thing that salespeople do. It is persuading people to buy. So where's the problem?

It is tempting to explain away the whole set of complexes people have about selling as an image problem, something which is immediately apparent and on the surface of things if you have an ounce of acuity. Happily enough, there are other reasons which are much seamier than image problems. Snobbery, hypocrisy, myopic self-contradiction, and – of course – the Ugly Raccoon Fuck all play a part. As well as selling's deep, secret heart of darkness, a secret that would have sent Joseph Conrad back to sea. Let's deal with them in order.

a) Image

Image is the alpha and omega of the selling business, yet the defining word 'sell' pushes the wrong buttons in the financial community. It carries more than a hint of ugliness around with it. Extraordinary, but true. Having got rid of the ambiguities in selling by the classic politician's device of alluding to them and then ignoring them, we come upon an ambivalence that cannot be explained away. Selling and the ability to sell are loved and loathed at the same time. How can it be that one of the fundaments of the financial universe, the sale, has this inbuilt fracturing of emotional response?

Well, look at the social evidence that tells us there's something not nice here. To call someone a good salesman is very much a double-edged compliment. To call someone a salesman's salesman, even more so. Think of the contrast with the unalloyed acclaim in the sporting world when athletes are accorded the title of 'Players' Player of the Year'. Yet to talk about a salesman's salesman definitely offers more than a hint of brickbat with the bouquet. There's no doubt about it: in a world of soft and obvious targets, the salesman is a marshmallow barn door.

This attitude is a combination of Victorian prudery and small-scale hypocrisy, the life-giving Vitamin H. It stems from the fact that – don't laugh – some salespeople are too honest. People who sell make a pitch on a product or a service, and they present whatever is being sold in the best possible light. The problem is twofold. First, they are too frank. They admit that, for the product or service they have just sold, there are other interpretations available than that accepted by the buyer. People hate this, especially if it is done in a self-congratulatory manner. Why? Because the salesperson is talking about work – something considered boring in many cultures – or perhaps it's just evidence of an unappetizing smugness, or again it may be because people recognize the false light of self-congratulation in their own lives all too clearly when they see it in others.

The second problem is more fundamental, and has a hint of moral rectitude about it. It is commonly felt that image alone is not enough, that a salesperson who deals in images deals in superficiality, and that this corresponds to something which is 'wrong' in some vague, communal moral universe (for communal moral universe read seething mass of irreconcilable prejudices) suspended out there in the ether. There is a strong gut feeling that people shouldn't be persuaded to buy things they don't want, even if they are too plain stupid to realize that what they are buying is good for them. Or bad for them. David Mamet puts his finger on the throbbing pulse of poison in the salesman's veins in *Glengarry, Glenross* when one of his characters cackles that his gift for the sale is so extraordinary, why he could sell people *cancer*.

This second objection has some merit to it. Although everyone is touched by marketing images and their apparently profound associative influence, no-one is supposed to buy just because of the clever image. At least in theory. The practical application of theory, however, creates all sorts of complications.

Let's start with the easy stuff. It's clear that only a cretin would buy a can of peas on the strength of the pretty photograph labelled 'serving suggestion'. This is an image which presents a somewhat idealized representation of the product, but will be more or less accurate as to what you will get when you open the can. Consumers attuned to this kind of heightened realism will make a comparative judgment based hardly at all on the prettiness of the label. More important criteria will be whether the various brands taste good, the price, etc. It's equally clear that some images have almost nothing to do with what the buyer is being asked to pay for, and are purely there to create a good 'feel' for the product or service. This is particularly the case in some sales cultures – if not, there's a vast, unnoticed white slave trade in naked French women (whose nudity is apparently deemed a useful 'serving suggestion' for an entire spectrum of products – from sanitary towels to heat-seeking missiles – but whose purchasability is non-existent, at least in hard currency western economies). The tricky bit is in the middle, where packaging and image are vitally important to the product. In the luxury goods sector this is so vital that some managements argue that packaging and image are part of the product itself. That reasoning makes sense, of a kind, of cosmetics companies' fondness for wrapping four dewdrops of scent in vast, day-glo banana boxes. If it looks good, it is good. The form is the content, the medium is the message.

The notion of image as product is perhaps best exemplified in the advertising industry. When companies employ an advertising agency they may be doing so for all kinds of subjective reasons. The management of the company might think it is simply trying to boost its turnover, that the advertisers will just help them to sell their own product by providing an imagistic sales tool. This, from the management's point of view, may be true. But the advertising agency sees it a different way. The company is going shopping for an image, an image that the agency will provide and sell to the company's management. So it's not surprising that the industry which offers image as product has produced some of the very best specimens of pure salesmanship.

Take the example of British Rail and the advertising account it awarded in the early 1980s.

At the time of this story British Rail (henceforward BR), the state-owned national rail system scheduled for dismemberment and return to the private sector, occupies a special place in the hearts and minds of the British people.

Special, but unpleasant. In the UK public's mind, BR is synonymous with laziness, inefficiency, uncaring incompetence and downright aggressive rudeness on a fabulously huge, positively gargantuan scale. Think of those foreign exchange turnover numbers, think of the number of atoms in the observable universe (around 10 to the power of 47), think of the number of possible variations in a game of chess (10 to the power of 110 – a genuinely silly number). Now add them all together, and double them. Add a few more zeroes if you're bored. Next, quantify the annoyance and irritation you feel if you miss a train or a shuttle plane or find yourself standing yet again in the slowest moving line at the post office. If each of those little moments of *ennui* counts as one unit of anger, boredom, rage and frustration, then that, multiplied by the earlier figure, is roughly how the British public perceives the mighty BR in the early 1980s. To say that BR stands for a wet brown ring on the psychic underwear of Britain is to insult the average wet fart, especially when you consider that wet farts have the common decency not to make you pay for the pleasure of inconveniencing you.

But the era of market worship is dawning. Already visionaries – or lunatics, depending on your political stance – think that BR should be slimmed down (shed jobs, junk rural services), toughened up (hire managers who enjoy firing people) and made ready to greet the new era in public transport (sold for a massive discount to the private sector). None of this can be said in the early 1980s, partly because the British are insanely proud of their national monument to decay and waste, and partly because it would be very difficult to find buyers for a wet fart at any price. BR is still a standing (not to mention all too frequently stationary) joke. It has become part of the national sense of humour.

The tardiness and unreliability of its service and the surly, uncommunicative incompetence of the staff are deeply entrenched in the public consciousness, but even less dearly cherished. So much so that, years later, under the revolutionary new policy of actually telling passengers why they aren't getting to where they want to be (a small but significant step along the really revolutionary path of actually getting them there) BR made a contribution to the English language. It once told the press that its trains weren't running because of a snowfall. BR had been expecting snow, but the type that fell was 'the wrong type'. 'The wrong type of snow' is now shorthand for ineptitude and laziness.

Anyway, things aren't too hot for BR in the 1980s, and the new management wants to spruce up the service. It also wants to persuade the consumer that – irrespective of any putative improvements – things aren't really that bad. Hence the visit to the advertising agency.

BR management arrives late, huddled together in a group of three (somewhat like its train service, but enough of that). At first they think they are in the wrong office. The reception area is completely unlike anything they expect from a front-line international advertising agency. Instead of the usual antiseptic post-modern nonsenses and soft, high-tech blister lighting, the place is an ill-designed mess. The lighting is harsh, the colours of the jumbled, ill-assorted furniture silently shriek mutual hostility at one another. And the place is, frankly, filthy. There are smeared hand prints on the wall. And in the corner there ... Isn't that ...? Could it be shit? Is it? If so, is it canine or human? To make matters worse, the receptionist is not exactly standard advertising agency issue either. You expect one of those women with tits like racing dogs straining at the leash, nipples pointing at the corners of the ceiling of every room she walks into, chocolate-box hair, gypsy-girl eyes and mail-order-underwear-catalogue demureness, but this one is different. She speaks in a barely intelligible cockney accent, appears not to have washed her hair for a month. She stubs her cigarette out in the overflowing plastic cup she is using for an ashtray, and picks up the phone as one of the BR team steps up to ask for the agency contact. It is a personal call, but clearly important enough to her to keep the BR guys waiting. She holds up a grubbily imperious palm as they fume in front of her. Eventually she finishes the call, takes their names with the enthusiasm you'd expect of a Persian quinquereme galley slave settling in for a day's oarsmanship, glances perfunctorily down a scribbled list and informs them that their names don't appear. Eventually, she corrects herself, but says that the agency executive will be late. No idea how long he'll be, no idea why he's late. She waves a hand in the general direction of the agency waiting room, and says they can sit there, if they feel like it. Coffee? Unfortunately the vending machine is out of order. The phone goes, and she starts on another personal call. The BR team is furious, and when it sees that the waiting area resembles a dog toilet even more closely than what they've seen already, they decide, as one, that they will leave there and then. They will never come back.

At which point, with perfect timing, enter the agency director. Immaculate in one of those suits that everyone else will be wearing five years later, he intercepts them at the exit. And he explains that he just wants them to see the kind of problem they are dealing with. Because the actress on reception and the carefully orchestrated filth, inefficiency and discourtesy they have just experienced are exactly how their research tells them that the public perceives BR. And those feelings of contempt and anger are pretty much what any image consultant will have to combat, divert and ultimately turn round.

The agency got the account. (I offer a deliberately skewed, exaggerated version of events. But why should I let the facts spoil the tale, and bear in mind we are talking about advertising here. What's the industry going to do, complain that I'm not telling the *truth?*)

But this is the exception rather than the rule. The BR team bought because it recognized a seller who had understood its needs and centred its presentation on them in a clever and creative way. No problem with the use of image in selling there, especially because image was the product.

b) Hypocrisy, snobbery, myopic self-contradiction

There is, however, another factor. Bravery. The selling process here didn't just demonstrate sensitivity, it was also honest about the most difficult thing of all to be honest to a buyer about – namely, how other people see the buyer. Of course, there was good business sense in this. After BR accepted its lowly standing with its public, it could hardly complain that its popularity wasn't soaring after a few TV commercials, could it? So this sale is extraordinary on two counts – for the completeness with which it demonstrates that image is a product, and for the absence of the usual hypocritical process of telling the client what it wants to hear, just to get a signature.

The stigma attached to selling exists for a complex set of partially raccoon-related reasons, but whatever the cause of all this negativity one consequence automatically flows from all this: those who are best at selling don't admit to doing it. Just as people who are geniuses at manipulating others are never clumsy enough to be called manipulative, so those who are the best at selling aren't called salesmen. And out of this hypocrisy, snobbery is born. Although everyone does it, those up at the top of the scale, the ones who sell millions of securities at a go, don't have to admit it.

There is, lamentably enough, a similarity between the unmitigated, feudal shabbiness of what the British call class, and the way financial markets operate. The markets are indeed classless, but they are also intensely hierarchical. And your position in the hierarchy depends on how much money you make. So money, as ever, equals respectability. A person who sells millions of dollars' worth of shares to a big pension fund is an institutional broker advising a client: a person who sells a life policy to an old lady is an insurance rep selling to a customer. The broker visits the bathroom. The rep takes a shit – one you can smell from here.

The hierarchy of money

The names change hue as you climb up the ladder of capital transactions, away from the latrine door. Pusher to hawker, hawker to pedlar, pedlar to salesman, salesman to broker, broker to adviser, adviser to consultant banker. They are all on the same rung of the evolutionary ladder – about three up from the amoeba. The difference is that the consultant banker is taking enough money from his client to persuade him that he is doing him a favour. The buying side of the equation has a similar cast: Junkie-John-punter-customer-client-private client-Your Worshipful Imperial Highness. All of which epithets are shorthand for 'Thanks for the cheque, but I'd prefer cash'.

So Willy Loman, Adnan Kashoggi and the head of a Swiss private bank are all basically the same creature. But those at the top end of this putative scale – the private bankers and stockbrokers – would rather die than admit it. However, the purpose of this book is expositional and descriptive, as opposed to expository and pre-scriptive. In other words, even though it might seem something of a soft option, it makes sense to go through the accepted scale of respectability. Just remember that these are basically the same animal with different markings. Let's start at the bottom and work our way up.

This type of 'bottom-up' analytical approach has been less than popular in recent years, since it actually requires analysts to do research, by visiting the companies in which they invest. This is irritating for those who prefer to take a 'top-down' approach – which mainly involves reading the papers (and blaming the media for the inaccuracy of its reporting) and scanning the latest pieces of gen-eralized, over-synthesized pieces of nonsense passing as research and published by entities like the Organization for Economic Co-Operation and Development.

Oh, and we'll take in the Ugly Raccoon Fuck along the way – for no extra charge.

i) Salespeople

Nowadays, the job title of 'sales representative' is essentially a standing invitation to slam the door on the encyclopaedia salesman's foot, put the receiver down on the Bible salesgirl in mid-spiel, and generally to start frothing at the mouth, screaming 'Fuck off, you stench hound' very, very loudly.

No, the invasion by clever marketing diction of late twentieth-century society has changed the whole semantic set-up in selling. If you are a sales rep, you're a wielder of the verbal blow torch, an applier of pressure, a cajoler, a pesterer, a nuisance. You're just one job away from living on the streets – which is similar work, really. Where you unsuccessfully try to grab people's attention all the time, and are told to fuck off a great deal. In this kind of sales job you're probably spending a lot of your time on the streets anyway, not making sales and not getting laid by housewives who don't want your double-glazing, your house cladding, or your overpriced insurance policies. You *are* Willy Loman, and probably better off dead – at least until you get yourself promoted and can send your own *gauleiter* brownshirts out to fight on the streets.

ii) Grocery store-type advisers

Now we are approaching the respectable. Advice is appropriately tangential to the idea of persuasion. And here, even in its humblest form, it allows the buyer the fiction that he is making up his own mind.

Bank managers, for example, typically know absolutely nothing about risk investments (a concept which arguably embraces all investments, but can be taken to mean products that leave your money exposed to the occasionally violent swings of the stock and, perhaps, bond markets). But they don't sell you these things. They offer you the product, the Thai Smaller Underdeveloped Companies

Mutual Fund which head office has informed them is readily available at its figurative financial warehouse, and which needs to be shipped out in bulk through the distribution system of bank branches on the street. If the bank manager can unload enough of these highly speculative products that he doesn't understand, can't explain, and can't even remember the name of without looking at the promotional material, he will win the in-house sales incentive trip to Bermuda for himself and his terminally bored wife. So the bank managers and the branch managers of insurance offices give you the brochure and settle back to watch, like some paunchy burgher allowing you to browse through his suburban store. These things are on offer. It's up to you to buy or not.

'Adviser' is a catch-all term for the very bottom end of this shopkeepers' echelon of selling. Bank managers and people who work for insurance companies are known as 'tied' advisers. This means that they can only advise you on services provided by their employers. In fact, the legislation in place prohibits them from even talking to you about funds and insurance policies offered by other companies. There are some other strange rules about what can be said, which mean that the buyer has virtually no idea what, if anything, the tied salesperson is going to get out of the deal (i.e. how much of the buyer's money will come directly to the adviser). This process is referred to, with the killing sense of irony for which the financial services industry is justly famed, as 'disclosure'.

iii) Tied agents – or pushy bastards

But the financial services industry is nothing if not adaptable. The lack of a real requirement to tell the buyer anything worthwhile about charges was a clear sales advantage, the narrowness of the buyer's choice less obviously so. But it has been turned into one by hard work and clever planning. What they couldn't offer in terms of choice tied agents made up for through intensive preparation, clever sales spiel invented to highlight the specific products they were entitled to sell, and teamwork. This produced a sales phenomenon perhaps beyond its best days – the tied agent factory farm.

Probably the definitive example of this was the merging of the sales team known as the Porchester group and the insurance company called Merchant Investors. They created an entity known in the retail investment world as MI, and they took offices based in one of the better parts of West London. The operation is now owned by CitiBank, but the good ship MI taking the high seas of salesmanship was an awesome sight to behold.

It is the late 1980s. Hundreds of fresh-faced young men and women are wearing suits of almost exactly the same colour. Focused across the tiny spectrum of tone between cinder grey and midnight black, each is an interpretation of the colour of contemporary power. These interpretative artists sit at desks arrayed across a vast, open-plan area, occupying an entire floor of the capacious office building. Hanging in the air is the subdued clamour of serious commerce. Smoked glass, chrome burnishing, bitumen-coloured plastic screens – apart from forty per cent wool in the business suiting, there isn't a natural fibre in sight.

Some of the MI crew are hitting the phones (you don't make a phone call, you hit the phones. If you're good, you punch your body weight.) Others have enticed 'prospects' into the building. The prospects are potential buyers whose names have been obtained from family, friends, or reluctant potential buyers who, in a desperate attempt to avoid a fourth or fifth bout of telephonic high-pressure sales torture, have opened their address books and betrayed their friends.

These people who sell are hard at work. Some of them are at different stages, but they are all following the same sales cycle. Make the contact ('Hi! JC! I'm a friend of Judas. He gave me your number and said I should call ...'), turn the contact into a prospect, get the prospect to come into the office, and convert the prospect into a sale. It is vital that the prospects come into the office for three reasons. There is the tiresome legal framework which gives the individual all sorts of rights, including the right to change his mind later, if a contract is signed in his home. Then again, it's much more efficient in terms of time (and therefore money) if the salesperson can stay in the office while the prospects waste their own time travelling. And last and most important, there's the vast, psychological stun-punch to the abdomen of doing business in a huge temple of selling.

To say the atmosphere of the MI office has been artfully

constructed is to understate the case. This is a three-Michelin-star restaurant for salespeople – an environment where nothing is left to chance. No, better (sorry, worse) than that, it is a two-star restaurant which is obsessively seeking its third star, the magic symbol which will open the portals of culinary/sales Nirvana. Every prospect is treated like a demi-god. You pick your nose and they nod appreciatively. Someone breaks wind and they pretend it's a witty musical reference. F sharp, how droll. So it's all seriousness, purposeful activity, deal-doing for the masses in liveried black and white.

The prospects look about them wide-eyed at the sleek whirrings of this particular capitalist machine. They are appreciative but unsure. Think of those cows in the abattoir, drugged for slaughter, pinned upside down to the moving rail that leads them to the rotating knives. For the first time in their lives they hear Mozart, the composer whom abattoir owners have discovered most consoles and comforts the distressed beasts. Think of that and you have the picture. (It is, by the way, a picture which somewhat confounds that Christmas cracker epithet propounded over many a Parisian dinner table '*le silence après le Mozart, c'est le Mozart*'. Not if you're a slaughterhouse cow it's not. The silence after Mozart, *c'est le filet mignon.*)

Anyway, this huge MI factory floor of besuited automata represents the process of persuasion pitched almost to the level of hypnosis. The soft warbling of disparate telephones, the understated certainty of the salespeople, the almost-uniform of the greys and the charcoals and the blacks. These are the worker ants of financial services, intent, as they say, on making their clients rich, on spreading the benefits of capitalism that little bit further.

And then somebody signs, a prospect is converted. A little group forms around the table. Other worker ants have come over to ask the converted prospect what he has signed for, to slap the convert on the back and say what a good deal he has done, how he is going to be rich one day. The salesperson is congratulated too – for his services to humanity. He is a virtual certainty for the next Nobel prize in personal finance. The little ripple of good feeling and approval spreads outwards across the factory floor. Other salespeople see it and try that little bit harder to persuade their hesitant prospects that the benefits of capitalism can be had through the simple expedients of hard work and paying large commissions to tied sales agents. The other prospects see the little flurry of hand-shaking and congratulation around the converted prospect, and suddenly they want it too. They want that approval, they want to do something which is good for themselves and will make them liked and lauded by these serious, attentive, obviously well-meaning people.

Occasionally, of course, it doesn't happen like that. Sometimes you get a stray financial journalist who comes in and points at the stick figures on the wall chart of the sales team's names and asks why they're chalked up there, like hunters' trophies or victims on the nosecones of World War II fighters. The journalist makes snide accusations that the selling philosophy is little better than brainwashing. The journalist asks if it's true that the salespeople, on days when no prospects are allowed into the office, stand on chairs to talk to difficult prospects, so as to produce a sense of mastery and psychological domination. The journalist doesn't believe that the MI product is a particularly good one from the consumer's point of view because research in investment journals, which compare the long-term performance of these products, reveals a very average return for the investor. The journalist creates his own little ripple, but this time it isn't one of approval. The journalist is asked why he is so hostile, and, when he explains that he doesn't believe a word of the sales spiel and he finds it an insult to his admittedly quite meagre intelligence, he is surrounded by large numbers of the team. And the frightening truth is that some of the team really believe that they are liberating the world through the sale of extremely expensive financial products. Poor bastards.

Much of the technique of selling is psychological, although most of it does not belong to the conversion/concentration-camp school of sales. Basic points, according to conventional sales wisdom, include positive body language (whatever that is) and generally being positive about things (another reason to dislike what selling things does to people – give me the company of a surly bastard any time). For example, even when dealing with a blatantly hostile contact like our journalist, the salesperson makes a point of taking him to the exit and – instead of doing the sensible thing and throwing him through the smoked glass revolving door – shaking his hand firmly, and making eye contact. Although this may not do too much for the salesperson's general air of positivism, since the journalist can then take the opportunity of underlining the point that he *really* thinks the salesperson is a piece of shit.

Even companies with solid, established reputations such as the Norwich Union, a vast concern that has been in business for over a hundred years with several billion dollars under management, and is generally well thought of apart from the occasional administrative mess, even the Norwich Union has produced some embarrassing pieces of nonsense with its tied sales force. Some six hundred tied Norwich Union agents had to be 're-trained' because they had been advising investors to do strange things such as cash in existing policies (not usually a good idea, see below) and take out lovely shining new Norwich Union policies. Very naughty. But no doubt all explicable as just over-enthusiasm on the part of the tied salespeople.

Although the embarrassments do keep coming in this area. The entire tied sales force (more than a thousand people) of the insurance arm of Barclays was suspended by the British regulators because of inadequate training and supervision. And – surprise – compliance shortcomings. Shortly afterwards SIB, the top UK regulatory body, issued a paper highly critical of the entire UK industry's selling practices. Use of confusing language in sales documents and failing to make clear how much a product would actually cost were the chief causes of concern.

On the whole, you are well advised to get rid of the pushy person who sells. To do this effectively there is nothing quite like genuine rudeness. But if you have time and the inclination, it can be quite fun to play them at their own game and deploy a few terrorist tactics. After all, they started the psychological war.

One of the pushy bastard's standard tactics is to ask bullshit questions in rapid succession. What's your favourite colour? Body of water? Animal? Your answers are supposed to reflect, say, what you think of yourself, your attitude to sex, how you would like others to see you. This way they think they are getting to know you – and (yawn) knowledge is power. When dealing with questions like this tactical rule number one must be to lie (of course). But the strategic objective is to unsettle and terrify the idiotic jerks. Make them think they're trying to sell overpriced crap to the antichrist, the nemesis of the twentieth century with the ethics of a Jimmy Swaggart or a Jim Bakker, the searing intellect of a Dan Quayle or a Sinead O'Connor, the tolerance and flexibility of Eugene Terre-Blanche, the warmth and wit of a separatist feminist, and the respect for human dignity of Adolf Hitler.

So don't say 'yellow, duck pond, and, er, koala bear'. Say 'magenta and shocking pink stripes cross-hatched with snot green, that water you get when you burst a blister, and ... oh, let's see, a stiletto-heeled pterodactyl in fishnet stockings, Chicago Bear linebacker shirt, barbed-wire nipple clamps and one of those luminous violet strap-on dildoes welded, unicorn-like, to the forehead'.

If that doesn't work, ask the adviser if he's discovered Jesus yet.

iv) Independent advisers

It would be grossly unfair (and fun) to say that all tied advisers are pushy bastards. The prosaic truth is that most aren't, but some are. The fact that they can't even talk about other companies' products is a real disadvantage. And many people, at the time of the implementation of the new laws, saw that tied agents had had their tongues ripped out and so decided that dialogue with a different kind of adviser might be more rewarding. The alternative was and is an 'independent' adviser, who can talk about any product on the market (and is obliged to consider all products in an attempt to find the best one for the buyer).

Some large and noble institutions are classified as independent advisers. The Bradford & Bingley Building Society, for example, is a major UK building society – the broad equivalent of a savings and loan institution, but without the greed and the grift. One benefit for its hundreds of thousands of home-loan borrowers is that they get a wider choice of savings plans and life policies, which are standard collateral in addition to the property in backing a UK home loan. The Bradford & Bingley is an unincorporated 'mutual' society that doesn't even officially make a profit but a 'surplus' to be applied for the benefit of its savers and borrowers who together constitute the society.

Unfortunately, independent advisers such as the B&B are rare indeed. Most independent advisers are autonomous businesses with just a few offices. This means they are either a) undercapitalized, very small and very greedy (in which case you have just a chance of getting some honest advice) or b) undercapitalized, very small and absolutely desperate (in which case you've no chance whatever). The key point to remember when dealing with creatures calling themselves independent financial advisers is that unless they sell you something they don't eat. That's because they make nearly all their money from commissions. So if you talk to an independent financial adviser, or rather if you let one talk at you, there's a near-certainty that the adviser will conclude that you need to buy one or several of those alarmingly titled products introduced to you by the cocktail party hostess. Because buried beneath that dense prose is a business structure which dictates that the person who sells the policy gets a nice fat commission from the company which provides them.

The product names, by the way, are deliberately mystifying. They give the adviser something to explain, they add an impressive, if counterfeit, authority and grandeur to what is basically a very simple job, namely helping people to save money, and occasionally to borrow it. This deliberate obfuscation of what should be a straightforward process has two other benefits for advisers. First, it allows them to operate pretty much unchecked by popular criticism. Naturally, the names provide a hermetically sealed barrier to public understanding of what the advisers are doing. This would normally be a disadvantage for the publicity-shy, it being an unwritten rule that a complete lack of public comprehension of any matter in art, politics or sport is a necessary pre-condition for the frenzied, ill-informed polemic which passes for public debate. No, these names do something else. True, a title like Convertible Term Maximum Capital Allocation Unitized Insurance Bond will certainly keep the Great Unwashed Public in its rightful place of complete ignorance, but it goes further. The clever bit is that these names confuse and, above all, *bore* the public. So the fat sweaty bald guy with the laptop may not get laid a lot, but he will probably get to take home a good salary. Why? The real reason is simple – because he can bear the grindingly dull necessity of having to decode the idiotic names that insurance and mutual fund companies choose as embellishments for an already somewhat unlovely industry.

The notion that financial advisers as a class are not just jerks but could jerk for the Northern Hemisphere was briefly challenged in 1993 with the newspaper publication of those famous topless shots of the Duchess of York. She was, you will remember, poolside, having her toes, among other things, sucked by her ... financial adviser. For a fleeting moment, financial advisers were almost sexy.

But sexiness is somewhat beside the point here. Commission is the vital diagnostic tool if you really want to know whether an adviser is any good or not.

In the UK, there is a distinction between financial advisers which bears directly on the kind of advice they are allowed to offer, and the amount of information they have to disclose. If advisers are classified as independent, they are obliged by the Financial Services Act 1986 to give 'best advice'. If you think that sounds like a ridiculous counsel of perfection, you are not alone. Who is to judge what 'best' is at any one time? What happens if the adviser, having read the words of so-called experts in newspapers and investment-house circulars, likes the look of Japan? He then puts the investor into a Japanese-invested mutual fund, and Tokyo stocks promptly plummet? There are hundreds of similar arguments to decry the idea that offering 'best' advice is possible or even practicable. But the intention at least is laudable – namely that independent advisers should shoot for the moon, and try to find the very best product across all the market for the happy recipient of their advice. There is a standard procedure to be gone through to facilitate a better kind of advice. The investor has to be interviewed and personal details and financial requirements ascertained. This interview is called, unhappily enough, a 'fact-find'. And then the entire market is surveyed, and a product selected. But not all products pay the same commission. So the investor is entitled to know, and indeed should ask, how much the adviser is making from each product. That way, the informed, reasonable – and undoubtedly objective – analysis of the adviser is subjected to the X-ray vision of pure financial analysis. Investors will have an extra layer of insight into the machine-gun burst of praise on the investment track record of one mutual fund or insurance company as opposed to others in the market. So what if this company pays fifteen per cent more commission than that one? This may just be one of those rare and happy coincidences between optimism and profit. Maybe.

It is sad but true that the accepted benchmark break-even point in the UK financial services industry is two years for a life policy-linked savings plan. The translation in English of all that is that it usually takes around two years of monthly saving before the investor is clear of all the commissions paid to the adviser. Of course, the saver doesn't see that when the savings plan comes to fruition ten years or more after inception. There is a fine piece of financial tightrope-walking performed by strange quasi-warlocks called actuaries, many of whom are professional mathematicians. It involves contingencies and escrow accounts, using which it can be shown that your money has been working for you all the time. But the inescapable fact is that if you cash in one of the life policy savings plans in the first couple of years you'll see very little of your money back. US investors are much better served in this area. SEC regulation requires that prospective buyers of investment plans be given hypothetical redemption values in the early years of their investment assuming a modest rate of capital growth.

The whole business of using a life policy as a savings medium is a typical piece of financial services fiction. It usually means that the investor pays money into what is supposedly a life insurance policy, but the insurance company's liability to pay out is limited to the value of the investor's contribution to a mutual fund (a pool of individuals' money lumped together for economies of scale and spread widely across (usually) a stock market or markets to lower the riskiness of the investment). Sometimes, so that they can pretend to the taxman that there really is an element of life cover, the insurance companies offer cover of the value of the contributions to the fund, plus one per cent.

So here's the key question. If all you get is the value of your contributions to the fund, why bother with a life policy at all? The answer has definite overtones of Marxism – history. There used to be some apparently good tax reasons to invest in life policies, but the tax incentive to invest in life insurance plans was abolished in 1984. Not that that made much difference to the individual investor anyway, since the advisers and the insurance companies made sure that they ate all the tax benefits up in commissions.

This part of the industry teems with custom-designed grandiloquence, the unsubtle verbal equivalent of ring-fencing the Johannesburg villa with razor-barbed wire and little signs saying 'No Blacks' (for 'black' read 'person kept in ignorance and exploited' or, more simply, 'buyer'). But no *tour d'horizon* would be complete without an examination of two old favourites which have convinced many a doubtful buyer – Maximum Allocation Units, and Capital Allocation Units. These phrases can mean whatever the companies putting together the savings plans want them to mean, but there is a common usage which lumps them together as part of the same incredibly gauche con-trick. The idea is to persuade the buyer that he is being credited with *more money than he is actually paying in*. Typically, one of these units will be credited to your account at 105, 106 or even 107 per cent of value received! Of course this is transparent nonsense, you say, reading it on the page. You laugh lightly, you titter at the feeble-mindedness of those who can't tell a high-pressure timeshare salesman from a phantom free prize automobile (if you sign the hundred-year lease now). But if certain types of salespeople get hold of you they can tell you any number of even bigger nonsenses.

A classic is the favourable interest rate climate that allows companies to benefit from positive cash flow (getting in lots of money instead of paying it out). The company passes on some of that benefit to its investors – and the result is jam for all. What they omit to tell you is that these magical units are the value allocated to the fund after your money has gone through that oh-so-necessary life policy (with its own set of charges and rake-offs, initial and annual). And then of course there's the little matter of the difference between the buy and sell value of the units. Buy and sell values (known as bid and offer prices) come into the equation when pooled investment funds operate in the second of the two currently fashionable ways.

Method one is broadly less fashionable, no doubt because it offers less scope for disingenuity. To reduce this method to the crudest of oversimplifications, the fund managers calculate the value of the assets they hold, divide this figure in proportion to the contributions made by the investors, and publish something known as a net asset value. From the investor's point of view this works beautifully. You invested $500 at a net asset value (NAV) of $2.50 five years ago, and through the undiluted genius of the fund managers (it's amazing how many geniuses there are when the markets are rising) the NAV has risen to $3.75. That means your investment has a value of $750. Simple. It works. Great. Not so great for those who run the funds, who want to make as much money as they can as quietly as they can possibly manage. Their problem is that using an NAV makes it easy for the investor to work out what he is losing in charges (a high percentage of which will go to an introducing independent adviser). So if the managers charge five per cent initially (this, incredibly, is the norm in Europe, though not in the US, where investors are more cost-conscious) the investor can work out how much he is paying. Clearly, this is most unsatisfactory for the fund managers and the advisers and insurance companies who bring them much of their business.

Enter into the lists system number two, which works on the basis of a bid-offer spread. The principle is that you buy a stake in the fund at a high price, but your stake is automatically valued at a lower one when you want to realize what you hope is a pleasant capital gain. The great advantage of the system is semantic gimmickry. The words 'spread' and 'bid price' are a lot more digestible than 'charge', a lot easier to sell to the buyers. So let's go back to our Maximum Allocation Unit which promises that 105 per cent of the bid value of the units in the underlying investment fund will be allocated to investors. The sums go something like this for $1,000 invested. Investment into a life policy – charge 1.5 per cent initially, 0.5 per cent annually. If the annual fee is taken in advance, that leaves $980 going through the life policy into the investment fund. Assume the bid-offer spread is seven per cent (i.e. only 93 per cent of the money is realizable when the investor wants his money back). So the bid value of the investor's cash is $911.40. And it is this lower figure which is subjected to the powerful magic of the 105 per cent factor. Thus the investor's cash is worth $956.70 – and the investor has only paid 4.33 per cent in charges. Clearly, not such a magnificent deal. Then again, maybe not such a blatant rip-off if the managers are good, and the fund does well.

But how many investors are going to understand that what happens to their money is a systematic trashing by the guys with the soft lead coshes, and that they are getting an extra five per cent of what has already been beaten up to the tune of more than 8.5 per cent?

Here, then, is further readily understandable cause for unease with the persuasive aspects of selling. The process is beginning to resemble a work of cheap fiction – what matters is the impression created, forget the reliability of the facts. Aside from dissimulation and pseudo-psychoanalysis, advisers have another cheap trick that does their reputation no good. This is, incredibly enough, moral pressure.

Many sales routines developed around exerting moral pressure on individuals who are reluctant to take out life insurance. Let's take one of them and nail it to a tree, shall we?

LACPAC is a systematic process whereby through asking a series of closed-ended questions, the salesperson draws the buyer into the logical cul-de-sac that unless the buyer takes out life cover the buyer is neglecting his/her family. And if the buyer still refuses to sign, the salesperson closes the latches of the (hopefully expensive) briefcase with a contemptuous snap and makes to walk off, saying that if the buyer is the kind of person who doesn't want to cater for the interests of his/her family after his/her death, then he/she is simply not worth knowing. The salesperson walks off in mock disgust before offering the buyer just one more opportunity of moral redemption in this world. Apparently, it works quite well. But which person do you think is probably less worth knowing?

v) Brokers – private client

Brokers sell shares. Here we meet once more the flimsy semantic barrier with which the selling process tries to defend itself. Brokers might protest that they broke shares. They do lots of research – at least they say they do – into lots of companies, and then they pick the ones that they like and let their clients know of the wonderful investment opportunities available. Which means they want to sell the client some shares.

This selling is done in a number of ways. The most important factor in determining how the selling is done is the identity of the client. Here, it's helpful to look at the crude dichotomy between the rich and the ultra-rich client. For practical purposes, ultra-rich clients are the professional investors, the vast American, Dutch and British pension funds. Individuals do feature, but the vast majority of ultra-rich money is institutional.

Let's start by slumming it with the poor old rich. Already we are breathing a sweeter air than that polluted by some ruthless, manipulative creature cajoling a white-haired old lady into investing for the long term. We are dealing with private clients, people who drive expensive cars – the antidote to all sympathy. We think for some crazy reason that if they have a turbo-charged Bentley then they must be better equipped to make decisions about the prospects of the Taiwanese semi-conductor company that the brokerage is touting in its circular.

Circulars, by the way, act as basic back-up sales material and crib sheets for the broking team. The brokerage will collate its analysts' views and publish them with lots of pretty graphics illustrating the argument of the analyst for that company – historical stock pricing, the ratio of the stock's price to its yield, the stock's price against the price of the general market, or companies with similar commercial activities. To make things simple there will be a recommendation against each stock – buy (probably for stocks not featured before), sell or hold (necessarily for stocks featured in earlier circulars). The circulars act as crib sheets for the broker whose client calls up wanting a view on a stock that the broker may know nothing about. And they act as a sales aid, because the broker can ring up special clients – and every client every broker has is a special client when the broker is on the line – and make a recommendation. The classic spiel is that the investment house's view on stock X is such-and-such, and the circular is going out into the market very soon. Of course, its pithy argument will sway market perception, and the share will probably rise if you're in early enough. And guess what, dear special client? You're in ahead of the game. Why not buy?

And then, sale made, the broker moves on to special client number 42.

You don't have to be a broker for many decades before you realize that there's a measure of personal and corporate wealth to be made here. After all, brokers are entitled to have their own accounts, and investment houses continue to take positions in companies to which they act as brokers (when acting as investment banks on the other side of a Chinese Wall fiercely guarded by the deaf, blind and toothless in-house compliance officer).

Incidentally, while the circular may move the market because of its learned and authoritative discourse on semi-conductors in Taiwan and rubber manufacture in Venezuela, it is comforting to know that the authors will almost certainly never have worked in the industries on which they comment, and many of them (especially if the analytical style is 'top-down') will not even have visited the company and asked the management searching questions about, say, the kind of wine the broker can expect to be served over lunch in the boardroom.

But the important point is that these circulars can affect the stock prices of the companies about which they pretend to know something. The investor's question must be: What is the real meaning of the circular, given that the person advising the client is also making money for himself?

One famous instance was a brokers' circular that smelled the rats in Maxwell's empire. But, fearful of the fat man's wrath and his litigious tendencies, the circular put out an apparently neutral comment on the company that made dramatic sense if you like acronyms – 'Can't Recommend A Purchase' was the verdict.

Beyond that, circulars in general have a special language that needs decoding. 'Sell' means either a) that the stock is a sick old dog, probably recommended a long time ago by a different investment team, and now it's time to fess up and say 'OK, let's all stop eating turkey' or b) it's already done quite well, we've already shorted it. And it always, always means c) we want the commission. Because brokers make a little turn whether their clients buy or sell. 'Hold' is pretty unequivocal. It usually means that an earlier recommendation is plainly wrong, the stock has fallen, but the brokerage is doggedly clinging on to what's left of its pride. And 'Buy' is the easiest to decode of all. It means 'we've just bought some'. It has to. Think of the quasi-insider opportunity the brokers are offering their clients – 'get in on this recommendation before the rest of the market'. But if it's the brokerage's recommendation in the first place, it's asking a lot of profit-oriented people to restrain themselves from filling their boots first, now, isn't it? Actually, it's asking them to be ethical and honest and to follow, at the very least, the strict set of house rules that every brokerage seems to like to talk about when issues like this come to prominence. But buying and then letting your clients lead the price up for you happens all the time. Sad, but inevitably true. You really do have to look very carefully at what's being said and sold to the buyer – alias the private client. Buy? Sell? Put both on hold.

vi) Institutional brokers

With institutional broking we are approaching the very top end of the market, the part where the salesman is invariably better dressed than the client. Here, no-one sells. What happens is the dispensation of pure advice, i.e. selling in its purest, subtlest form. The buyer is getting advice like a skilled magician gives the stooge from the audience free choice of playing card – whatever happens the stooge chooses the four of clubs, and all of them are hammering the corporate bank account.

Spy on the process without the benefit of a long-range hearing device, and what you see is a low-key conversation in which that nice, quiet, well-dressed man does marginally more of the talking. What the buyer might be getting is a mild-mannered child abductor whose big turn-on in life is offering fund managers' investment strategies a packet of sweeties and the opportunity to climb into his turbo-charged Audi Quattro and stroke his non-existent pet rabbit. If the managers decide they want him to drive into a remote field and play doctors and nurses, despite the fact he's frothing at the mouth and drivelling on about nothing in a language that is a cross between algebra and esperanto, that's their problem. It is they, apparently, who want this to happen. It's their choice, they're just taking his advice on what to do with someone else's money.

The institutional broker selling to his client is a financial version of a Hollywood meeting (as though all Hollywood meetings weren't financial). All right, eavesdropping on the broker-trustee meeting might not quite live up to a Kim Basinger/Uma Thurman Bel Air love tryst. Agreed. Come the day you're filling in your dating agency form, putting down 'Occupation – pension fund trustee' may not automatically set off the jaguars' love calls in your averagely verdant delta of Venus. Agreed. But trustees and the fund managers they use to spend their money for them are pretty damn sexy if you're a broker.

Take the case of a relatively small part of the UK, bearing in mind that the British industry is dwarfed by its US counterpart. The figures are already sexy (i.e. big). Scottish pension and mutual funds, according to statistics from Scottish Financial Enterprise, an investment industry group, had more than $1.1 trillion under management at the end of 1993. Fixed commissions were abolished in May 1975 in the United States and in October 1986 in Britain. That means that the client who is advised – the punter who buys the shares – can negotiate the commission down. The more money the buyer has, the lower the percentage. But even 0.1 of a percentage point on a significant purchase of say $100 million runs out at $100,000 for just one transaction.

Already the distant but frenzied cries of mating jaguars are audible in the background ...

So let's spy on the paradigmatic example of brokers dispensing advice, the perfect financial sales pitch. This is perhaps best evinced in the UK when the American broker meets the Scottish fund manager or – on the unlikely assumption that the broker can get near enough – pension fund trustee. The broker will almost certainly be meeting a fund manager, because pension fund trustees have so much money under their control, and are burdened by such onerous fiduciary duties, that they find themselves with an entourage of consultants (as tangible evidence of complying with the duty to exercise 'due diligence' in their administration of assets) and fund managers (officially labelled 'experts' in investment, and as such apparently fit to manage the trustees' money). Brokers, being people who sell, are kept out of their presence. If the trustee sounds like a fairytale princess, constantly chaperoned and surrounded by syco-phantic courtiers, that's probably fair enough. So a meeting between a trustee and a broker would be like the poor fisher boy getting his leg over the lovely, golden-haired Princess Miranda without having to pay the usual forfeit of being pulled apart by wild horses. There will be more of Princess Miranda and her travelling boudoir later. For the moment let's content ourselves with the broker and his fund manager, perched as they are at the top of the financial food chain.

Before we go and sit at their table, let's start with a few basics. Naturally enough, the American broker isn't a broker and he isn't American. The people who run American brokerages are not stupid. They recognize what's needed to make a sale, and what's needed when dealing with a Scottish pension fund manager isn't usually an American. And he certainly isn't going to use a crude cover name like 'broker'. Nor even marketing director. Investment strategist or director contains enough apparent substance to satisfy most trustees or fund managers.

The problem for American firms selling in Scotland isn't lingusitic, despite George Bernard Shaw's one worthwhile joke. It isn't even cultural. It's temporal. You see, Scottish pension fund managers, if they're enlightened, live in the late eighteenth century (most are fairly enlightened, the really primitive ones go south to make a living in the media as professional purveyors of caricature Scottishness). These managers have a vast amount of money under their control, thanks to a long tradition of thrift and clever acquisitions and, above all, hard work. They are direct descendants of a time when the word industry simultaneously had both a macro-economic and an intensely personal impact. Individual industry produced a thriving industrial society – and great trading and financial companies arose as a consequence: Jardine Matheson, the Asian trader and multi-national; Robert Fleming, a tobacco merchant prince, whose name now graces a bank; the great Scottish thrift societies, founded on a principle of communality of spirit, shared benefit, the safe keeping of hard-won gain. The Scottish financial community is the sole true remnant of the economic majesty of the British Empire, discounting, of course, such minor imbecilities as the British presence in the Falkland Islands and Northern Ireland. All in all, what our American broker is dealing with is a lot of money that subscribes to the preposterous fiction that it has been purely acquired.

So the American brokerage sends along what the Scottish pension fund trustee wants to see – a fresh-faced young man with good manners, a good degree from a good university, and an appropriately adoring attitude to the Protestant work ethic.

Let's have lunch with them.

They are eating in the Caledonian Hotel at the nether end of Princes Street in Edinburgh. Georgian beauty and rolling grey cloudbank swell in through the windows. The waitress, an inexperienced teenage wage-slave, brings their drinks. The trustee is a big man, a bison in a chain-store pin-stripe. He reaches for a glass of whisky, which he takes with water. He nods.

Our broker works for one of the big 'name' American houses. His employer may be Salomon Brothers, Goldman Sachs, or Morgan Stanley – one of the very biggest firms, each of which imagines that it has a 'style', sometimes referred to without a trace of irony as a 'culture', vitally different from the rest. He is on the cusp of thirty, fifteen years younger than his luncheon guest, and much, much better dressed. Without, of course, being flamboyant. Cufflinks with clever designs and little sparkly stones in them would not do. Our broker has played some totally unimportant sport – field hockey would be ideal – to a very high standard, and represented British Universities at the game. This is a good thing to be modest about. He can consistently fail to mention his sporting history and so gain a reputation for a much-prized Caledonian virtue, modesty. He is English. This has three advantages. First, he cannot be quite so easily judged by his client. While the English class system engenders much nastiness, Scotland has its own culture of pathetic judgmentalism based on religion. Advantage number two is that on some level, the client acknowledges that he has the broker in his thrall. This is part of the selling process called advice on asset allocation, or spreading risk, or diversification. But basically, there are rites of obeisance to be gone through before the client will agree to buy, and it feels good to have a fine young member of the English establishment perform those rituals. This is not because the Scots dislike the English. It is because they have a vast, unstinting, metaphysical grudge against them. The third advantage the broker has is that he's English – all he has to do is smile and keep his mouth shut.

And he will, if he wants the commission on $100 million worth of high-yielding Telefonica shares. Just like he isn't going to be talking too much about his $400,000 bonus if he makes his $400 million turnover target that year. The manager who places the buy order and makes this boy-man so rich would disapprove; he would think it immoral that the broker should earn so much. Not just because the ceiling of permissibility is conveniently positioned just above what the manager is earning. No, the real reason is the nature of the broker's job. It's somehow wrong that he should be so richly rewarded for doing ... What, exactly?

This is the deep, dark secret that is the sale. The two are murmuring together like monks in prayer. What is being said? They are taking it in turns to smile and nod. What is the mystical Act of Sale?

Those of you who found Conrad's *Heart of Darkness* a bit of an anti-climax will probably have guessed already. The horror is the vacuum in culture, the notion that the supposedly 'barbarous' and the 'civilized' are the same. It is not just that they are interchangeable, nor is it that they have equal value (a shocking enough notion in its time. Conrad was way ahead of the multi-cultural game.) No, the terrible I-never-saw-it-coming horror was their identity, in the quasi-mathematical sense of identity of value. They were the same thing. And this is the secret of the successful person who sells. Our stockbroker isn't talking finance at all. Dividend yields and price-earnings ratios are not spilling out of his mouth like stale biscuit crumbs. All our broker is doing is being pleasant, cultivating the manager's trust. It's all about the continuity and credibility of their relationship. It's simply a friendship where the parties give and take, buy and sell one another their ideas. The only difference from normal friendships is that one party occasionally gives the other multi-million-dollar-trade orders, and so makes him extremely wealthy. Ah, the horror! The horror!

vii) Private bankers

Private bankers have succeeded where Euclid and a host of hack theologians failed.

How big is the tiniest point imaginable? Imaginary, said Euclid. You have to imagine it has no physical mass whatever. Otherwise it spoils the theoretical basis of his geometry. How many angels can you get on a pinhead? This one produced innumerable idiotic answers from theologians of a low enough cast of mind to concern themselves with the question.

Next in the pinprick file is the following question. Which, of all the thousands in the financial universe, is the single cleverest, best and safest institution to invest with? 'Mine,' says the private banker, and, if the client agrees, the question is satisfactorily answered. If, as Metternich argued, truth is that which is confidently asserted and plausibly maintained, the answer will even be true. Metternich, with his desire for achieving his goals with the minimum of ostentation, would have made an excellent private banker. But any private banker, no matter how humdrum, will tell his client with professionally honed certainty that the client has been wise or lucky enough to come to the snow-tipped apex of financial services wisdom. There is only one Everest peak and, incredibly, the client has managed to force his millions up there, without even the aid of a Sherpa.

So what is it that private bankers do? What is it that they are selling? Their great cleverness is reflected in the fact that the answers to these questions aren't really known. Some would say that the answers aren't even knowable. In most cases, individual clients will be more or less aware of what is happening to their millions, but private bankers like to stress the personal nature of their business, how they analyse each individual's wealth, how they plan custom-made investment strategies. Consequently, any attempt to build up a picture of what private bankers do from a succession of almost impossible-to-obtain case histories would be, at best, casuistic. That's shoddy, inaccurate and incurably partial, by any other string of epithets.

That said, this is what they do. They take your money and do two things which are at the opposite ends of the limited spectrum of financial possibilities. First, they keep it safe. Second, they make it grow. These two objectives are in fundamental opposition to one another, since there really is no such thing as profit without risk. But that's what they aim to do – as do just about all other managers and advisers. The key difference is that private bankers take your money and don't really tell you, and certainly not anyone else, what they're doing with it. This self-appointed licence to do whatever they want is called discretion.

'We are like the stewards entrusted with the Talents in the biblical parable,' said one private banker, taking the habitual guise of Mr Unquotable of Zurich. 'Only God knows who the good stewards are.'

So what is the consequence of this somewhat unusual – in that it is virtually non-existent – accounting and reporting system? Are consumers seeking out transparency, looking for advisers and institutions that actually account regularly, openly and clearly for what is happening to the money in their custody? Just the opposite. According to what are, admittedly, best-guess statistics (but aren't they all?) private bankers have some $16 trillion in their coffers. But given that we are talking about discretion (i.e. pathological secretiveness) this figure is even less reliable than most. One thing is clear, however. No-one with less than $5 million of liquid, immediately investable cash should apply (there are many banks who will take less, but you aren't getting much more than a glorified mutual fund advice service for that kind of money). And the extraordinary thing is that there is a long line of people queuing up to give their money to God, the private banker. This is marketing genius. These are People Who Sell at their most exquisite.

Not only that, but – as you must have suspected – private bankers are the undisputed masters of the Ugly Raccoon Fuck.

The Ugly Raccoon Fuck is, simply, stiffing the buyer. It is the point where persuasion completely overreaches substance, where the illusion that the seller is purveying good and worthwhile things to the buyer can no longer be sustained. The image is widely known. A raccoon goes out clubbing and scores. It allows itself to be dragged back to a strange raccoon's for drunken sex and temporary oblivion. And then it wakes up the next morning, and – the horror, the horror (of a different sort) – sees what its partner looks like. It has to leave at all costs before the still sleeping Ugly Raccoon wakes up. But there's a technical problem. The first raccoon's arm is trapped under the Ugly Raccoon's head. To move the head will waken the ugly partner. Rather than face that, the raccoon gnaws its own arm off and runs away leaving it under the pillow – just as raccoons in the wild do when trapped.

The applications are obvious for the seller who has overstepped the mark. Too much selling, too little value, and you have an angry buyer, a buyer who wants explanations, who feels cheated that the seller abused the trust in their relationship to sell the buyer worthless crap. The defining moment arrives when the seller refuses to acknowledge the buyer. Rather than lose face and admit that the client has bought junk, the seller no longer takes the buyer's calls. The seller denies any relationship with the buyer. It is, to borrow a phrase from Woody Allen (a man who appears to know something about power in relationships) worse than a dog-eat-dog world, it's a dog-does-not-return-other-dog's-phone-call world.

Sadly, it happens all the time. It happens with little old ladies buying plastic items from suitcases, it happens with brokers' private clients all too frequently – in a moment of boredom, a broker will pick up the phone and get rid of something that's been kicking around on the books for a while, or it may be that the broker just feels like selling something, anything. It happens less often with institutional clients because a) there's more money to be made from only selling the good stuff and b) the institutional world is vast in monetary terms but has few inhabitants. Any broker unloading a truckload of turkeys on a client will soon find real poultry farming among a remarkably narrow range of career options.

But how can private banking, the apogee of smartness in selling, where the bankers emphasize the importance of the personal relationship, how can this possibly be the home ground of the definitive client disappointment?

You just have to remember that private banking is a triumph for reverse marketing. The real private banks are concerned with their images only in the negative sense. What pleases them most is the idea that they don't in fact have an image, that no-one really knows about them. They want the private bank to exist only as the hushed name whispered by one rich person into another rich person's ear, only as balances against numbered accounts, only as impassive Swiss faces silently receiving suitcases full of cash, only as a coded entry in God's cash ledger.

That anti-image extends to the client relationship. All clients are told that they are special. The services sometimes are. They can range from arranging billion-lire loans in a single working day, to checking the work of the domestic staff in each of a client's dozen villas around the world, to arranging a touching, discreet little birthday party for a client's illegitimate daughter. But the clients are not special, nor are the relationships. What's special is the money. So the client, the buyer, is stiffed because he thinks he's buying a relationship, and what he's getting is an attentive service shrouded in secrecy. The private banker's Ugly Raccoon Fuck is the definitive version because the banker comes supplied with a whole sackful of false arms to stick under the pillow. Every time the client walks out of the Geneva office he ceases to exist, although he can keep coming back for another session of reassurance and another false arm to wake up to. The private banker, at the top of the tree of selling, never lets the client know how he's perceived. Compare that with the advertising agency pitch to its rail company client and you begin to see what an outrageous compliment and risk it is to let a buyer know how others see him. Set against the private banker, the advertising agency looks positively benign. Which just goes to show that you *can* do anything if you have enough money.

CHAPTER IV

Banks – Ivory Towers in Transition

'Our banking system grew by accident; and whenever something happens by accident, it becomes a religion,' – Walter Wriston, ex-chairman of Citibank, quoted in *Business Week*, 20 January 1975

'What is robbing a bank compared with founding a bank?' – Bertolt Brecht, *The Threepenny Opera*

In search of an identity. Banks and self-transformative emptiness – why saying 'bank' is like hitting people with peas. History as an irrelevant factor in the content of banking practice, but a vital part of banking form (alias the bullshit that you pay for). The non-institutional nature of banking offices. One immutable banking tradition – gratuitous sex. Why central bankers aren't bankers at all. Retail bankers – storekeepers in cheap suits. Custodian bankers – so boring, other bankers think they're dull. Commercial bankers. Investment and merchant bankers. Insider deals. How to find a chainsaw when insider dealers claim to be trees in a rain forest. Why insider trading really is a crime. Non-bank bankers. Rock star or mutant snail? – The ultimate banking question. Bankers as cultural imperialists – how Tom Wolfe got it right without really knowing why.

In search of an identity. Banks and self-transformative emptiness – why saying 'bank' is like hitting people with peas

The terms 'bank' and 'banking' are almost lost to us. Once upon a time, before vegetarian dog food had even been invented, these were easily identifiable terms. A banker was someone you went to see if you wanted money. All right, he was someone who would only lend it to you if you could prove that you didn't need it, but you knew what he was there for. A banker would look into the viability of your project, investigate the value of your house, assess you as a person, weigh all the factors in the balance, and say 'no'. A bank was the imposing, stony palace, the intimidating cathedral of money, the emporium of minor humiliations in which the banker worked.

Nowadays, things are a little more complex. Which is to say that the term 'bank' is almost completely devoid of meaning. As a generic usage, calling something a bank is about as useful as calling a massage parlour, a funeral home and a twenty-four-hour liquor outlet by the umbrella term 'store'.

So what are banks? The answer to that question today lies exclusively in what they do with their own or, if they can possibly organize it that way, other people's, capital. There are the occasional, rather pathetic claims to an identity centred on banks being institutions – solid and unchanging both in their physical home, and in their business activities. Again, there are those banks who say that they have a style, a distinctively graceful way of doing what the others do ordinarily, and that this marks them out.

All of which is specious nonsense. Today's financial markets are vast, semi-rational mixtures of forces radiant with life – capital reacting to rumour, mathematical trading models, central bank interest-rate decisions, triple witching hour statistics, tighter or looser monetary policies, marginal propensity to consume (alias the feel-good, spend-more factor) to name just a few. And these forces all act together to produce little bumps and hollows in the credit, mortgage, deposit, foreign exchange, interest rate swap, current account, mutual fund, household insurance, thirty-year T-bond markets. Banks are creatures of the gigantic, febrile markets which are their environment. They live in a world of semi-tangible mathematical force fields, they are creatures of the vector drives of capitalism. Banks are functions of profit, a study in financial motion. They can be defined – like vector forces – solely in terms of their strength and their direction.

If mathematical analogy doesn't set you humming, think of banks as vast killer sharks, but with chameleon tendencies. They swim along – and they have to swim, because it's a choice between swimming and dying for sharks – and they are quite content in their thermal current or their trail of pheromones. And then they scent an opportunity for profit – which is swiftly acquired and devoured. Here the chameleon takes over. As soon as the shark eats a baby squid and bites on that ink sac, it changes colour and becomes black itself. Similarly, by acquiring a mutual fund or an insurance company, the bank changes its identity, and becomes a financial services supermarket. If it sets up a capital markets division to trade in bonds or swap commodity, share or interest rate contracts, it becomes an investment house. If it does good business as an acquisition and merger specialist it becomes an investment bank, king of the hostile bid scene. If it forms an alliance with an insurance company to pool office networks and sell savings plans at high street branches you end up with a hybrid entity that the French call *bancassurance*.

The thing acquired *is* the bank's identity, until it sells that acquisition or hives off a division of its business for a nice meaty profit and swims along with its new, slim-line profile to bite off and digest another chunk of the financial world. So, in fact, banks are not so much chameleons, which merely change colour, but something even more malleable – banks are gigantic icons of self-transformative emptiness. They are little more than brand names. Banks are empty, profit-seeking containers that take on the form of the thing contained.

Which offers us a linguistic nicety, an unusual kind of inverse metonymy. Current idiom typically names the container for the thing contained. It is, for example, more common to talk about the kettle boiling than to say the water in the kettle is boiling. Inverse metonymy, on the other hand, names the thing contained for the container. In most cases, this produces nonsense. To ask someone to plug in the water, for example, just because you've filled a kettle, is utter gibberish.

When you say 'bank' (meaning investment house or financial services group, depending on the latest business developed or acquired) you are, metaphorically (more precisely, metonymically) speaking, hitting people with peas.

To elucidate. Modern banking has made a generous donation to an arcane niche of the English language previously explored only by pioneers like the American humorist James Thurber. Thurber produced a fine example of inverse metonymy: Wife, angrily, to husband, as she picks up a can of peas: 'I'm going to hit you with the peas.' Again, more prosaically, if a decanter is filled with port, you ask someone to pass the port, not the decanter filled with port.

History as an irrelevant factor in the content of banking practice, but a vital part of banking form (alias the bullshit that you pay for)

This underscores the point that for the agglomeration of money-making businesses that call themselves banks, change is all. Their identities turn on financial evolution and self-transformation towards ever-bigger profit. For banks, to do is to be. Now is all, and history is bunk, an irrelevant factor in the content of banking practice.

But if the content of banking practice is self-defining, history is relevant – indeed vital – to the *form* of banking. Why is it that we, the consumers, give banks our money? It's for historical reasons only – a bank is a bank is an entity that we've always revered and paid good money to. Part of the reason for this is legal history. The second, more interestingly, is that we have for too long believed what we have been told. Even if we know so much of the banking aura is just bullshit, it's bullshit that historically we appear to like and have been prepared to pay for.

The appellation 'bank' is legalistic – a legal and semantic technicality of almost no importance. Typically, an entity will be referred to as a bank if the organism at the centre of the seething mass of financial protein is licensed by a country's central bank, and keeps a small percentage of its assets on deposit as a 'reserve'. There are also some rudimentary stipulations as to 'liquidity' – central banks want to see plenty of cash flushing through the system, and expect the banks they license to have a range of deposit accounts, etc, on offer. Of this, more later.

The essential point, however, is the store analogy. To be called a bank means that part of the group of businesses transacts its affairs on premises licensed by the government's bank, the central bank. Once upon a time when banks did more or less the same things – lending money, offering clever ideas on how corporations could restructure their finances or raise money – it was just about possible to guess what sort of activity something calling itself a bank might be engaged in. But deregulation has changed all that. The situation in financial services is essentially that everyone is chasing after profit, and will buy and sell businesses to make the most money possible. Modern banking is basically opportunism with lots of capital backing. And, to reiterate, the more the capital backing is OPM – Other People's Money – the happier the bankers will be. The result has been such a wide diffusion of activities – drawn together only by the common thread of profitability – that if a corporate grouping is called a bank, it is merely an accident of history.

But by far the most interesting aspect of history in banking is the fact that bankers themselves constantly lay claim to it. A sense of history feeds false notions of a continuity beyond the profit motive, creates a bogus aura of permanence, perhaps seduces the foolish into believing that 'old money' (very much a bankers' phrase) is to be respected. In other words, history is relevant to banking since many bankers like to use it as a prop for their vanities and pomposities. A well-manicured finger pointed in the direction of History justifies the banker's claim to be part of an 'institution', or to have a mysterious identity drawn from 'corporate culture' – the latter concept being another fine addition to the large and growing collection of late twentieth-century oxymorons.

The notion of bank as institution has several interpretations. The first concerns the physical entity, the building, which used to be a necessary implication of using the word institution. An institution used to be something instantly locatable, with a significant physical presence – an institute. This sense of institutional is much diminished, for good reason. The second version of bank as institution is figurative. It is the idea of the banking industry and bankers as part of a financial and social elite. The essence of institutionality here is the historical continuity bankers claim for their work. Thus, even though they may like to be thought of as financial pioneers, bankers will say that they are really following in the fine entrepreneurial tradition of some founding father or other. This, it is frequently imagined, imbues their work with an historic dignity and also masks the truly impressive streak of avarice that runs through this heterogeneous group of financial buskers.

So let's look at the idea of bank as institution in both senses, starting with the place of business.

The non-institutional nature of banking offices

Forget the fine buildings that used to constitute a bank's traditional home and be concrete evidence of its standing as an institution. A combination of the surge in western property prices and the short-term, profit-obsessed mentality of the west's banks has taken care of all that. The steep rise in property values in the 1980s was at first welcomed, but then became an increasing embarrassment to bankers as their auditors insisted on marking up the value of their offices. The problem is clear. If the board of a bank can't depress the balance-sheet value of its prestigious building, shareholders are apt to ask what benefit they are getting from this expensive chunk of stone. If the board can't show some immediate benefit the building has an honorary classification as a 'non-performing asset'. This means something that the bank is stuck with, but which doesn't do it any good. For example, loans to people who can't or won't pay are classified as non-performing assets. Another good example of a non-performing asset would be the many billions of dollars' worth of junk bonds that the US thrift institutions were stuck with in the late 1980s. That was a non-performing asset carnival to make New Orleans during Mardi Gras look like a collection of Cistercian monks at prayer. Estimates vary, even now, but some put the total cost to the US taxpayer at $500 billion.

Anyway, the banks decided that the clever thing to do with their buildings, seeing that they had become such big items on their balance sheets, would be to sell them. The profit-seeking mentality has its own logic – realize the capital value (i.e. get money), boost capital reserves (put the money on deposit), and reduce outgoings through judicious relocation (rent cheaper office space).

But this attitude is confined to western banks. In Japan – specifically Tokyo – property values are, despite a little softness in the early years of the 1990s, breathtakingly high. And they have been that way for decades. For example, in the 1970s the Australian government reportedly sold off its embassy and repaid its national debt. Again, depending on the dollar/yen rate and the fluctuations of the two property markets in their various currencies, it has been estimated that the value of the Emperor's Palace and grounds is roughly equivalent to what it would cost to buy California, the entire State of California, the one in America. Really.

Naturally enough these prices create problems for ordinary Japanese families, some of whom like the idea of owning the place they live in. So the white-coated boffins of the financial world got their heads down and invented the one-hundred-year mortgage – it was only through the device of having a fantastically long term that repayment levels could be fixed within the range of working people. This means that the person buying a house takes on not just a lifetime's debt, but commits three entire generations of the family to paying monthly mortgage bills. All so that the family may eventually own a tiny apartment. Property is expensive in Japan.

So you might expect that the Japanese banks have all sold up so as to manicure their balance sheets. Not so. The Japanese obsession is with control and power rather than profit, which is important but comes a poor third in the pecking order. If you ever have lunch in a Japanese bank's boardroom ask what the building – which the bank invariably owns – is worth, and you are treated as an amusing westerner. Ho, ho, the western mind asking its strange, abstruse impractical questions. It is inevitably very difficult to get an answer. This is partly because of the extreme vulgarity of discussing figures with a Japanese banker, especially if you are talking about his workplace (he spends most of his life there, so it's like home). But the real reason you won't get an answer is because these experts in asset evaluation and collateral credit risk analysis (finding out whether a property is good backing for a loan), these geniuses of capital manipulation *don't even know* what their own building is worth. Why? Because it's a purely abstract, theoretical question to put to pragmatic people. The stark and simple truth is that they have never considered moving, nor are they likely to do so. So the hypothetical value of the building is of precious little relevance.

Plus there are the imperatives of Japanese business culture, which centres on power and control of the market. The idea is to dominate through gaining market share, and then, once control has been established, to push prices up and create healthy profit margins. This basic thinking has proven successful through the range of Japanese exports to the western world. It started with radios, and moved up through stereos and videos to cars. Now, having made their billions, the Japanese are exporting their capital. Or perhaps they are returning the west's capital – if you've looked at Japan's current account trade surplus (the figure that tells you how many more billions of dollars' worth of goods are exported than are imported) recently, it is difficult not to see it that way. In any event, the latest Japanese export to the west is capital, which comes to us through the banks.

But a vital difference between western and Japanese business culture is the primacy of control over profitability. And if it is vital to the mainstream businesses such as car and electronic goods manufacturers, it is absolutely vital to the ultra-conservative banks. And the first thing they control is their own environment. Which means that buildings are owned. The homes of Japan's banks are physically quite big, stupendously expensive Tokyo tower blocks.

Their presence, physical and financial, makes them monuments to the pride and power of capitalism, eastern style. That the offices of a Japanese bank, a major institution, should be rented is utterly inconceivable. Renting is an activity associated with sexually frustrated single people who, thanks to the prohibitive cost of Tokyo property, find themselves in their late twenties and still living with their parents. The result is that, for obvious reasons, they rent rooms by the hour in places known as 'love houses'. No, no, renting is not something a Japanese bank would do.

Western banks, however, have no such problems. At least, they have no worries about their status being diminished through renting. Whether their employees like it is another matter. When the London arm of US bank Morgan Stanley relocated from central London to a vast, unremittingly unpleasant office block in Canary Wharf miles to the east, there was much distress. Many of Morgan Stanley's employees hate the place, not least because a large number of them have smart addresses fifteen miles to the west (this is the commuter's equivalent of a trans-Siberian trek, thanks to London's ancient and rotting transportation system). The building itself is unexceptionable. Its interior conforms to the distorted notions of banking normality – high-tech dealing rooms, lots of smoked glass, space-age technologies and insanely incongruous and anachronistic dining rooms of heavily varnished portraits and antique furniture. But these little cocoons of nineteenth-century culture are the only physical concessions to tradition, or the idea that a bank should be an institution with an aura of gravitas. The fact is that the place is rented, and this underlines perfectly the transience of modern banking. Just as western banks move from business to business, from market to market, by thinking on their feet and constantly changing, so their places of business reek of impermanence. The Morgan Stanley London office is a paradigm of modern banking – many outer layers of turbo-charged technology dedicated to movement and change, with a tiny inner core of bogus stillness. Stillness does not exist in the modern banking world. At the eye of every financial storm is a banker with a wind machine.

One immutable banking tradition – gratuitous sex

Some traditions, however, have proved immutable, and are indeed perfectly intact. Chief among these is the time-honoured practice of fucking on the boardroom table. The banking industry has a long and illustrious history of gratuitous sex and generally wild rutting on the altar of financial decision-making. In this respect, the industry has preserved and respected one of its noblest traditions. This ancient practice is still carried out frequently today, although just how frequently is difficult to say because human beings – uniquely among primates – tend to copulate in private. Nevertheless, some fine examples of the boardroom beast-with-two-backs (or should that be banks?) have survived to embellish the annals of banking posterity. Some of the stories – such as those of the Italian Stallion and the Culpable Table – have already passed into legend.

The essential ingredients in any boardroom game of Wobbly Willy Plays Bury The Helmet are fear and lust (they feed one another in definitive symbiosis). This is why the boardroom table, the very public emblem of financial sanctity and respectability, is also one enormous sexual aid. An unusual sexual aid, in that it is likely to be made of French rosewood and hand-crafted by Hepplewhite or Chippendale (the cabinet maker, not the male stripper) as opposed to being a battery-operated piece of rubberized vinyl, but it is a sexual aid nevertheless. Another vital component of high-level drilling stories is that, if the lust has overpowered the fear to such an extent that the couple is discovered, someone has to be sacked. And the more dramatically the better. The best stories feature instant dismissals, security guards sweeping belongings into plastic bags, and company Porsche keys being petulantly tossed down storm drains. But these are just side dishes to the main course, which is always fear, lust, and unemployment.

There are hundreds of these stories. Two will serve as well as any to illustrate the universal nature of the themes involved. The first concerns the Italian Stallion.

The Stallion is a self-proclaimed stud of, guess what, Italian extraction. He works in the foreign exchange dealing room of a London bank. And, the level of maturity and good judgment being what it is in such places, he accepts a bet that he will be able to seduce one of the support staff, and, moreover, have sex with her in the boardroom. The deed done, he returns to work the next day ready to claim his magnum of Louis Roederer Cristal. Only to find his desk cleared and security guards waiting to escort him from the premises. The moral of the tale is never to embark upon a horizontal jog when security cameras are about. Incidentally, video tapes of the Italian Stallion in action are rumoured still to be circulating the City of London. Who said banking was dull?

Perhaps more famous is the Culpable Table. The table in question is sited in one of the biggest and best-known banks in London. This bank is contesting a takeover bid. The bank has a tough job, since contested bids are notoriously more difficult to defend than to launch. It is serious, in-depth strategy discussion time as a deadline on the hostile offer nears. Senior directors of the bank pore over proposals to undermine the market in the bidding company's shares, thus reducing the value of its offer and making it less attractive to the defending company's shareholders. There is a break for food, and everyone leaves the boardroom apart from two directors who send out for sandwiches and mineral water. Both are married and in their early forties, both have children, and both, more to the point, are valued members of the board and are vital to the merger and acquisitions operation – then deemed to be the bank's core business.

They have been friends for years, and are both stone-cold sober. So when their friendship blossoms into something meaningless at half past nine on a cold spring night, both are surprised. Not quite as surprised, however, as the managing director and chairman of the bank when they return. She is wearing her ankles as earrings. He has a rosiness of buttock to put the average gibbon to shame.

The chairman and managing director look at one another. What to do? Company policy is quite explicit in forbidding in-house rumpy-pumpy, and tradition states that a sacking is compulsory. Tradition and sexual chauvinism dictate that the woman go. Yet she is so vital to the operation, and is even more senior than he. So the man must leave. But he is crucial to the success of this high-profile battle, upon which millions in future business and the prestige and reputation of the bank depend. Neither can possibly leave, yet there has to be a sacking.

The way through this little impasse comes to the chairman in a blinding inspirational flash. They call an emergency board meeting, barring the nonplussed members of the bid team from returning to work after their hurried supper. The emergency board meeting has a swift and decisive result. The chairman advances the theory that the table is to blame. It incited them to irresponsible thrutching, he argues. The board agrees. The table must go. And it does. In true brutalist style, the table is instantly dismissed for gross misconduct. The security guards are called, and the table leaves the building (in disgrace) that night.

All right, so much for one cherished banking tradition. But whatever happens over the boardroom table, does it matter that fewer banks do their business from big, old stone buildings than used to be the case? In that narrow sense they have lost historical continuity and are less 'institutional'. What about the more complex and difficult (and more important) idea of an institution?

The central concept is that bankers form a cohesive professional group which is an institution of itself, with its own accepted codes of behaviour and practice, minute deviations from which are thought of as being unique identifiers, style-points of a given bank. Beyond the idea of solid, historically evolved business practice the institution of the banking industry has a place among the other institutions in society – banking and bankers lay claim to be part of an elite, power-broking set, referred to in many western societies as the Establishment.

But already the identifying criteria for bankers who would lay claim to elite status have narrowed the area of analysis to investment, merchant and central bankers – the merchant princes of the profession. Given that the set of people calling themselves bankers is pretty disparate, it makes sense to take them category by category, and determine what they actually do (if anything) to justify those salaries and bonuses. In their business practices the true value of their claims to respectability and continuity will be revealed. Sorry (but not very) if the notion of bankers having to justify themselves is shocking.

Why central bankers aren't bankers at all

If you're British and into Spoonerisms, you probably already know that the collective noun for bankers is a wunch. If you're not

British, or just have an adult sense of humour, the first sensible question you should ask yourself is whether central bankers are really bankers at all.

Central bankers do lots of jobs within the framework of a democratic society. It's just that most of the jobs resemble very closely the functions of a civil servant or a politician. The two most important roles of central banks are the implementation of monetary policy, and supervision of a country's banking system. There are other functions, such as keeping the government's books balanced (or at least keeping the government informed of the books' state of imbalance), and being an impressive-sounding and mysterious 'lender of last resort'. All of which is a long way from the role of swashbuckling profiteer athwart the great oceans of modern finance.

In western countries, and a few other places where economic policy is not habitually implemented at gun point, the biggest single variable among central banks is their supposed independence or otherwise from the local government. Although some central banks, such as the Bundesbank, insist that they are independent of their governments, this is on the whole just a question of nomenclature. All right, the board of the Bundesbank doesn't take orders from the German government, but it's about as independent of the German government as your mouth is from your hand.

The simple fact is that no central bank is really independent of its government. This situation occurs for an obvious reason. It is politically expedient to have a group of subservient people in dark suits to blame for implementing the policies which the politicians have told them to devise.

It was, for example, extremely convenient for the German government to have the Bundesbank to blame for the exquisite torture the member countries of the EU were forced to undergo in the late 1980s and early 1990s. The other EU countries did not want high interest rates, but the Germans, mentally scarred by the hyperinflation after World War I, most certainly did. The result was that the other EU countries were forced to raise them to maintain parity with the German currency. When thousands of homeowners had been dispossessed of their properties and the screaming became a little loud, the German government could point to the council of the Bundesbank and say 'It's not our fault. The central bank works independently.'

Right. Just like the central bank of France, which became 'independent' at the beginning of 1994. For those who enjoy a nice meaty triumph of political will over language, the 'independence' of the French central bank is a veritable chateaubriand for several people with healthy appetites. The French central bank has not one, but two masters. First, it is an instrument of its government's financial policy in just as transparent a way as the Bundesbank of German political will. But the real puppet master of the French central bank is the master of all European financial policy, the Bundesbank (i.e. the German government, but without the Bundesbank's famous sense of humour). Irrespective of French domestic needs, the French bank slavishly follows the interest rate moves of Big Brother within a week or two. For French central bank read *Bundesbanque*.

The Federal Reserve System probably has the most independence of any central bank, although far less of a fuss is made of this sacred concept. The system mixes the private and the public, has about forty per cent of the commercial banks in its membership, and subjects nearly all the rest to its regulation and control. Beneath the Fed are twelve regional federal reserves. The monetary and regulatory functions of central banking are carried out in Washington, while the foreign exchange functions (the sharp end of policy implementation) are performed – at least, officially – by the Federal Reserve bank of New York. The effectiveness (or otherwise) of central banks in dealing with the foreign exchanges was dealt with in Chapter II.

The situation is more complicated than this, but not much. The broad truth is that central bankers are really just another form of civil servant. They certainly are if you at all accept the notion of banker as vector force-cum-self-transformative shark.

What would a *real* banker want to know about regulation, for example? Or licensing other banks to do business? Licence awards are a wonderful banking placebo in that they offer the illusion of a uniformly regulated system, while the substantive controls and checks they provide are almost non-existent.

Admittedly, the controls look quite impressive at first. The terms of the Basle Accord, a lofty document by which the world's central banks agreed common standards, states that banks must pass quite fierce-looking capital adequacy tests. The key provisions concern capital 'adequacy' requirements that the share capital of a bank be equal to at least eight per cent of its total assets (this created terrible problems for the Japanese banks whose share prices were savaged by falls in their stock on the Tokyo market in the early 1990s). There are also stipulations as to how much of these reserves can be in equity and disclosed reserves, and how much in hidden reserves, general provisions and other pieces of accounting wizardry such as 'subordinated debt'. The idea was to create an internationally level playing field, so that the financial position of each bank could be assessed on the same criteria, and the central banks could then begin to set about the business of international regulation in earnest.

The fact is, however, that banks can avoid international regulators with extreme ease. Look, for example, at the fiasco which was the Bank of Credit and Commerce International (BCCI) saga. Although the accounting is still not finished, the best guess is that this international 'bank' was able to conceal a hole in its accounts of some $10 billion.

Scandalously, if not surprisingly, it wasn't that difficult to do. Whenever a central bank wanted to see the reserves of BCCI (famously named 'Bank of Crooks and Criminals' in a remark attributed to former CIA director, Robert Gates) funds would be surreptitiously transferred.

Many books have already been written about the extreme unpleasantness of the BCCI affair. The client list reads like a roll-call of late twentieth-century villains – Saddam Hussein, Noriega and the Colombian drug barons. Here we can examine, very briefly, the minuscule role of central banker as regulator.

You see, there is no effective system of international regulation. None whatever. The regulating central bank cannot look beyond the bank branches presenting themselves for inspection in their own country. It has to rely on information sharing. And given the secretive nature of most bankers (even these strange central banking creatures) and the fact that they don't like to reveal the deep mysteries of their preferred audit trail (the way they analyse documents and accounts) not a lot of information tends to be shared.

As regulators go central bankers do have a tradition – one of minimal competence and a general lack of vigilance. This may qualify them as being an institution, but if so, it is an institution terminally overloaded with irony. One certain conclusion of the BCCI affair is that if you want to have a bank efficiently regulated, don't look to the Cayman Islands or Luxembourg to share the responsibility of being principal regulators. The Bank of England, considered by some to be the real 'moral' villain of the piece, is one central bank being aggressively pursued in law by defrauded investors. We shall see if they are successful.

As wise a comment on the regulator's function as any was offered by Richard C. Breeden, the ex-chairman of the top US watchdog, the Securities and Exchange Commission, just before his retirement in 1993. 'It's better to have market evolution and regulators adjust to what the market is doing rather than have regulators set rules by which the markets have to operate.'

In other words, regulation is not about leading, but necessarily about following (as the very phrase 'audit trail' implies). These people are civil servants, not bankers.

Retail bankers – storekeepers in cheap suits

Now we embark upon a brief survey of the real players in the banking profession. Beginning with retail, graduating to custodial, commercial, merchant, investment, and ultimately non-bank banking, we shall see that the industry of banking describes a perfect circle.

So. Retail banking is the street-level version. The kind of thing that ordinary people without the millions to buy a little counterfeit respect experience daily. This is the financial supermarket end of the profession, and these bankers know it. They are the lowest of the low, storekeepers in grey suits. The galley slaves of capitalism, high street bankers do not have their hands on the levers of high finance. They are, as a group, much more interested in getting their hands on the cashiers' tits/into his pants than anything remotely financial.

There is a certain continuity about what they do – the continuing tradition of bad value, drudgery and astounding impertinence.

Everyone will have plenty of tales of his own after half a dozen visits to a high street bank in any country in the world (although I suspect Britain and France have a close hold on the title of champion). It is, if nothing else, evidence for the proposition that money is a universal language. And the language is that of pure alienation.

Who do you think coined the old adage that, even if a person's teeth were on fire, you wouldn't cross the road to piss in his mouth?

In fact, you wouldn't even let him have the *steam* from your urine. Might not this cheery little phrase have first been produced by a high street banker speaking of a cherished customer? Forget all that stuff about New Yorkers having attitude. The pissed-off, late, naturally aggressive, got-to-truck-to-survive New York subway commuter has nothing on a British bank clerk when it comes to snappy, vicious ill-humour. But then a professionally goaded, amphetamine-crazed pit bull terrier comes in a pretty poor second, too.

It's not even as though there's a vivid culture of discourtesy. There are no subtle textures to the vapid look, the dismissive shrug of the shoulders. There are no greys shading into cinereous charcoal for the dead-eyed, closed-ended statements telling you that you've queued in the wrong line for forty minutes, hard luck. There's no quiet clerical ululation by which the bank employees communicate to one another above the turbid hum of the air conditioning precisely which rich seam of life-hating tedium they are mining now. There is no special vocabulary – no seventeen different words for humdrum, no fantastic Mandarin-style tonal subtlety in the saying of 'paper clip' to indicate that there will be glue-sniffing and an oral sex fest in the stationery cupboard after work. Nothing. Just the same blank expression on different faces, the same 'position closed' sign being turned in your direction – just as you are about to step up to the little plastic rabbit hutch and transact your business. And you don't even get discount stamps to set off against your next purchase.

Anyway, this position is closed.

Custodian bankers – so boring, other bankers think they're dull

Their work is custodial, but they are not prison guards. Maybe they ought to be. It might bring a little joy into their lives. They execute trades for fund managers and send out bits of paper and cheques for the correct amount of money to lots of small investors. Except that frequently they don't send out the cheques to the right people, and every now and then they get the amounts wrong. Custodian bankers are so boring, other bankers think they're dull.

Commercial bankers

The first point to note about commercial banking is that it has nothing whatsoever to do with commerce. These people exist primarily to oil the wheels of the banking system, to manipulate liquidity and help ensure that everybody's books balance at every close. They are the definitive money lenders, and if they run out, the central banks step in as lenders of last resort.

Investment and merchant bankers

Pick a name, any name. Whether the creature on the other side of the thick glass panelling is an investment or merchant banker, the attitude is the same: sleeves rolled up, elbow-deep in the trough, looking to climb in if possible. Pure remorselessness harnessed to the pursuit of money. Money chasing after money is a life force with a human shell, and that shell is quite often called a banker.

Despite the differing names, there's really only the one species. Investment bankers and merchant bankers are pretty much the same thing. It's just that merchant banking used to be a more usual term in Britain for a bank that bought stakes in other companies. But the British dialect of the English language has been much influenced by its American cousin. As the US banks have become more powerful and better established in the UK, so the American financial dialect has become more usual. It's a microcosm of the success story of the English language itself. Over the last two hundred years, thanks first to the British Empire, then to the irresistibility of the dollar for most of this century, one linguistic certainty emerged. If you wanted to make money in international trade or finance, you spoke English. So, the US banks have been successful, and nowadays the term 'investment bank' is usual in Britain, and pretty much interchangeable with 'merchant bank'. In the US, however, where British banks are known but are far from dominant, merchant banking is something quaint that Europeans do. Convicted felon Ivan Boesky was known to be fond of the term, and wanted to adopt it as a pretty name for his ruthless and predatory activities in corporate America.

None of which has got us very far in determining the difference between a banker and, say, a foreign exchange dealer – another surfer on the ebbing and flowing network of capitalist forces. This time it's slightly more than pure nomenclature, although a dealer might easily be called a banker, if the dealing room is owned by a bank. It's not remuneration – at least not if you take the view that after a certain level all salaries are the same. There is, however, an important attitudinal difference. If you ask a foreign exchange dealer to distinguish his professional activity from the vast bet of the eighteenth-century nobleman who famously wagered on the outcome of a 'race' between two drops of rain on the window pane of his Pall Mall club, the foreign exchange dealer will probably not see too much difference. The self-styled banker probably will.

There are plenty of arguments as to the usefulness and necessity of foreign exchange dealing rooms and the people who inhabit them. They have already been well ventilated. But the crucial point is this: whether the foreign exchange dealer takes a highbrow approach (the market is a function of the flexibility of the international finance system, a corollary of economic liberalism, a form of re-insuring exchange rate risk) or is simply facetious (the difference from the aristocratic high-roller is that foreign exchange dealers need banks of computer equipment to wager vast sums on the outcome of obscure events), the response you will receive is likely to be contaminated by honesty. God knows why, but despite (maybe because of) the lousy image they have, foreign exchange dealers have some hint of a redeeming humility. They know that they are playing with money chasing after itself, and the standard response is that it's a tough job, but – wry little grin, shrug of Armani-draped shoulders – someone's got to do it, someone's got to be marinaded in money.

Ask a banker whether the job isn't really a number puzzle game with huge cash prizes, and you get a different response. Bankers will typically try to justify it all. They will try and pretend that what they do is a fundament of the capitalist system, the very cornerstone of what is making us all (some of them, anyway) so very prosperous.

The key concept is the bank as institution, the bank as a strand of continuity in an ever-changing world. This differentiates the banker from the dealer – an ugly word, when you think about it, redolent of casuistry and opportunism.

But where *is* the continuity in modern banking practice? Do the modern banks lend money any more? Apart from those isolated moments of rutting, is there another serious purpose to those boardroom tables – the making of loans to strengthen the fabric of society, to create the equivalent of the nineteenth century's railroads?

Some hope. Banks don't lend money any more – for a variety of reasons, some of which have been touched on already.

First, regulation, such as it is, requires them to be sensible. If they take the Basle Accord seriously, significant assets have to be held in reserve. The US and UK banks complained that the accord reduced the scope for making loans. But the facts are that the timing was bad. The implementation of the accord coincided with a period of low interest rates for US banks (which made it less lucrative to lend) and an ERM-inspired crisis in the UK economy that meant that even if the banks had wanted to lend, they would have had a tough time finding a UK corporate sector to lend to.

Second, and more important, is the increased competition from other institutions. Credit lines from endowment funds, insurance companies and others looking to make a steady return over long periods has shaved margins right down. It has required exceptional ingenuity, or an exceptional market, to induce bankers to make loans in the last two decades. And when the loans have been made they have often gone bad.

Take the experience of CitiCorp and its former chairman Walter Wriston. On the back of the high returns for a higher than usual risk, he pretty much single-handedly committed billions of CitiCorp's credit to Latin American banks in the 1970s and early 1980s. And then the Latin American countries began to default – or, if you prefer, to unilaterally re-schedule their debts. Which left CitiCorp with a problem. By the time Wriston was through it was unclear who owned whom. CitiCorp's loan book was a substantial chunk of South American industry and government indebtedness. What was the bank going to do for the next tranche of money that Bolivia or Peru was refusing to pay? Manage the industrial base of a continent all by itself? Install its directors as finance ministers? Invade? Not even banks – or most banks, anyway – have loan officers who double up as paratroopers. CitiCorp's Latin American experience, and the distinct possibility that the bank might go under, taking with it much of the western banking system, meant that bankers have been shy of lending money ever since.

Make that *should* have been shy. Because just a few years later one bank was shovelling shit over its own head again and screaming with joy as it did so. The structure of the tale is familiar. After a cautious beginning there follows a massive extension of credit to a particular market. The bank then takes a position on this market, about which it feels territorial and of whose inflated asset values it is proud. The position is closer to two macho cretins fighting over a bar-room floosie than anything we are supposed to recognize as the cool, rational world of high finance. The pride overcomes prudence, and the bank keeps lending more and more money to players in that market. In the short term, the availability of funds keeps things buoyant, but after a while somebody gets an attack of common sense and starts to sell. And then the scales fall from the speculators' eyes and everyone starts to sell. The market folds. This phenomenon is covered in more detail in Chapter XI, Living With the Lunatic. For now, let's guess what the market is, and who was silly enough to bankroll this particular bubble.

The market? US real estate. The banker? John Reed – chairman of CitiCorp!

Here's a quote from the *Financial Times* of 17 October 1991 – 'Mr Reed began eating humble pie last November when he admitted he was "damn embarrassed because the critics were right and we were wrong". At the time he was referring to how Citibank continued to build up its commercial property loan book well into 1990 in spite of clear warnings that the sector was heading for trouble.' Clear, maybe. It depends who's doing the looking.

Three months after that article appeared it became clear that more than forty per cent of Citibank's commercial property portfolio was classified as 'non-performing' (i.e. crap). Before the full folly of this was exposed, Reed said, with perhaps a hint of understatement, 'We are guilty of having run this business a bit cavalierly.' If that's cavalier, bring on Oliver Cromwell.

The third and most fundamental reason that banks don't lend money any more is that they have significantly changed they way they operate. The OPM (Other People's Money) mentality now reigns. Compare and contrast the conquering of North America in the nineteenth century with what's happening on the new frontiers of capitalism and industrial change today. The nineteenth-century story is simple enough. Railroads were built, and after them came commerce and the rest of the capitalist system nestling in the infrastructure. A major source of funding for the railroads was loans from the banks. The modern version of the tale is very different.

The standard wisdom is that the railroads of today are information superhighways – conduits of information allowing householders access to a vast variety of digitally stored information in the form of television, music, film, library archive, and the rest. And the householder will be able to receive as well as transmit. All kinds of possibilities exist. It's already possible to edit your own television programme in high-definition-quality picture with superlatively good sound using nothing more unusual than an Apple Mac lap-top computer. Imagine the possibilities for noticeboard-style television. Television programmes made of home-edited audio-visual inserts are the radio phone-in shows of tomorrow, some say. All that's needed is the information highways – alias the right cable system – and we have that slightly frightening situation where everyone is connected to everyone else.

And who is paying for all this? Apart from empty gestures on the part of the White House, the companies themselves. Aided by the banks, who are, of course, not lending the money, but arranging for other people to lend it. The information technology companies raise the finance through bond issues organized by the banks. Already we are one step down the road to OPM Shangri-La. Instead of lending its own capital a bank provides a service which enables a client to borrow from someone else. Step number two comes when the bank trades the debt. It may simply make a market in AT&T bonds, or perhaps swap them for something else (in which case the bank is exchanging one obligation to pay for another, and so taking an investment position itself). In all cases the golden rule is that OPM is king. Why risk your own capital if someone else is going to be foolish enough to do so? That is the spirit of today's banker.

OK, it's perfectly reasonable to ask what's the big deal. Does this present a problem at all? Should it? Financially speaking, there is no problem. No problem at all. Financial markets change, and a bank that helps a company raise billions of dollars in exchange for its promise to pay at a set rate over the following few years is surely doing all of us and our society a favour. Agreed, more or less. But why pretend, when you're simply facilitating and then speculating on the debt issue you've helped to create, that what you're doing is in some way part of a noble tradition?

Some bankers *are* noble. Right. And some poodles can use a knife and fork – it can be done, but it's messy, and deeply unnatural. Banking is speculation with other people's money. The difference from other speculative areas of finance, apart from an accident of history, is that there's usually a part-time bordello of a boardroom somewhere in the building, and bankers are so po-faced they refuse to admit they are just as grubby as the rest of the marketplace. And of course they are not just as grubby as the rest of the marketplace. The very falsity of their superior air lends them a quality of pure hypocrisy that locates bankers – after those who peddle 'ethical' investments (see Chapter VII) – at the very top of the league table of hypocrisy.

Early in the second half of the century there may have been some substance to the claim that bankers were the inheritors of a tradition. It was, for example, 'traditional' attitudes that engendered such vicious anti-semitism toward Sigmund Warburg when he established a merchant bank in London.

Warburg really established himself as a force to be reckoned with in 1958–9 when he successfully acquired a stake in British Aluminium for an American client, TI-Reynolds, against British opposition.

'Unlike his opponents, Warburg had grasped that the nineteenth-century traffic in British capital was now flowing the other way. American industrial investment in Europe ... was unstoppable,' wrote Dominic Hobson in his book, *The Pride of Lucifer*, a study of the UK bank Morgan Grenfell. 'Warburg had made fools of the establishment by the simple expedient of taking the battle to the shareholders rather than the management and offering them more money, and the City loathed him for it.'

(But the City had clearly forgiven him by December of 1994, when the American investment bank Morgan Stanley moved to acquire the bank. There was much shocked talk of British banking culture, much fussing over the potential loss of part of Britain's financial heritage. In fact, the Americans didn't give a fart in a hurricane for the precious banking operation. What they wanted was the asset management division (loosely speaking, this means mutual funds – see Chapter V). The acquisition failed when it became clear that asset management was a separate part of the business that Morgan Stanley would not be able to control. So the Americans walked away, leaving British banking 'culture' intact.)

The conduct of Morgan Grenfell well illustrates the continuity and integrity in UK banking culture that was to be found in the late 1980s. Morgan Grenfell was once centred at the heart of the British establishment. Some would say it still is – but it is at least arguable that the bank's image has been tarnished by its involvement in Guinness' fiercely contested takeover of Distillers in 1986. One of the bank's senior officers, Roger Seelig, was found guilty of insider dealings, fined and given a suspended jail sentence. And – perhaps even more damagingly in the view of the City's chauvinistic establishment – Morgan Grenfell is now owned by the German giant, Deutsche Bank.

Some would argue that the nastiness surrounding Guinness was the ineluctable conclusion to the slow revolution in acquisitions begun by Warburg. Although money was a vital factor, until the 1980s the UK banks had played their acquisitions games according to a set of rules that did not have the force of law. Business had been something of a gentleman's game with conduct dictated by the Takeover Panel's rule code. Then Morgan Grenfell began to distinguish itself as the outstanding UK merchant bank in the contested takeover field. Although the bank had had little notable success as an acquisitions specialist before the 1970s, it had a few major victories in the early 1980s.

Then came a series of hostile, contested bids such as the struggle between industrial conglomerates Thomas Tilling and BTR, and the electrical retailers' dogfight between Dixon's and Curry's. These were marked by attempts at media manipulation, an increasing reliance on press relations officers and 'spin doctors', aggressive advertising aimed directly at shareholders, and lots and lots of pressure on institutional investors to provide support. It culminated in the Guinness affair, with wholesale illegality, share price support schemes, guarantees, success fees and market manipulation.

The result of the Guinness trials has been less than cheering. While it would be beneath the scruples of the average lynch mob to complain about value of money per conviction, there was plainly something very wrong in the conduct of the Guinness takeover. Yet miraculously, very few of the main players have been nailed.

Perhaps it's better to confine oneself to an observation about investment/merchant banking in general. It's a rather sordid game played exclusively and ruthlessly for profit. The profit motive has led many to overstep the bounds of legality. There is no tradition involved, except perhaps that of denying culpability and not getting caught.

Nor have the US banks covered themselves in financial glory. The theme is a familiar one. The relentless pursuit of profit leads to a departure from familiar practices. At first, this is best termed innovation. The new activity leads to spectacular wealth, cachet in the marketplace, and the feeling of a God-given right to make a handsome profit. And eventually that arrogance leads to a deluded notion of infallibility. The banker who has discovered and popularized a new market becomes a financial version of the Pope. With one crucial difference. The Catholic church has it that the Pope is only infallible when pronouncing *ex cathedra* on matters of doctrine. A successful banker, apparently, becomes incapable of making an error at any time. And this article of faith applies even if the banker is stretching the concept of innovation so far that some people would be tempted to say he is breaking the law. It especially applies if the banking law in question is allegedly being broken by a 6' 3", cigar-smoking, whiskey-drinking, golf-playing tough guy from Cicero, Illinois, who happens to be the Pope's bodyguard and wears the scarlet silk robes of a cardinal. But of that, more later.

Insider deals. How to find a chainsaw when insider dealers claim to be trees in a rain forest. Why insider trading really is a crime

Back to the investment banks. What other explanation than delusions of infallibility can there be for the hubris that led to the insider trading scandals of the 1980s junk bond market? Multi-billionaire Michael Milken, seated like some Californian version of the antichrist at the centre of a huge X-shaped bank of trading desks in his Hollywood office, started off by exploiting a clever idea. He saw research papers that argued an interesting case for a sector of the bond market. (To reiterate, to buy a bond is basically to lend a company or government money for a fixed period of time. What you get in return is a stream of income, and then your capital back. So when you buy a bond you're lending money in the way that banks used to do.) The paper argued that bonds issued by companies with low credit ratings, in other words, small companies, or companies with a financial problem or two, were better investments. Why? Because to attract investors the companies offered more return on investment, and, despite their supposed riskiness, the research indicated that relatively few of the companies went bust in the long term. Milken sold the idea brilliantly, and then – yet more brilliantly – sold it not just as a sexy investment, but as a weapon in an increasingly aggressive takeover market.

The logic went like this. If a company can promise attractive returns for its high-risk investment, it can raise lots of money. If it uses that money to acquire another company, and if by clever management it can then sell all or parts of that company for a better price than it paid using the junk bond capital, everyone is happy. Perhaps not everyone. The corporate predators of the 1980s had a bad reputation as disassemblers and destroyers of companies. A lot of that, of course, was because of some sensationalistic, ill-informed reporting by the press. Their image was not helped by having a series of annual conferences of increasing extravagance and ostentatious bad taste (Frank Sinatra, Diana Ross in cabaret, models in Barbie Doll outfits, custom-made videos, deafening rock music – all the trappings of a Mammon worshippers' convention). The annual conference became known as 'The Predators' Ball', by which time it was definitely too late to hire an image consultant. But whatever the merits of the corporate predators' position, the financial cleverness of the junk bond as corporate takeover weapon was undisputed. The beauty of it was that the market appeared to be limitless, both as to buyers and targets. No buyer of Milken's junk bond services was too small, no target too big. If it could raise the capital through a junk bond, a company with a turnover of $1 billion could swallow whole a corporation five or six times its size.

The corporate world bought the idea, and a feeding frenzy of unparalleled intensity followed, as corporation devoured corporation. And Milken, who for practical (i.e. income-generating) purposes had become almost the entire firm of Drexel Burnham Lambert, was the man that ambitious corporate predators needed to approach. With his connections and power, he could at one stage virtually ensure that a corporation would get its money, simply by formally certifying a high level of confidence that this would be the case. In other words, a letter from Milken about what he thought would happen became effectively as good as a properly underwritten guarantee by a bank that if the bonds weren't bought in the market, the bank itself would buy.

Milken had become a market force. This was only partly because he was rigging the market. There were many outside the circle of the guilty who innocently – all too innocently – watched his every move, followed his every word. If he said something would happen, it did, because the market expected what he said to come true. And yet, incredibly, it wasn't enough. Despite the hitherto unmatched greed of the fees charged for his junk bond services, Milken and a ring of investment bankers wanted more (some, such as would-be 'merchant' banker Ivan Boesky, were professional speculators known as 'arbitrageurs' – but this is only a semantic difference from aggressive investment banking). They wanted butter and jam on both sides of their bread. So that when one of the insider ring was approached to find funds for a raid on a given corporation, that person would let someone else in the ring know that the corporation was 'in play'. Typically, the share price of a corporation in play will rise. And knowing this, the 'arbs' and others in the ring could make spectacular profit by buying heavily, often using options, of which more later, to enhance their gain. It was, of course, illegal to profit in such a way, and eventually there were fines and jail sentences for the key players. For Milken there were public tears and – great cultural cliché of our times – the inevitable finding of God.

There is one particularly pathetic line peddled by many a criminal when caught trading on inside information. The argument is that insider trading, if it is a crime, is one with no victims. Which brings to mind the old philosophical conundrum of the tree falling in the distant rain forest, hundreds of miles from the nearest human. If the tree falls and there's no-one to hear the fall, can it be meaningfully said that there is a sound? The parallel positions are that there can be no sound without a listener and that there can be no crime without a victim. The philosophical issue is an extreme interpretation of Heisenberg's Uncertainty Principle (that the observer has a qualitative impact on the data observed). The criminal issue is purely one of law – if the rules are clear, and they are breached, and this can be proved, it's a crime. Let the bastards swing. Aside from the somewhat neutral reasoning that says 'you knew the rules, so tough luck,' there are all sorts of good reasons – reasons with substance – as to why insider dealing really is a crime.

First is the whole idea of The Market as something substantial. The concept of The Market has been grotesquely misunderstood and given an undue respect born of ignorance (a recurring theme in finance – one of the few areas of human activity where incomprehension does not generate foolish laughter, but awed respect). The idea of The Market has been adapted by many, many governments starting with the US and the UK and moving into Europe and around the world. These governments, from Portugal to Vietnam, have encouraged the spread and the dissemination of The Market as ideological hot brand of the last quarter century. They have donned the notion of privatization like a pubescent girl grabbing a pair of flared pants from a '90s (or a '60s) store rail. And this plank of economic and social policy is vitally underpinned by the assumption that The Market is something which is free and fair. Forget collectively planned misery. Let's get back to nature with an elemental economic force – the impartial, objective, ruthless certainty of the unbuckable markets. All of which is hardly consistent with a few greedy men getting greedier and richer through their ability to manipulate The Market through controlling price-sensitive information.

Second, stupidity should be punished (or at least not actively rewarded), and the greedy insiders had to be pretty dumb to get caught. Why? Because the wind is basically in their favour. You have to try hard to get caught insider dealing. Consider the difficulties. Inside information is one thing, rumour another. People trade on rumour, perfect market or no perfect market. Rumour – alias the unofficial news, alternative data to discount in the market – is an actual, acknowledged force in persuading individuals to trade. Regulators know and accept this, partly because it suits them to. Their jobs are technically impossible in most cases, so they let the minor abuses go. They have to, because they are always over-worked, under-staffed and slightly behind The Market. Their task would become overwhelmingly, practically impossible if they looked at all the suspicious trades. So they are not monitoring everything as it happens, merely chasing the biggest, most obvious abuses after the event. They do not direct market price moves, they correct manipulations of them.

So the game is naturally tilted toward a discreet, smart insider dealer. To get caught means there has been a systematic, gross and obvious abuse of the law, for whatever reason – pride, arrogance, the simple thrill of believing yourself smarter than the rest. Greed usually plays a significant part after the initial thrill of the first insider trade or two has worn off. Whatever. One thing is for certain – the detected insider breaks the inviolable eleventh commandment by getting caught. And because he is the visible beachhead of a small sub-continent of vice, let an example be made of him. Let him sit in the eternal crucible of flame, and let no tears be shed.

Third, and perhaps most important, they're guilty of very bad bullshit. Bear in mind that bankers and analysts are paid to have opinions. Whether they're wrong or right doesn't really matter most of the time. In fact, lots of chief executives like a certain kind of elegance in a faulty call. It reminds them that the smart guy is right fifty-one per cent of the time.

So, in a world where a good argument and a persuasive opinion are all, what kind of a defence to a criminal charge is it to pretend you're a *tree*? The no-listener no-sound line is just about tolerable when expounded by a lunatic with an arborial fixation, or perhaps Wittgenstein or Bertrand Russell, fresh from their inconclusive debates about whether there is a green rhinoceros in the corner of the Cambridge University lecture room. But insider dealing sees criminally minded bankers make millions of dollars. And are we to believe that it's not a crime because we can't point to someone in the street they've physically beaten up and mugged? When these people use the victimless crime argument they are pretending that they, who spend their lives engaged in the intensely practical world of finance, are to be treated like the philosopher's toppling tree. When the SEC officers come to their desks and they plead for their allegorical arboreal status, you've got to hope a) that the handcuffs go on nice and tight, and b) that the prosecuting attorney has brought his chainsaw.

Fourth, there really are victims anyway. Here's a concrete example. Drexel Burnham Lambert, Milken's firm, was punished so heavily for its misdemeanours that it went out of business. Unfortunately, there is little evidence that the firm's collapse did anything to lift standards of conduct in the investment banking business. What the demise of Drexel did do was hasten the collapse of the junk bond market. And that meant that the thrift institutions – which had been major buyers of junk bonds – were left with worthless paper. Which in turn meant that the US government – alias the taxpayer – was left with billions of dollars more liability to reimburse savers through government bailout. And of course there's the not insignificant fact that a by-product of breaking up and selling off bits of corporations has invariably been a lot of unemployed people. So much for that errant nonsense about insider trading being a victimless crime.

Non-bank bankers

The most celebrated example of non-bank banking made its first claim on public attention with the discovery in June 1982, of Roberto Calvi, hanged under Blackfriars Bridge in London. It was a sordid end. Calvi, who was found with $10,000 in the pockets of his suit, controlled Banco Ambrosiano, the biggest private bank in Italy. His presence at social functions was solicited by the good and the great, he was welcomed across the thresholds of the most powerful people in the land. One of them was Pope John Paul II. Soon Calvi's habit of trotting in and out of the Holy See earned him the soubriquet of 'God's banker'.

But God's banker had been finding life a little difficult before his sudden end. Charges of fraud and larceny were in hand, a scandal was breaking. The audit trail of $1.3 billion in payments by the 'Vatican Bank' to dummy corporations in lightly regulated environments such as the Bahamas and Peru began to lead to the senior management of that bank, and its advisers – including Calvi.

The Vatican Bank is essentially the bankroll of the Catholic church. It is otherwise known as the IOR (Istituto per le Opere di Religio). The head of the bank is Paul Marcinkus, cardinal and papal para-trooper. Marcinkus grew up in a tough neighbourhood in Cicero, Illinois. He is of Lithuanian origin and has the reputation of being a tough guy. His fondness for whiskey, cigars and the golf course do not detract from this image (well, maybe the golf course does – but not much).

As a result of Calvi's death the allegations that the illegal payments were in some way connected to Mafia money-laundering could not be substantiated. The provenance of the money and the advice given or received could not be discovered (partly because there is a piece of legislation that confers immunity on Vatican employees if they choose to invoke it).

There were two inquests into the cause of Calvi's death. At first it looked like suicide, but doubts grew. A second inquest was held, and the London jury recorded an open verdict.

But one certainty does emerge from all this. The revenues from the Pope's book – the first to be written by a Pope while actually being God's vicar on earth – will go to the Vatican Bank. The millions it will produce be channelled into a special account there. The account will not be numbered, but it will not have a personal name. The account will be named after the title of the book *Crossing the Threshold of Hope*. So the Vatican Bank, which was the subject of allegations about processing money for the Mafia, will now receive its cash directly from one of the purest sources of all – being a hit on the *New York Times* bestseller list.

And, let's not forget, the Vatican Bank is really the IOR, which isn't a bank at all. This is non-bank banking.

It is also exceptional. The more usual, more downmarket version of non-bank banking comprises elements such as electronic funds transfer using the television set and an alphanumeric key-pad hooked up to the telephone. The entity on the other end may call itself a bank, but then again it may not. Merrill Lynch, for example, has always been dedicated to the idea of bringing finance to the masses. Now the firm is one of many that offer personal counselling on stocks and fund selection, and they will take your money and pay you interest if you keep it on deposit with them. Many of the companies doing this have not previously been engaged in finance. It's just that they have had to develop sophisticated electronic data-processing systems for stock control and payroll management, so it's easy for them to offer an extra product that happens to be a financial service. Automotive manufacturers, retail department stores and other heavy hitters from the industrial base of the US now offer their own money market accounts, credit cards and checking account facilities. So the next time you go into a supermarket, remember that deposit accounts and checking facilities are available on the shelves too. This is, in a peculiarly literal sense, 'retail banking'. Which is where we came in.

Rock star or mutant snail? – The ultimate banking question

What does it take to be a banker, apart from an ability to feel comfortable about large sums of money being credited to your personal account? Who *are* these people?

The genuine article – the inheritor of banking tradition – is to be found at American banks. This is not because these banks have a longer, more illustrious history. It is because they have more money.

It is undoubtedly the large American firms that do their best to preserve the myth of unchanging tradition and profit with honour. Salomon Brothers, which still has a UK office in central London as well as its own tower at the World Trade Center in Manhattan, is among the most valiant subscribers to the fiction. Take lunch in the firm's vast Victoria offices and you see state-of-the-art financial compromise in action.

While the boardroom is tucked away from the vast, football-pitch-size trading area, there are a number of cosy executive dining rooms that overlook it. Once within the boxes you find yourself in the familiar cockpit of ersatz antiquity – antique furniture, crystal decanters, liveried service, stupendously heavy cutlery. Through the heavily tinted glass you can look down on the traders, but they can't see you. So the fake past can see the real present, but not vice versa – a neat little model of the way finance likes to ignore its sordid history of errors and catastrophes. The failures of yesterday are in truth forgotten if today is a big, profitable success. Continuity? What continuity?

The Salomon employees point out the desk at which Michael Lewis wrote his bestselling book *Liar's Poker*, all about Salomon Brothers. They are quick to say that there are several errors in the book – but accept that these are not so egregious as to provoke a lawsuit, nor will they go into detail as to which trivial alleged inaccuracies they most dislike. You get the impression that Lewis' biggest error was not mentioning the people you're having lunch with, thus failing to import a little glamour, albeit in the form of notoriety, into their lives.

The firm itself has had plenty of notoriety in recent years. But it has been good, solid, old-fashioned ill-repute. Salomons was found guilty of illegally rigging a market as well-established and dull as the US government bond market. Two of the firm's traders were fired, and one received a jail sentence, for buying more bonds than the thirty-five per cent allowed. The traders put in bids for the securities on behalf of others who had not authorized them to do so. The result was that they artificially inflated the demand, and therefore the price, of securities which they controlled and could then sell on for a profit. The chairman and two other senior executives left the firm in the wake of the scandal.

That scandal was in 1992. It appears that misconduct was not unknown in the bond market well before that date. In 1985, for example, Goldman Sachs – another well-respected firm – illegally pre-arranged the purchase and sale of bonds without incurring any risk so as to realize tax losses of more than $36 million. The SEC, which brought charges against Goldman Sachs, also alleged that the firm had helped Salomon Brothers to carry out a similar plan.

The balance sheets of these unimaginative but huge frauds make interesting reading. Let's take the Goldman case first. Liabilities – a tiny fine of $250,000, plus a slapped wrist administered by the authorities on condition that the firm promised to re-vamp its reporting procedures and never to be naughty again. Assets – the fact that the firm basically got away with it. Who appears weak, who appears strong? Goldman or the authorities?

On the liabilities side in the Salomon affair are the fines exacted for its violation of US Treasury rules – $290 million were paid out in 1992. Then there is the settlement with litigants – shareholders and holders of debt suing for economic loss. A further $54.5 million was agreed out of court in 1993. Heading up the asset side is the fact, astounding when you think about it, that there was only *one* jail sentence, one fine of $300,000 and a handful of resignations. Those who resigned just walked away from a situation which involved a felony that they had – at the very least – clearly failed to monitor properly. Talk about power without responsibility. Then there is the ability of the firm itself to walk away from it all. Salomon Brothers recorded a modest profit in the first quarter of 1994. The firm actually lost money on some of the services it provided for its clients because of difficult markets. Yet it recorded a profit overall, thanks to a $212 million profit from taking its own positions. Or as *Bloomberg Business News*, with uncharacteristic clarity, put it, 'betting its own capital'.

This is what today's investment banks do – they advise clients, and they invest their own money. There is of course a theoretically strict division between the two activities, demarcated by Chinese Walls to control information flows, overseen by compliance officers ('Helens', remember?). And, of course, trading on an individual account is carefully watched. There are black lists of proscribed shares in which the bank has an interest. The theory is that trading in any share on the list was forbidden, and would, at the very least, incur severe disciplinary action. The practice was that these lists were much sought-after during the 1980s orgy of insider dealing. A share on the blacklist was almost certainly going to rise in value. So the blacklist was an important document to obtain and use, the logic of the times being that that which is naughty is nice. As a consequence, firms began to produce 'grey lists' of corporations in which no merger activity had been definitely planned, but which were the subject of 'discussion' among the self-styled elite. Grey lists were even more desirable but riskier, since trading in those shares would be further away from any bid announcement, and so even more difficult for the authorities to trace. Fraught as it is with conflicts of interest, personal account trading is not quite banned. The banks want their people to stay, as it is so felicitously put, 'sharp'. When you consider how carefully watched all these individual account trades are it is perhaps surprising that almost all the major scandals involve large sums put through personal accounts. It makes you wonder whether the working definition of 'sharp' might not be 'stupidly greedy'.

Despite the examples set by punishing the big players, small-scale greed and general shadiness are still extremely common. Think of the New York investment banker who invites his accountant friend to place a couple of thousand dollars with him, or the London institutional broker who invites his lawyer friend to add a thousand pounds to his personal trading account 'to see what we can do'. The self-deceiving logic is to drag in the lawyer, the accountant, the friends and the family in the hope of somehow legitimizing dubious trades. The trader may even hope to make himself popular by spreading some of his questionable gains around. And so the insider spreads a little illegal profit to a grateful outsider, and feels good about it. It happens all the time. If it isn't happening in a bar in the upper East Side or a public house in Fulham as you read this, it will tonight.

But don't forget, in the matt black world of profit, greed is just another shade of bitumen. The litany of hideousness is long, and has a rising cadence. For example, there's the investment bank (the much-admired Morgan Stanley) fined for its lax handling of pension funds as Robert Maxwell stole the savings of current and elderly former employees from under the bank's nose. The bank in the same year awards its employees vast bonuses, many hundreds of times bigger than the fine. It was, after all, a good year for the bank. Again, there's the acute sense of justice and the deft timing of the bank (Barclays – an erstwhile investor in the South Africa of apartheid) which announced 432 redundancies in one division followed, two days later, by the distribution of more than $150 million in bonuses for employees in another division. And Goldman Sachs announced million-dollar bonuses for dozens of employees in its London office in the same year as it was fined for securities violations.

It's not pleasant, but it's also not surprising. In the world of pure greed only the strongest and darkest of emotions can survive. There's always a place in the throne room for fear, of course, since fear helps to stoke the market boiler and also offers an adrenal high that not even the finest, financial-district-wine-bar-bought cocaine can match. And then of course there's lust, which complements the other two perfectly. Most of the banking industry's jokes combine at least two of these elements. For example, a greed-lust combo. *Q. What's the difference between a penis and a bonus? A. You can be sure that your wife's going to blow your bonus.* Not exactly Dryden or Pope, but definitely one for the social historian's archive.

You might think that this is all a bit tough on the poor old banker. So what if the banker is making money? Isn't everybody else in finance? Maybe, but not everybody else sees the job as an entrée into fashionable WASP social clubs. Not everybody requires the wife (let's be fair, it's almost always the wife) to organize 'charity events' – whatever the fuck that means when bankers are involved. This is done, in the UK at least, in the hope of buying the banker a knighthood.

So let's sum up the modern banker, starting with the good points. As financial innovators bankers are excellent. They work out new ways to climb the Eiger every day. Good luck to them. It's almost possible to feel sorry for them. For example, their latest invention, the effective successor to junk bonds as the hot spot of the financial markets, has almost got away from them. It was bankers who grew the swap market to its present awesome size. It was they who found that the secret of making real money is not knowledge in a perfect market, but ignorance in an erratic one. It was they who understood that the ultimate in opportunism is to look not for the absolute worth of something in a market, but to find its value relative to what a buyer – even one will do – is prepared to pay. It is the bankers who have let the power and the secret of 'smart money' slip from their grasp to small, immensely powerful firms who call themselves hedge or derivative fund managers. This secret of the sweet, arcane centre of money-making was nurtured by bankers and has passed to these sorcerers wreathed in smoke, the gurus of the derivatives markets. Of them, more later.

The dark side of bankers is, as Scrooge would say, Bah Humbug. Humourlessness, pretentiousness, overweening self-seriousness are the principal qualities of the modern banking industry.

Individually, you can meet many a fine person who happens to be a banker. As a group they provide an experience almost as amusing as being strip-searched at Siberian work camp.

For instance, I know a banker in his mid-thirties, who, despite being on the UK board of a major US bank, has his lighter moments, if you can catch him alone. He still hasn't quite given up his student naughtiness of smoking dope (those drug tests aren't as frequent as the bank press departments would like us to believe. And anyway, it's possible to buy sachets of dry, powdered urine, so all the druggie banker has to do is add water and he's 'clean'. Scrapings from hair follicles are much more difficult to get round, but such tests are rare in the extreme.) All right, this banker's music collection stops in 1985. OK, so he's unimaginative, fat, and looks like a younger Yasser Arafat, but lots of very nice people are like that, more or less. We all need friends like this. You can think about them when you feel depressed. The point is that on his own, he's tolerable – not a vegetarian, doesn't give a flying fuck in a hurricane about the environment, never been seen with alcohol-free beer in his hand. But put him in a room with another banker and it's time to play the financial anthropologist. Suddenly he's part of a great tradition, a rising executive with a role to play – get this – *in society*. He's suddenly got clever views on the way the world turns. That's this world, our world, the one that some of us just love to laze around in and lightly pollute while making completely unnecessary mildly sarcastic comments about everyone else.

One story counts for all. With his banker's head on (if he sounds like a Minotaur, that's probably fair) he once volunteered the information that, given the choice of identity, he would rather be Leon Brittan (this is pre-knighthood) than Rod Stewart. Readers who don't know who Leon Brittan is might feel that whatever his identity it is probably better than that of a man whose youthful looks have transmogrified to an artist's impression of Mother Teresa of Calcutta after a night on the tequila and altar wine cocktails. For pity's sake, not only is Rod's voice nowadays like listening to a badly tuned lawnmower, but his electrified porcupine hairstyle has gone, and he's demented enough to pretend to be, of all things, *Scottish*.

But the option of being Leon Brittan (who is in fact very slightly older than Rod Stewart) is *really* unappetizing. Brittan has looked a solid fifty-five-year-old for the last twenty years. Moreover his voice is an unctuous, high-pitched Uriah Heep-ish bleat, and his hairstyle is unreconstructed SDB (Self-Deluding Baldie). The top of Leon's head looks like an adolescent, heavily pomaded hedgehog crawled across it and died. It's like he's been in a kitsch Chinese restaurant where the hot towels are made of oil-slicky black shiny stuff, and Leon's so pleased with his hot towel that he decides to wear it over his head. Permanently. You get the picture – Leon is a slaphead. Moreover, for breathy pomposity he takes some beating. As a commissioner, he presides over the ghastly idiocies of the European Union from the bureaucrats' power centre in Brussels. And gives every appearance of enjoying himself.

Now bear in mind that when the schoolboy conversation about whether Leon or Rod has the better existence takes place we are in the early 1980s. Rod is snake-hipped, rich, and sleeping with Britt Ekland. Leon already looks like his mother, except that he probably takes a bigger dress size. Who would you rather be? Why, Leon, of course, raps out Yasser for the benefit of one of his banker colleagues. Why, oh why? Because he has better expectations. Rod is on the way down, Leon on the way up (Or not. Brittan was a minister in Margaret Thatcher's government at the time, although he shortly afterwards resigned for reasons whose validity he subsequently chose to impugn from the obscurity – to British politics at least – of Brussels.)

So there you have a key question, a banking litmus test. Would you rather be a) a globe-trotting, Ekland-rogering, having-access-to-lots-of-interesting-substances-if-you-want-them kind of person with a creative bent and a half-decent voice or b) a humourless Conservative politician with a Groucho Marx moustache for a hairstyle and the ability to create the uneasy feeling in people that you might be not too distantly related to a snail?

If the answer is b), go into banking. After all, it's an institution.

Bankers as cultural imperialists – how Tom Wolfe got it right without really knowing why

But there is a more serious side to this. There is a real call to be made on modern banking, once you strip aside the social vanity. Let's just leave it this way. Financially, banking is a creative powerhouse. Socially, the condition of the banker is that of the genuinely transparent aspiring to the opaque. But societally? What of the sociological analysis of bankers and their role in society, the impact that they have on shaping attitudes, creating employment?

Tom Wolfe, in his book *Bonfire of the Vanities*, more or less got it right, but for reasons which he either didn't appreciate or just didn't bother to expound. Essentially bankers really are Masters of the Universe, but in a real, profound way, not just because some of them are arrogant and most of them have plenty of money.

Consider what a banker does in a broader context than that of mere money, the profit and loss sides of the balance sheet. What does the banker do apart from generate revenue? Essentially, the banker, by creating a leveraged management buy-out of a company, by hedging the oil corporation's Swiss franc liability into yen, by managing pension money in a swap fund, is saying 'this is mine'.

The empire-building is undoubtedly true in a financial sense. Banks are the definitive predators, ultimately flexible in the acquisition, right up to the point of changing identity. This means that everything is capable of being touched by a bank, of becoming part of the banker's empire.

The imprint of banking on business and society is similar – light but indelible. Through its manipulation of capital, and its ability to spread its tentacles to every corner of business, banking directly affects us all. This is *das Kapital* that enthralled Marx's imagination so. But today's bankers don't control the means of production, they have a gentler, surer hold. What they control is the means to control the means of production. After all, who needs to own a factory when you can buy and sell (or, better yet, *threaten* to buy and sell) the company that owns it many times over? Essentially, the bankers have marked out everything in the store as available for purchase by themselves. They are the financial equivalent of a special kind of cultural imperialist – the extinct nineteenth-century white male kind, the kind that has provided an excuse for the sad fragmentation and implosion of cultural life into thinly veiled ethnic hatred.

But this is money culture, and it's different from the more tangible things of culture like books, pictures and icons. This kind of culture doesn't wither and die if it turns inward. In 'regular' culture, an exhibition of, say, Tang dynasty pottery will be beautiful and no doubt much appreciated. But it would be as relevant to contemporary society as a poem by Horace. *Vivamus atque amemus, mea Lesbia* has life, wit and beauty for Latin scholars, but it tells us little about the times in which we live. So a Tang exhibition tells us about Tang pottery and very little about the society that finds the money to put the show on. Whereas an exhibition by Chinese American artists or a book by UK author Timothy Mo might say a lot about the life of people of Chinese ethnicity in the UK and the US – and about those countries themselves. Separateness and a retreat into ethnicity will lead to sterility in culture.

In money culture, however, just the opposite is true. Keeping things separate is a good idea. Keep the fund managers away from the mergers and acquisitions departments. Keep client and company money separate. Be brave, make up your mind where the line is, and keep as clear a distinction as possible between right and wrong.

Good idea or not, the truth is that money is everywhere. Bankers have brought, or are attempting to bring, the culture of money to every aspect of human life – the company for which you work needs the protective guidance of bankers for its finances, the school that your children attend requires a banker to advise on its charitable status and the quality of its investments, the new job your sister has might not exist if the bankers advise the launch of a hostile bid, the tap from which the water runs would dry up if it were not for the bonds the bankers arrange. Thus everything becomes dependent on orderly finance, everything is an annex of the infinite universe of banking. It is a universe that the banker does not own. But, frighteningly enough, he is the master of it.

And the Word Was Made Flesh – Mutual Fund Managers, Pension Fund Managers and Trustees and Their Investment Consultants. With a Nod to Venture Capital Funds

The most important difference between a divine, universally present non-corporeal being who is the fundament of creation, and a fund manager. The vast majority of the world's population dismissed in 381 words. Mutual fund statistics as a one-way ticket to Toy Town. Are fund managers good at what they do? Indices and their magical effect – managers become foetal balls of wailing pinstripe. Four pieces of rhetoric (including Specious Nonsense in a Ballgown, Mark II) and two pieces of action. Public comprehension of financial management – somebody else's air crash. Pension fund managers and the promotion of child slavery. The next link in the chain – investment consultants. Venture capitalists' strange physiques – three eyes and no balls.

The important difference between a divine, universally present non-corporeal being who is the fundament of creation, and a fund manager

How many angels fit on the head of a pin? How much silicone is there in the average movie starlet's chest? Who is God's vicar on earth?

The answers to the first two questions require deep, dark and dangerous knowledge, but question three is easy. God's representative on earth is to be found deep in the panting heart of the financial services industry. God's representative is the manager of a mutual fund. The manager is a golden inhabitant of Arcadia, a fleet-footed creature capering nimbly along the iridescent walls of paradise, a confident, downy-cheeked youth who sits astride the partition between the mortal and the divine.

For fund managers inhabit a world more perfect even than the land where French deodorant commercials are made. They are the porters of capitalism, the noble beasts of burden whose mission it is to transform our personal finances by enlightening us. Give your money to the fund manager and the fund manager will make you rich. That is the message, conveyed in thousands of ways, to all who have any money to part with. It used to be the middle classes – doctors, dentists, the moneyed and intelligent but financially unsophisticated, whose money was targeted by the fund industry. But in the last twenty years the net has spread ever wider. Nowadays you don't need to be rich to have your soul saved by the evangelical forces of capitalism, you don't even need to be 'comfortable', all that's required is a small lump sum. Not even that! A few zlotys a month will do, and you can subscribe to your own salvation. You can become the owner of a stake in a mutual fund. Allelujah!

Actually, it is possible to subscribe without shaking uncontrollably, frothing at the mouth and being wholly immersed in a muddy river. But you must remember that we are talking about the evangelical forces of capitalism here – the mission to save the financial souls of the masses. Have you discovered mutual funds? Mutual funds love you. They love us all. Even those of us who have strayed from the path of righteousness and left money mouldering in a bank deposit account. Expose your breast to the market. Sing out in praise of God the Father, God the Son, God the Extremely Smart Fund Manager. Great Stock Picker In The Sky – dark-suited, white-shirted – He is staring into that humming screen on our behalf. He is negotiating our entrance into the inner sanctum of financial Nirvana. His computer screen is awash with the Mediterranean-blue of the rising stock price, with the goodness of the upwardly moving, Heaven-bound market. Thanks to him we are all imbued with financial grace. Mutual funds love you, they love us all, brothers and sisters. Allelujah!

Yeah, right. Welcome to the cult of equity.

In fact, although they share many of the outwards signs – sorry, stigmata – of crank Christianity, mutual funds are considerably less injurious to you. True, both will take all your money and keep asking for more – but the mutual fund manager only wants a relatively small percentage. The rest goes into a pool with other people's money. The idea is that the manager uses his superior knowledge and skill to invest wisely for everyone's mutual benefit. He is a mutual fund manager.

Another difference is that if you give your money to a crank preacher it's gone for good. Give it to a fund manager and you can always ask for it back. It's even possible that you will receive more than you gave (further proof of sanity – in mutual funds it is definitely better to receive than to give).

Both religious zealot and fund manager encourage and promote the abandonment of independent thought, but mutual fund investment doesn't usually lead to estrangement from your family or wild scenes of group sex (although I did hear something about an offshore fund conference in Bermuda once ...). Above all, both actively promote the cult of the patriarch, God the Stock Picker with his white beard of pure algorithm, and his flowing robe of market cyclicality. Entrust your destiny to Him, my child, and He will bestow His love on you. For He has said: 'Suffer little investors to come unto me.'

Actually, there are a couple of quibbles with the concept of fund manager as patriarch, and a big, important difference between the fund manager as deity and the non-spiritual, very concrete reality of fund management performance.

The quibbles are swiftly dealt with. First is a theological objection to the very idea of the Christian God as male. For the Christian God is being relentlessly reinterpreted and feminized. Christian prayer is increasingly cast in language termed 'inclusive' – i.e. it excludes men instead of women. Nothing wrong with that, except that it's a complete waste of time and energy.

Sexual equality and equality of opportunity are things that every rational human being should want. If feminism is to agitate for the political, social and economic equality of men and women, it's basically impossible not to be a feminist. But the items on the agenda are things that work on a rational plane – jobs, education, healthcare, political power. Whereas religion has nothing whatever to do with rationality. Trying to abolish the guy with the beard and re-invent a hermaphrodite just won't work. The Jews and the Catholics have been running their businesses, also known as the Judeo-Christian ethic, for longest, and they have got it right. If you're going to sell religion, sell the full, unadulterated product. Offer the punters the entire mystical, all-singing, all-dancing, totally scary, emergent-from-the-distant-mists-of-time, unaltered, real McCoy. Which is to say white beards, terrible wrath, burning bushes, menstrual cleansing rituals, incense, silk robes, secret one-on-one confessionals with God (*brilliant* marketing concept, that one), special diets, sung Latin Masses, live performances of Bach's St Matthew Passion in large, echoic cathedrals – the whole irrational works, the full slap in the face and knee in the groin to Intellect in favour of uncompromising Belief. If you don't believe me, ask a Rabbi with a sense of humour or a Jesuit with a couple of glasses of Irish whiskey inside him.

It is perfectly rational and fair, if you're inventing a god, that God should be neuter, or sexless, or at least non-gender specific. But since when is religion rational and fair? God is a patriarch with white hair and a beard, that is, when he's not being his own son or the Holy Ghost. And the Devil is a horny guy with cloven hooves and a pitchfork. So religion is an unfair, 'he' environment. And in this, religion unfortunately mirrors the rest of the world, which is very 'he'-dominated. Except, of course, for slimming magazines, where the default form of the third person singular pronoun is invariably 'she'. Isn't life, er, a bitch?

All that guy stuff might not seem like much of a product, by the way, but it's sold consistently well. Take a look at St Peter's and the Vatican City. Not a bad corporate headquarters for a two-thousand-year-old business.

Minor flaw number two in the idea of fund manager as patriarch is the fact that a lot of fund managers are women. Fund Research, a London-based firm specializing in the worldwide analysis of fund performance and the assessment of fund management skills, estimates that 'close to one fund manager in three' was female in mid-1994. And the number of women managers is apparently rising.

But in terms of personality worship, the cult of fund manager as minor deity, the gods are nearly all men. Nowadays most of the leading names, such as Robertson, Steinhart, Theime, Yacktman – belong to men. Before that it was Peter Lynch at Fidelity, and before that another Fidelity fund manager, Gerald Tsai.

Consider those who have really made it, who satisfy the one true criterion of superstar status – those in the financial sector who have made television commercials. They too are nearly all men.

Before he became chairman of the US Federal Reserve, Alan Greenspan showed us on television how easy it was to calculate your financial statement on your Apple personal computer. Then, deadpan, Greenspan intoned: 'If you've got any money left over you're doing better than the government.' Quite.

Again, there was Lawrence Kudlow, chief economist for investment bankers and brokers Bear Sterns, who explained the status involved in having a Cadillac (although he somehow forgot to mention the huge, never explicitly stated kudos that comes with having your face on television – even in a cruddy commercial).

But the fund industry has struck a blow for equality here. The only internationally prominent woman to have made the televisual grade with the men is Elaine Garzarelli. Garzarelli is renowned for having predicted the 1987 crash. She sold most of her stock portfolio just days before the curtain came down, and achieved considerable fame as a consequence. On the tails of that fame came a $1 million a year job at what used to be Shearson Lehman in New York and, at last, genuine success – a television panty-hose commercial. The camera follows Garzarelli's legs as she strides about her office advising clients on the phone. The product, by the way, was No Nonsense panty-hose. Go out and buy some now.

But Ms Garzarelli, who has since moved on from her Lehman job, is most definitely the exception rather than the rule. Call it glass ceiling, call it plain prejudice, but the truth is that most of the investment deities are men. The women are present in the sylvan grove all right, but they are nymphs rather than Dianas.

And so to the most important difference between a divine, universally present non-corporeal being who is the fundament of creation, and a fund manager. Basically, you can sack the fund manager, whereas God is self-employed.

The chief reason for sacking a fund manager – or, if you are an investor as opposed to the manager of a fund company, withdrawing your investment – is because he's not very good (or should that be god?). Fortunately, it is relatively easy to determine whether a fund manager is good at the business of fund management. There are lots of fund monitoring services out there who track the performances of funds, and sometimes even individual investment decisions to buy and sell stocks within a fund. The result is that fund managers are watched, measured and continually evaluated.

So who is the best manager, according to the fund monitoring services? Ask that question and you'll typically find yourself on the receiving end of dithering equivocation. The spiel usually takes in the difficulty of comparing funds with slightly different investment remits – some funds, for example, have trust deeds that restrict the manager's choice of investment. There may be some talk of the risk implicit in the fund, of whether the manager has managed to maintain a smooth investment performance, as opposed to one that jumps around erratically. You might also hear something about the state of the market, and what a tough time it's been for utilities recently, so a fund investing in electricals is surely not going to be doing so well. All of which is worth listening to, before you ask the telling question. Which is how much your money is worth now. This, don't forget, is the money you have entrusted to a person with supposedly superior knowledge. That person is paid – often very well paid – by you and your fellow investors to make your money grow. How well he has performed that task is largely a function of the net value (net of the charges that pay the manager's wages) of your investment.

Before we get to the criteria we should use in determining how good or otherwise the fund manager is, it's worth understanding the magnitude of this issue. In other words, how many people are asking the same question? And just how much money are we talking about here?

The vast majority of the world's population dismissed in 381 words

In a global context we can dismiss Africa, since the people are too poor to be paid much attention, even by the mass-marketing-orientated, wolverine-appetited fund industry. That will change soon enough. Capitalism is working its early little charm tricks on the Dark Continent – the tobacco industry has already discovered a new and enthusiastic market for its products, and once it has its addicted target market, just watch the prices rise and rise.

Fund managers are interested in Africa, all right. But mainly in skimming a little of the speculative froth from the continent for the benefit of western markets. The obverse side of the coin that the African people are too poor to be investors is that they make excellent wage slaves – see the chapter on ethical investment for the financial euphemism for this shameless exploitation of the poor. Anyway, the net result is that some of the more advanced economies in Africa should soon make attractive markets to sell to enthusiastic 'emerging market' investors. But, for the moment, the Africans are safe from marketing literature promising miraculous wealth.

Pretty much the same can be said for the people and countries of Latin America. Except that the food's a lot better.

Asian investors are basically resistant to the concept of investing in funds. Asians (Japan has a developed fund market and is excluded from this) are smart enough to realize that paying someone else to play with your money is a) often quite expensive and b) possibly counter-productive. Because, the thinking goes, when you get to a balls-to-the-wall situation these fund manager people are dealing with someone else's money (and don't ask what a balls-to-the-wall situation might be, I don't think I've ever been in one).

So Asian investors, if they have the money to spare, like to keep much of it in ultra-safe bank deposit accounts. Or, if they have been drinking too much cognac, they like to speculate wildly, betting thousands on horse races, or fish or cock fights, or a new factory in Shenzhen. The point is that however contradictory the investing mentality of Asian individual investors might be, they do like to do it for themselves. If their money is going to be badly handled and grotesquely misapplied, Asian investors, on the whole, like to do the misapplying.

Mutual fund statistics as a one-way ticket to Toy Town

Right, that's the vast majority of the world's population dealt with in 381 words, so let's concentrate on the size of the markets in North America and Europe, and the idiocies perpetrated on the peoples of these continents in the name of popular capitalism.

The US mutual fund industry grows and grows and grows. According to the Investment Company Institute (ICI), the Washington, DC-based trade association of the US mutual fund industry, net flow into US mutual funds in June 1994 was $19.7 billion, up 44 per cent from June 1992. In addition, there are now a total of 4,224 funds operating in the United States containing assets of $1.8 trillion (one thousand billion). Ten years ago, there were 857 funds with total assets of $297 billion. Every year, it seems, a new record is set.

DWS, the mutual fund arm of the giant German bank, Deutsche Bank, concurs with those figures for the US industry, and adds data for the Europeans and the Japanese. The European industry rose from $1.07 trillion to $1.44 trillion, and Japanese funds grew to $523 billion from $374 billion. 'Eliminating currency movements, the increase in the larger mutual fund industries was approximately 30 per cent,' concludes the bank.

These are the kinds of figures to send anybody who stops for a moment to reflect on them on a one-way ticket to Toy Town. It isn't a question of the inability of words to describe just how absolutely, unnecessarily big that figure is. It is, yet again, a failure of numbers. As savings go, those statistics represent a lot of pennies in a lot of bulging piggy banks.

In short, the mutual fund industry has sold itself well, and continues to do so. Not all of the money under its control is going into high-risk investment like the stock market. According to DWS figures, just over one third of assets under management in the US mutual fund industry is committed to shares, compared to 38 per cent of Japanese funds, 27 per cent of Swiss funds, 16 per cent of German, and 14 per cent of French funds. The British industry, in comparison, looks ludicrously overweight in equities, with 97 per cent of all mutual fund assets committed to the stock market.

There are all sorts of explanations for these wide discrepancies. The French have 59 per cent of their mutual fund money in money market funds because these are as close as you can come to a bank deposit account yielding a fair return. And fair returns on bank deposit accounts are unheard of in France, a country whose bankers have a long and illustrious tradition of shamelessly ripping off their customers. The Germans put 76 per cent of their mutual fund money into bond funds. Why? Well, pick a cheap chauvinistic slur against German people, and say that this kind of humourlessness/lack of imagination/obsession with officialdom (if we're talking government bonds) is typical of 'the German mentality'. Whatever that might be. The truth is, they invest in bonds because they always have. As for the British, you might be tempted to say the almost exclusive concentration on equity exposure is proof positive that Thatcherism has converted Britain to a casino economy. Maybe, maybe not. But the truth of the matter is that a lot of money has been placed with managers who are committing it to the febrile stock markets of the world. More than $1.44 trillion. This is a staggering gesture of faith on behalf of the world's small investors.

Because – let's not forget the fundamental point – this isn't the manager's money that the manager is taking risks with. Just about every country in which risk-oriented mutual funds are sold insists that the fund industry point out that the price of mutual funds can go down as well as up, and that past performance is not a guarantee of how a fund will perform in the future, etc, etc. But who pays attention to that kind of warning? These little bits of fine print are treated with the mild contempt and calculated indifference normally reserved for those monotonously spieled safety instructions on plane flights. Yeah, sure planes fall out of the sky. But it's always somebody else's plane, just like it's always somebody else's fund that's going to nosedive.

Except that it isn't. Mutual funds are one hell of a lot more liable to pitch into the sea than jumbo jets. That means we are talking about the far from remote possibility of millions of investors going blue in the face and scrabbling for their oxygen masks.

So, all in all, the question of whether fund managers are managing our money well is pretty important.

Are fund managers good at what they do?

Now we've got to the sticking point. How do you know whether the fund manager is any good? There are lots of tests, and – guess what? – most of them are entirely inconclusive. Picking a good fund manager is like picking a good stock, is like predicting whether it will rain tomorrow.

In retrospect it looks great. We have a splendid set of ready-made arguments formed within a system that shapes our understanding of the world, a crude instrument that imperfectly but satisfactorily explains what happened yesterday, and yet is hopeless at predicting what will happen tomorrow. If you enjoy *ex post facto* rationalizations read an interview, any interview, with a successful fund manager. Hagiographic articles in the financial press are as close as you can come to perfectly reliable leading negative indicators (for an explanation of that piece of algebra see Chapter X and the Calabrian traffic light theory of journalists as leading negative indicators).

Whatever. The sequence of events goes like this.

'How do you do it, Champ?'

'The secret's in the wrist action.'

Exit Champ, pursued by a bear.

Or to move closer to the real world. Once they've finally caught the attention of the media, they are well and truly fucked, the poor bastards (the word 'poor' here is used in a violently oxymoronic sense. It means 'grotesquely overpaid'). Essentially, media praise is a professional death sentence. Journalists do these things for reasons that merit explanation, and indeed are explained in Chapter X.

The solution must be to ignore reputation, especially if it's built on media hype. The most important element in deciding whether a fund manager is good or not must, surely, be the figures.

And, aye, there's the rub. Against what, exactly, should we judge those figures?

Indices and their magical effect – managers become foetal balls of wailing pinstripe

There is an important point to be made here. This may be an over-used phrase, but really, it is an important point. So hang on to it. The single most significant benchmark for the individual investor must be inflation. If the fund manager beats inflation, if you are able to buy more (more cars, more stockings, more – if you really must – *Best of Gregorian Chants, Volume II*, to complement *Volume I* of which you're only just beginning to get bored), if you can buy just plain *more* than you would have been able to with your original investment five years ago, then you have not been badly served.

Incredibly enough, the German authorities refuse to allow investment companies to market their products by comparing fund performance against inflation. Why this should be really is a mystery. What is clear is that it's unfair on the German investor, who keeps squirrelling money into that boring old bond fund.

So if your money holds or even increases its purchasing power over five years you haven't really got a case for throwing the fund manager in jail.

But, but, but, and quadruple but. Open a financial magazine, read a newspaper, look at those marketing claims. Investors are being offered just about everything this side of financial paradise. Just because your savings aren't being eaten alive doesn't mean that you're getting a good deal.

Which brings us to criterion of assessment number two. This is the one that causes all the trouble. This is the one that has those managers curling up into little foetal balls of wailing pinstripe. This is the market index.

Market indices, in the words of one of the world's leading index compilers, Morgan Stanley Capital International, 'serve a number of important purposes. They serve as an unbiased measure of markets enabling investors to understand the opportunities in each market. They serve as benchmarks for professional managers against which their portfolio management abilities are measured.'

Essentially, they are the thing that all the managers want to beat. It's inherent in the very nature of their jobs. They are paid to be smarter than the average. That means not just the average individual, who typically knows very little about stocks. No, to make their way as professional asset managers, to climb the professional ladder all the way up to panty-hose commercial status, they need to be better than the market.

But the figures from the statisticians show that most of them are failing to achieve that objective. The result has been a frenzy of often entirely contradictory acts of self-justification. The failure of the majority of fund managers to outperform the market over the past decade and more has offered us high farce and low comedy. An industry on two continents has been trying and failing to prevent its underwear from being seen in public. As yet there is surprisingly little popular awareness that the industry isn't wearing any underwear at all – just the Emperor's Clothes brand.

So let's look at the figures that make the asset management industry so unhappy. Then we can see the hybrid mass of justification, explanation, machination, and old-fashioned shit-eating the fund management industry has been putting itself through in order to preserve its business.

The numbers provided by statistical firms Micropal (a London-based fund performance monitor, it has the biggest international database) and Lipper Analytical (the dominant statistics firm in the

US fund market) both show that year in, year out, most mutual funds don't do as well as the market average. The proportion of funds outperforming the index varies a little, but not much. According to figures provided by Micropal, over the decade beginning in January 1983 no more than 34 per cent of mutual funds beat the main market indices in either the UK or the US.

Not only are those figures depressing for the failing majority, they are *consistently* depressing. When the fund management arm of Morgan Grenfell, the UK investment bank owned by Deutsche Bank, was looking to launch mutual funds at the back end of the 1980s, its research showed that not one manager had managed to beat the market every year for ten years. Even the very best managers failed to beat the market average at least once. Morgan Grenfell concluded that its best option was to launch funds that tracked the market. At least that way they could be sure of having funds that were consistently ranked in the top third of all mutual funds.

'Why are we launching index trackers?' asked the then-managing director of the firm. 'Three reasons – performance, performance and performance!' He was right. If you can't beat the index, join it – but what an indictment of contemporary management skills!

Morgan Grenfell was not alone in adopting this solution, and the growth of index funds – vehicles designed simply to mirror the performance of a market index – has been one of the most important developments in modern asset management. Indexation now accounts for a huge percentage of the industry's assets under management. According to statistics from Chicago-based fund monitor, Morningstar, the number of US index funds available to individual investors rose from 4 to 41 in the decade beginning 1 January 1983. The amount managed in those funds grew by a factor of more than twelve to nearly $13 billion. The US institutional index fund market experienced similar growth over the same period. Large investors like pension funds saw the number of funds climb from 1 to 21, while assets under management more than quintupled to almost $6 billion. While in the UK there are more than $7 billion under management, as opposed to less than $500,000 ten years ago.

The existence of these funds is an undoubted service to individual investors. Not only do they benefit from generally superior performance, they do not have to worship at the altar of God the

Stockpicker – although the fund management industry is trying very hard to preserve its mystique.

The arguments it uses to preserve its image would do credit to an expert in criminal pleading. The sort of rhetoric used is that which is prepared to dump any inconvenient fact at any given moment. To the charge of extreme ordinariness and an inability to perform the essential task of being smart, the fund management industry responds with the equivalent of a flimsy alibi – it didn't do it because it wasn't there. But if we see through that and get the industry to confess that it did do it, it tells us that it only did so because it had no choice. Guilty as charged, but please take account of mitigating circumstances.

Four pieces of rhetoric (including Specious Nonsense in a Ballgown, Mark II) and ...

The uncomfortable truth about fund managers' inability to beat the indices produced four wonderful pieces of self-serving rhetoric, and two concrete pieces of action entirely independent of the white noise generated by the flacks (press officers) and the spokesmen.

Argument number one was a long technical whine. Of course managers have a hard time beating the index, argued the industry. The index doesn't have to pay fees and charges on real trades. The index is a mathematical abstraction and it doesn't live in the real world where there are costs. Fund managers have to do real trades, and those expenses are reflected in lower performance figures.

Which is a fair point. But if we allow, say, a generous two per cent of assets to take care of administrative and dealing costs, are we really being told that the managers can't make that up? They are supposed to be smart people, remember. The figures show that even if you pare a couple of points off the index performance the vast majority of fund managers still fail to beat it. And in any event, two percentage points is a generous allowance. Fund managers have lots of financial muscle, and therefore a great bargaining position. They can negotiate trade commissions down to tiny fractions of a per cent. They can also make use of the highly liquid (and inexpensive) derivatives market. This can and does keep trading costs right down.

Specious Nonsense in a Ballgown Mark II was the industry's

sudden devotion to an apparently new thing called stock picking. In the mid- and late '80s, there was a collective shift of emphasis in the story the industry was putting out to its public. We were told that stock picking was a difficult and dangerous job, a skilled craft – nay, an art. Stock picking was the sexy bit of a portfolio, the 'satellite' round the 'core' which might be an index fund.

But what else are managers supposed to do, if not pick stocks? What did they *think* they were being paid for? To look at screens all day and then *not* pick stocks? The very idea of a stock-picking fund manager is a gigantic redundancy – or at least it should be. It's like talking about selective journalism. Surely, surely, people can see that all journalism is selective. The journalist is paid to select the relevant, interesting, sexy bits and package them all up in an article or a television piece. It's only called selective if someone else doesn't like the bits the journalist has chosen. The whole process of journalism is selection, just as the whole concept of managing a fund involves picking some stocks and not others. Or have I missed something?

Anyway, the idea of stock picking as a sexy little add-on to the fund manager's job – as opposed to being the central plank of his existence, the prime reason for being there in the first place – does seem to have caught on. It is a major public relations victory for the fund managers.

The third bit of frippery concerned the methods of indexing. Paraded as deep scientific knowledge discovered somewhere in the fathomless well of fund management industry expertise, we were told that indexing was a tricky business. It was, we learned, a difficult skill, this indexed investment stuff.

For example, some index followers favoured 'stratified sampling'. Which sounds impressive enough until you realize it means picking a few stocks from each sector of an index – a few retailers, some heavy industry stocks, a couple of banks, a drug company or two, a computer giant and some bio-technology corporations and you have a portfolio that will probably react in much the same way as a recognized standard US market index, such as the S&P 500.

It's as simple as going to a stall that's offering four varieties of fruit for sale and buying a pound of apples, pears, cherries and bananas. If you or I do that, we've bought some fruit. But if you're a fund manager you've modified your quantitative approach to this particular problem, and have taken a stratified sampling of the fruit stall.

There are other methods of indexation, but they're just as empty and pathetic. But before we pass on, an honourable mention for pure horse shit must be made of one particular indexation technique. This one's called 'full replication'. Which means buying all the shares in the index. Not too difficult to follow, is it? Not even for the technically naive who pay these managers' salaries.

But what's the managers' alternative to this empty obsession with nomenclature? How do managers fight against the fact that some people – the wicked cynics – call this type of investing 'passive'. There are those who refer to index funds as 'no-brainers'. Which is fair. Once you've bought your computer and you've made your investment what else is there for a fund manager to do? Except, maybe, vegetate and wait – passively – for the next pay cheque.

With argument four it's time to bring out the rapier, baseball bat, AK-47 assault rifle, Howitzer, and that oh-so-useful hand-held thermo-nuclear device all over again. This argument must be resisted above all others, but it is a many-headed beast. The more you slay the Hydra of Perfect Market Theory (aka Paradigmatic Market Silliness) the more it comes back at you.

The argument that the markets are far from perfect is already made. But to deal with advocates of the PMT/S in a fund context it will have to be stated here again, as briefly as possible.

The Market is, essentially, a forum for the exercise of collective trading instincts. These instincts are drawn towards profit, towards making a sale to the hypothetical Biggest Fool. Above all The Market is a creature of the warm side of the mind. It is coded language, not a science. Even the numbers that we use in indices are a form of metaphor. This is why psychological barriers, the quasi-magical double zero closing points that the markets often shimmy away from and then break free of, really do exist – as statistical evidence indicates. And this refutes any notion of a perfect market discounting only rationally relevant information into its prices.

Thankfully, few people take the vanity and pomposity of the PMT/S seriously any more. It has fallen from intellectual fashion, just as Reagan and Thatcher have faded into richly merited obscurity. But put yourself in the position of a fund manager. If you are the hypothetical 'average' fund manager, your average fund performance consistently fails to beat the market index. Isn't the idea that The Market is this perfect entity suddenly very appealing indeed?

Too right it is. It offers you two stunning advantages.

First, you have an impregnable excuse for failing to beat the market index. For God's sake, you're dealing with what is effectively a force of nature. It is the unconquerable perfection of The Market against which you're struggling. It would be unreasonable almost to the point of, well, extreme unreasonableness, to expect you to be better than something which is already perfect.

And then there's the already familiar gatekeeper factor. The notion of fund manager as God's Vicar on Earth can only be reinforced by the fact that the fund manager is the intermediary between the great, unwashed public, and the perfect market. It's perhaps not quite so alluring as the earlier version, where God the Stock Picker sat at his screen and offered divine wisdom. But being demoted from one of the archangels in the throne room to St Peter at the pearly gates deciding who shall have admittance is not so bad. It's certainly much, much better than looking for another job.

These are the reasons why the fund management industry held aloft the PMT/S, its arms raised in triumph. The PMT/S was both marketing sword and criticism-deflecting shield.

So the failure of many managers to beat the index is not evidence of the perfection of The Market, merely a fact that tends to support the not terribly controversial theory that a lot of fund managers really aren't very good at taking care of the money that is entrusted to them.

When they are good, we hear about it soon enough. In pre-panty-hose commercial days, there was a celebrated set of American fund managers who regularly got excellent returns in the bull market of the 1960s. They were (surprise, surprise) young, aggressive etc, and many wore sideburns. They were dubbed 'the gunslingers' by the press. Embarrassing, isn't it? But many of them consistently beat the market, which just was not thought of as a perfect entity. Nor will it be again when another generation of talented fund managers comes around.

... Two pieces of action

So much for the rhetoric. The decisive action taken by the industry has been the adoption and the quiet subversion of indexation. The growth of assets under management has already been remarked upon. But something else has grown hand-in-hand with that. There is now a whole industry of 'customized indexation' out there.

Managers of, say, funds specializing in smaller companies (quoted corporations doing a lot less business than a corporate giant like IBM), didn't like being compared to an index that included mainly big businesses. So the investment houses decided to invent their own benchmark against which they could be measured. The result has been huge growth in indices of all kinds – small cap, mid-sized cap, utilities, Japanese smaller companies. Just about everything short of the Thai whorehouse sector has its very own index.

So the fund industry has been smart once again in getting its hands on the levers of power. It now controls the benchmarks against which it allows itself to be measured. And it makes quite sure that the stocks it uses in the indices are those which it finds convenient to buy and trade.

But the fund management industry's struggle is not just against the supposed force of nature, alias The Market, that they have such a tough time measuring up to. No, fund managers have more problems than their demotion to grade-B angels. In assessing whether they do a good job or not, you have to take account of the difficulties they face.

They have an increasingly sophisticated and demanding public to cater for, a difficult industry to run cleanly because of the frequent conflict between an individual manager's interest and those of the fund, and – of course – they face stiff competition from each other.

Let's begin with how the industry has addressed the problem of competition. If you are strong, competition is a benign, inspiring thing. Competition also helps you to look good if the quality of your competitors is low. While it may be tough to beat the market, it may not be quite so difficult to do better than your fellow professionals.

But the fund industry is not a dog-eat-dog operation. Fund managers want to accommodate one another. They like the sense of community. Or at least they like having someone else around whose fund performances are demonstrably poorer than their own. But it would be bad publicity to point at a competitor and identify him as a loser. Apart from the extra irritant of possibly facing a law suit for defamation, it's hardly a claim to make the punters come running, is it? *Shake hands with me, I'm less diseased than the leper in the corner.* To make the life of the broad church of fund management just that little bit easier the industry has found a way of making everyone a winner.

Parents of small children know how this is done.

The specially hired clown is stationed by the door, and when each little bundle of toddling selfishness arrives it has a balloon, a colouring book, a cake and a drink thrust into its grubby little hands. It is then insincerely congratulated on the loveliness of its present.

Well, the fund management industry has opted for insincere praise and the simple expedient of having lots and lots of prizes. Prizes are doled out by the fund-monitoring firms, by specialist trade magazines (often in shameless barter for promises of advertising), sometimes even by industry representative bodies. There are, for example, some seventeen different categories of funds in the UK industry alone. That's seventeen different first, second and third prizes.

So now you know. When you pick up a newspaper and see '2nd in sector, UK growth' set in aggressive type in some advert, you'll see something that's quite impressive. But perhaps it isn't quite as impressive as it might at first appear – '2nd' and 'UK' will be easily visible. All that stuff about sectors, and so on, may not be. Still, if the fund is second out of a sector of 150 funds, as opposed to the 3,500 registered with that country's financial authorities, why worry?

If UK growth stocks have had a bad year, and their investors have lost money, *that* might be a reason why. ('Growth', by the way, is a euphemism meaning that the share probably pays lousy income. Anything with a half-respectable dividend is enthusiastically ticketed as 'income' or 'high-yield' – which is another category of fund, with a whole new set of prizes to be won.)

The result of this pluralistic prize-winning is indeed that everyone is a winner. It's just important to remember that some managers win bigger than others.

When they win for themselves rather than their fund and their investors, the issue of the quality of service offered by fund managers takes on a wholly different, more sinister aspect.

Fund managers have any number of ways of abusing the trust placed in them by their investors. But few would accuse the fund management industry as a whole of being overburdened with a vivid imagination, and one particular and obvious malpractice stands out as by far the most common.

The trick is to use the purchasing power of a fund for the manager's own purposes – or, only slightly less disreputably, for the benefit of another fund. Imagine that you are in control of a modern fund. It's fairly big. It has around $750 million in assets, and it has performed pretty well since you took control. You like to let it be known that you have a buccaneering (maybe even gunslinging) management style. You take big positions in stocks, sell as and when you please, and enjoy making your profit. You identify a good investment prospect in a smaller company that has a market capitalization of around $500 million. You're going to wait for the price to ease, maybe just a little bit, and then you're going to press the button in your own inimitable style. Using several brokers to try to disguise your interest and obtain the shares as inexpensively as possible, you have decided to take a $50 million stake in the company. You know as surely as you know the sun will rise tomorrow that the company's share price will also rise, because you are big enough to be a major force in the market for that share. Your sudden demand for these shares will see the supply of them priced more expensively.

Now, isn't it tempting just to buy in a couple of thousand of those shares for yourself? After all, you're the one who identified the opportunity. Why shouldn't you do a little of what some people like to call 'pre-buying'?

Well, apart from the moral obloquy of abusing the trust of the investors whose pooled assets you manage, there's the not inconsiderable fact that the law in both the US and the UK takes a very dim view of that kind of trade. In the US rule 17-j of the Company Act 1940 prescribes fund managers 'from engaging in fraudulent, manipulative or deceptive conduct in connection with their personal trading of securities held or to be acquired by the fund.' In the UK, legislation and regulation are in a state of flux, but it's clear that this type of trade is at least subject to swingeing penalties from within the UK regulators' disciplinary code. It is also possibly a breach of criminal law – if not outright theft, perhaps obtaining a pecuniary advantage by deception.

Yet despite the unequivocally wrong nature of the act, fund

managers do it, time and time again. If not for themselves or their families, there is always the temptation to back up their personal judgment on a specially loved fund. Perhaps there's a new fund that a manager has nurtured into existence. Perhaps the manager has argued hard for the fund management company to go to the expense of setting up the fund, and perhaps the success or otherwise of this fund is therefore linked to the manager's personal standing within the firm. All the manager has to do is lead the little fund into the stock, step by step, softly, softly. And then a few days or weeks after the little fund's position is secured, in comes the big fund. Up goes the price of the stock, up goes the performance of the little fund, up goes the manager's reputation. Even though it is a blatant fraud on the shareholders of the large fund, this happens frequently. Bear in mind that we only know about the ones who get caught.

And for those seeking personal gain, it doesn't require financial genius, or even very much money, to open up a Bahamian or Swiss account. It is easy to execute trades anonymously through these accounts – partly because the criminal codes of Switzerland and the Bahamas provide for jail sentences for bankers who breach the strict terms of client confidentiality written in to those countries' banking laws.

One of the most recent cases is not yet proven. But whether impropriety is involved or not, stupidity most certainly is. A manager with one of the world's biggest fund management groups purchased several thousand shares for members of his family. He did not follow the management group's notification procedures for share purchases of this type. Shortly after the purchases were made the company filed for a public stock offering.

In a separate incident that occurred around about the same time, Fidelity Investments, the biggest fund group in the world, announced that some of its employees had purchased stock for personal accounts which rose in value after the firm's funds purchased the same shares. Fidelity said that it was changing its procedures on personal trading. Which is fine and dandy, but Fidelity is the grandaddy of the mutual fund business. Fidelity's so big, has been around for so long, and is generally so Old Money and respectable that its shit is supposed not to stink.

Well, I don't know about you, but it doesn't smell too good to me.

There is one last area that causes concern in the mutual fund industry. In this case, mutual fund managers are victims of their own success in their mission to educate the public in finance. The notion of spreading the gospel of personal financial management is perhaps something of a high view of the industry, but many claim to believe that this is what mutual funds are all about.

Public comprehension of financial management – somebody else's air crash

Unfortunately for fund managers, the level of public comprehension of financial management is, shall we say, uneven. On the one hand, the investing public clearly fails to understand that if it puts money into a fund that invests in shares there is a distinct possibility of loss. Prices can go down as well as up – that's somebody else's air crash, right? On the other hand, the concept of getting value for money is readily understood. While UK investors still passively accept initial charges of five or six per cent and annual fees of 1.5 per cent, their American cousins balk at such costs. They will negotiate charges down, or maybe shop around to find a more keenly priced service. That might seem like plain nickel-and-diming, but for a mutual fund investor it counts as a pretty sophisticated attitude.

Now the mutual fund industry is not lacking in business acumen. If it sees what its customers want, that product will be provided. This is why the back-load fund was born. 'Back-load', as you've probably guessed, doesn't mean that there are no charges, it means that there are no charges in the form that you might expect to find them. In most cases, this boils down to low charges that are evenly spread through the duration of an investor's keeping money in a fund. That can present serious cash-flow problems for fund managers, as explained in an article in 1994 in the *International Herald Tribune's* quarterly magazine, *International Fund Investment*.

> With shares [that levy front-end charges, the managers] simply split the commission with the brokerage that sells the fund. With [back-load] shares, they collect no commission, but they must still pay the brokerage, usually 4 per cent. This is no small piece of change: [back-load] share commissions will likely total more than $1 billion [in 1993]. Fund purveyors recoup this advance over time by charging shareholders a steeper annual fee.

There is something quite healthy about a mindset in which levying an initial charge of five or six per cent would probably be accepted as grounds for justifiable homicide. It betokens an attitude of vigilance and questioning which requires the fund management industry to behave properly and professionally.

Financially, however, the US mutual fund industry is in some danger. Although the industry has more money under management than ever before, despite the fact that the capital keeps pouring in, mutual fund companies are going to find themselves in serious trouble if investors keep insisting on paying no up-front charges.

Let's not forget this. For all their pomposities, posturings and general naughtiness, fund managers have mommies that love them. Fund management, particularly equity fund management, really *is* a good thing, especially if you do it over the long term. Regular saving is one of the few reliable ways of building capital and – over the second half of the twentieth century, at least – of beating inflation. So for all their wickednesses, fund managers are providing a valuable service. They do offer access to the inner workings of the high markets of capitalism. But they will not be able to do so if they are starved of income. They too have businesses to run.

Devices have been used to circumvent the cash-flow starvation of not levying initial charges. Some companies have simply taken out bank loans and matched repayments against the income stream they lock into as their investors stay in the funds. Others have borrowed money from the capital markets, offering bond investors the opportunity to buy that income from investment fees as a securitized package, otherwise known as a bond.

Now that's all very well, but if the industry chooses to go down the bond route it is flirting with catastrophe. What will happen, for example, if interest rates turn up sharply? First, no capital markets investors would want the bonds, since alternative investments – namely, interest on deposit accounts – would be that much more attractive. Second, it's entirely conceivable that the equity markets, which notoriously detest high interest rates, would tumble. That would leave fund management groups with, successively, no income and no business. The conclusion must be that while fund managers do a pretty average job in most cases and do not deserve – at all – to be thought of gods, there is still no need to cast them out into darkness.

Pension fund managers and the promotion of child slavery

Pension fund managers do more or less the same thing as mutual fund managers, except they do it much more conservatively. This is because of the onerous responsibility of trying to provide an income stream for an increasingly large constituency of elderly people who have developed the extremely inconvenient habit of living longer and longer. Speculation is not the fund managers' thing. They are all about grandfather clocks, measured views of the markets, long-termism, one small whisky before bed, and an anal retentiveness quotient that enables them to play complex jazz-funk tunes with their colonic ducts. Many pension fund managers are actuaries. Some are Scottish (thought you should know).

They are part of the equity cult, but are in the middle of the chain of worship. Pension fund managers almost never have to deal with their pensioners the way that fund managers sometimes have to get their hands dirty dealing with the public. The main contact they have with things other than mathematical formulae is professional. Lower down the chain is the broker. Upstream is the investment consultant, and ultimately the pension fund trustee.

Let's go downstream first.

Pension fund managers are to brokers what a Macy's dress buyer is to a garment manufacturer – i.e. for all practical purposes, God.

Anyway, in the not inconsiderable US pension market, the role of the fund manager is increasingly prominent. According to Investment Company Institute statistics, the number of Individual Retirement Accounts (self-pay pension plans) rose from 4 million in 1983 to 29.3 million in 1993, with assets under management rocketing from $10.8 billion to a 1993 figure of $283 billion. Meanwhile, in the even bigger arena of company pension schemes, the mutual fund industry's share of the market almost doubled over the five years to 1993, rising from 14 per cent to 26 per cent of the total corporate plan industry, according to statistics provided by Access, Inc. Over this period the fund industry took market share from both the banks (which declined from 32 to 27 per cent) and the insurance companies (down from 40 to 34 per cent).

There are good reasons why this should be so. They are to be found upstream. But the practical effect is clear. Even if one or two brokers might once upon a time have shown some resistance to selling their nine-year-old daughters into slavery at the fund manager's behest, there's no question of that happening now. *Ladies and gentlemen, here's Anne-Sophie, my younger child, ten next birthday. What am I bid?*

The commission percentages may be minute, but if you're processing orders for a manager for the Californian State Employees pension fund (known by its acronym, CALPERS, it has $85 billion under management) you don't need a large percentage share of the pie to have a very full plate indeed.

So why do pensions use pension fund managers (remember, pension fund managers do the same job as mutual fund managers, but the money they manage is for the longer term and is distributed to people called pensioners as opposed to investors)?

The next link in the chain – investment consultants

It's happened for a variety of official reasons, but really because of the next link up in the chain. These are the people whom the mutual fund managers must please. These people have a very favourable mix of power (a great deal) and responsibility (almost zero).

They are called investment consultants. What they do is advise the trustees of pension funds how to fulfil the onerous duties placed on them by trust law.

Pension fund trustees are obliged to exercise 'due diligence' in the care and control of the assets of a fund. Given the litigious nature of American society it is clearly a desirable thing to employ a professional investment consultant so that the board of trustees can say that it has acted responsibly in carrying out those duties.

So the investment consultant is approached, and is asked whether the trustees are discharging the investment management side of their duties as fully as they might. For this the consultant is paid a fee.

What will the consultant's response to the question be? Will it be a) 'Yes you're doing a great job. Here's my invoice.'? or b) 'Well, it looks OK, but you could perhaps do better with a little asset diversification – investing in, say, international bonds and stocks with a specialist non-US manager. By the way, we can help you find the best manager by doing a search. For which, of course, there will be an additional fee.'?

There is strong evidence to support the argument that US pension funds have been too conservatively managed over the years. Trustees have been so scared of losing money that they have not hired managers who will try to boost fund performance by putting at least some assets into international bonds and shares. Enter the investment consultant, who is in the very happy position of being able to say that the trustee should do just that.

And then the consultant can help the trustee with step two in the process of finding the right fund manager for the trustees' investment objectives (as stated, usually, in some antedeluvian trust deed). This part of the business has been nicknamed the Beauty Contest or the Beauty Pageant.

Trustees, in taking their duties seriously, look very carefully at the financial credentials of a manager, as presented by the investment consultant. After the consultant has submitted a detailed written questionnaire to managers considered (by the consultant) to be suitable, the trustees will receive a shortlist, usually of three to five firms. They may then whittle that list down yet further themselves, or they may call the candidate fund managers to come and make a presentation to them. It is that last, presentational element of the selection process that has earned the procedure the soubriquet beauty contest − an anachronistic name, perhaps, but some attitudes die hard in the financial world.

Like modern-day beauty contests, the decision will often rest not just on beautiful figures but on whether the contestant can argue convincingly that giving several hundred million dollars to the firm will significantly promote the cause of world peace. But the importance of non-financial considerations − such as the nationality or sex of the fund manager − is relatively unimportant. True, some US pension funds hand out small portions of money (sometimes as little as $1 million a time) to fund managers forming part of a minority group. But this kind of money is insignificant, and the whole process might be seen as pure tokenism. Nevertheless, the biggest chunk of money ever allocated internationally by a US pension fund was grabbed by a management team from the mutual fund arm of the French bank, Paribas. Paribas plainly knew its Californian client, the 800-pound gorilla of the pension world, CALPERS. Its four-strong team was composed entirely of women.

The investment benefits of the trend to move a small percentage of US pension fund assets abroad will only be determined in the long term. But it is already clear that the process must be lauded for its openness. US pension trustees hold public meetings which the beneficiaries of the fund – the pensioners – can attend. So the trustees have to be well briefed to answer awkward questions, and have to know how and why the assets of the fund have been invested. Compare that openness with the pathetic inadequacy of European – and particularly UK – trust law, and you quickly know which side of the Atlantic you'd like your own assets to be domiciled.

Europe is the home of the closed door and the po-faced Swiss banker. It is the secrecy attached to entities such as Liechtenstein trusts that has proved a fertile breeding ground for outrageous fraud on pension fund beneficiaries. When the pensioners of the Mirror Group – a newspaper concern owned by the late Robert Maxwell – were being defrauded, none of them really knew what was happening. The occasional difficult question was put, but thanks to the European obsession with secrecy, Maxwell was able to steal tens of millions and ruin many retirements. That he managed to do so almost entirely unchallenged is a cause for great shame to the British government, the ramshackle system of financial regulation it introduced and is belatedly overhauling, and the UK financial press which was cowed by Maxwell's teams of attack-dog libel lawyers.

So perhaps it can be accepted after all, this system that, as a by-product of openness and extreme seriousness of purpose, creates a little power without responsibility. Even though it is, in reality, a great deal of power without responsibility.

Consultants choose the managers whom the trustees see. They advise (i.e. tell) the trustees about questioning, they are frequently involved in the committee discussions on the merits of individual firms. They are the conduit between the trustees and the people who will manage the pension fund's money. Investment consultants will not allow fund managers independent access to the trustees. The trustees, when they are deciding to whom they will entrust pension fund money, go into a kind of financial purdah – it is considered improper for them even to be seen eating in the same restaurant as a candidate fund manager. It is the investment consultant who plays the role of the 220-pound eunuch, the brothel-keeper-cum-bodyguard-cum-*eminence grise* in this scenario.

For the fund manager, the question of whether the investment consultant is doing a good job is completely immaterial. All the fund manager wants is to be liked. But the trustees are at the top of the tree. If they don't take a critical look at investment consultants, no one does. So what criteria do they use?

Obviously, given that the trustee hires the consultant to demonstrate a high level of compliance with their duties to improve investment performance, the single most important factor will be whether the consultant has led them to a good manager. If the consultant has advised them to hire a poorly performing manager, then both adviser and manager go. That much at least can be taken for granted.

But, yes, you guessed it. Manager performance is among the very least most important reasons for firing an investment consultant, according to research conducted by Greenwich Associates, an international research firm based in Connecticut. The research covers the most important pension funds in the US and the UK, and reveals that, in 1992, the most important reason by far for changing an investment consultant was 'poor client service', cited as the top of the hate list by 49 per cent of the several hundred funds surveyed. For poor client service read minimal after-sales service.

Consultants, once they have talked themselves into a job, need to keep talking, or else they are in real trouble. It isn't the quality of the discourse that counts, because many trustees – bless their hearts – are easily impressed by people who appear to have knowledge. So it's keep talking or die – consultants are the investment equivalent of Yasser Arafat. Except they have an easier life than Arafat. If Arafat screws up, the Israelis, or more probably a faction within the PLO, will permanently remove his power of speech. Investment consultants, apart from not having to dodge bullets if they get things wrong, don't have any worthwhile check on their power.

They have it within their gift to send billions of dollars swooshing round the world – just because they say so. And if they send it to the wrong place, to some smooth-talking Brit with a pretty accent and a Gieves & Hawkes pinstripe who can pontificate mystifyingly about asset allocation modules but couldn't recognize a good investment opportunity if it pinned him to the ground and shat in his mouth, if they do that and the value of the fund's millions nosedives, what then?

Nothing. Unless, that is, the torrent of financial white noise dries up. In which case, the consultant is fired for providing poor client service. Incredible, but true. Consultants have it all – maximum power, minimum responsibility. In this, and their dependence on empty rhetoric, they share an identity with a group wider than just Yasser Arafat. They are very similar to – whisper it gently – that frequently and rightly vilified set, financial journalists. Which is another story (or at least another chapter) entirely.

Venture capitalists' strange physiques – three eyes and no balls

No tour of the fund world would be complete without a look at the role of the venture capitalists. Strictly speaking, venture capitalists are not necessarily fund managers, but they have been using the technique of pooling their investments in funds for some time.

The industry has grown hugely over the last two decades. According to the *New York Times,* venture capital funds in the US had expanded from something close to a cottage industry to an important financial sector with some $32 billion invested in small business by around 600 venture capital firms by the end of 1992. European venture capital is about half the size of the US industry, with the bulk of business being done in the UK.

The phrase 'venture capital', by the way, is another worthy entrant in the lists for the prize of Financial Redundancy of the Year. After stock-picking fund managers and selective journalism, few things can live on the same level of daftness. What venture capitalists do is invest in or lend money to small business people. So they venture their capital to 'start-ups' which have never traded, or newly established businesses in need of money to expand and survive. These businesses are too small or too young to have access to the usual sources of capital investment, such as the stock market (although whether that is really a form of raising capital or a high-stakes form of roulette is still an open question). From the capital backer's point of view, the hope is of a higher than usual return for investment in a relatively untried business. But there's truth in the old cliché, nothing ventured, nothing gained. No profit without risk, etc. Which offers us this interesting conundrum. Given that you're lending capital with the prospect of profit, you are necessarily taking some kind of risk. So why specify that the capital is being ventured?

Well, maybe the name refers to project financing, the injection of liquidity into a venture. Maybe. Whatever the linguistic nicety, the business reality is that venture capitalists do what bankers used to do – they advance money for profit. The rationale for development of the phrase 'venture capitalism' is analogous to the sly marketing acumen that has successfully promoted the idea of the stock-picking fund manager. As banks evolved into opportunistic seekers after profit and stopped lending money to corporations that were a credit risk, there was a need to invent a new term for lending money that made the old equation of risk and return seem magical and special, somehow outside the normal run of affairs for the banker.

Venture capitalism fitted the bill nicely. The banks, which had been running away from genuine, ground-level risk for years, consigned the taking of stakes in small businesses to this neat little pigeon hole. Banks were much more interested in betting their own capital for profit, either on the international capital markets or through playing bid games of buying and selling shareholdings in their own clients. (The latter activity, as we have seen, has had the gracious epithet of 'investment banking' bestowed upon it.)

Venture capitalists are, on the whole, no worse at their jobs than most other sectors of the financial services industry. But then, few of them are much better. A number of them actually believe that, because they ask small businessmen to go through the ritual of producing projections (venture capitalist slang for guesswork), they have some kind of genuine insight, that they can make some genuine prospective progress into what will happen tomorrow. Which is rubbish. The future trading prospects of the business, its viability in the economic conditions of its market niche, and the general possibility of success are all subject to the universal rule that anyone who claims to know what will happen tomorrow in any market is either a charlatan for telling you secret information, or a fool for treating what is unknowable as certain.

Which makes venture capitalists sound like economists, doesn't it?

But the most important difference between economists and venture capitalists is that despite their common addiction to pure theory, venture capitalists actually go out and act on their conclusions. Money changes hands, risks are taken. They are real people doing real jobs that provide a driving force for capitalist enterprise.

What is unreal to the point of being downright fantastic is the actual substance of what guides their decision-making. Essentially, there is an even bigger gap between the theory of what is supposed to guide venture capitalists and the practical art of their business. The rules of official venture capital theory, being a kind of applied economic theory, are necessarily unrelated to what happens in day-to-day life. The practice can be reduced to a few essentials. And if these are not provided by the person seeking capital, all the sensitivity analyses, all the market research surveys, all the quantitative, bottom-up research in the world will count for nothing.

Practical point number one, then, is the business plan. Business plans must be pretty and have lots of pie charts. They must contain the words 'quantitative', meaning that the company has sent a letter to everyone in its market soliciting information. The fact that the letters are nearly always ignored is irrelevant. The word 'qualitative' must also appear. This means that a few people who know something vaguely related to the market in which the company is seeking to operate have been fed drinks in a bar somewhere until they eventually said something optimistic about the company's prospects. These comments are then quoted and dotted about the business plan at various points, usually where the pie charts are especially dull reading.

It is also vital that the venture capitalist see a certain rate of return. The current vogue is for a rate of return of 35 per cent (or more) compounded over five years. Let's pause a moment to consider why venture capitalists impose this ludicrously high figure. The short answer is, surprise, pure profit. The venture capitalist offers the backers of its funds – typically institutional investors – a premium return over risk-free returns. In other words, the venture capitalist gets business from his clients by saying that money invested will return, say, double the prevailing deposit account rate. To achieve that, in the knowledge that some companies are bound to fail, the venture capitalist hikes up the returns that the fledgling businesses must achieve. So far from being a noble facilitator of burgeoning enterprise, the venture capitalist stands between capital and entrepreneur. The venture capitalist is in fact a hurdle to be overcome, a cruel man with a clipboard and a stopwatch requiring superhuman performance from the exhausted entrepreneur. As far as the venture capitalist is concerned, ventures and capitalism are irrelevant, all that matters is the financial returns of the companies that are bringing in the cash. And those companies exist solely as cash cows – sources of income – for the venture capitalist. Forget enterprise, these are just profit centres.

But, like him or not, the venture capitalist is there. So how do you meet his requirement for an annual return of 35 per cent or more? The good part is that you don't have to do it, all you need do is say that you can do it. Then you get the money, and then things change. With the advent of spread-sheet programmes, achieving a high hypothetical return is laughably easy. You just tone down an assumption here, trim a cost there, boost that estimate of earnings in the top left-hand corner, and the figures represent the current norm for this type of investment. Spread sheets also make it easier to deal with another key requirement – sensitivity analyses. These are just sets of figures with various assumptions radically altered, known at street level as 'what ifs'. What if the price of oil quadruples? What if interest rates halve? What if the moon stops orbiting the earth? The more you think of, the better. Almost nothing is too silly.

Why? Because the business plan isn't a serious attempt to guess what will happen to the venture capitalist fund's $2 million. It is a road test for the viability of the operators of the company. Have they done their homework? Do they know the market really well? Are they conscientious, clean-living people who can draw a nice pie chart and spell correctly? Projections and applied economics in a business sector has no relevance.

And so to point number two. The would-be entrepreneurs must be nice boys and girls.

Good track records, a family which risks destitution if the business fails, a personal commitment of capital, and good taste in business apparel are all very important. To have at least two of the four is essential.

Factor number three is greed. There's no point in asking for too little. That's because the venture capital industry just isn't geared up to lend small, really useful amounts of money, like $100,000 or so.

Venture capitalists are professional people, often accountants, and they have to be around large sums of money or they wither away and die. Or their BMW gets taken away from them, which is much the same thing. A study commissioned before World War II by the British government identified a vast gap in the market for small businesses looking to expand. Named 'the Macmillan Gap', it still exists. Of course, you could always try and get a bank to lend you the money, but, to reiterate, that really isn't what banks do these days.

Point number four is plain luck. Anyone seeking a capital injection has to hope to find the venture capitalist in a good mood, and above all in the frame of mind to take a risk. Otherwise, you may end up with the kind of criticism of the industry made by one entrepreneur who had just had his proposal – pie charts, discounted cash flow, et al – turned down by one of the industry's biggest players, formerly known as Investors In Industry, alias 3is. '3is? Well, that may be the case. It's just a shame they haven't got any balls.'

CHAPTER VI

Hedge, Swap, Derivative Fund Managers – The Left Hand of God

The multi-billion-dollar video game. Level one – who are these people? And why should we care? Level two – the wall. Level three – technical torture. Level four – blind man's buff. Level five – beat the market, Part I. Level six – the hall of mirrors. Level seven – the genius factor.

The multi-billion-dollar video game

B race yourself. The unpalatable truth is that we need to know who these people are. Why? Because if the financial world is a giant electronic game played by and for the benefit of the young (and that's as good a position to start from as any) these are the Teenage Mutant Ninja Turtles, the Super Marios, the Sonic the Hedgehogs of our era. They have their own coded language of success – Feeling fractal, Michaelangelo? Happy with your delta range parameters, Mario? Bent your risk distribution curve to a pleasingly fat oxbow, Sonic? Yo! Respect! Cowa-low-equity-index-correlation-bunga!!!

If you try to explain this antipodean part of the financial imagination in more mundane language it doesn't get any easier. For the truth is that those who can even begin to address themselves to the concepts in those jejune questions are probably mathematicians interested in investment theory, actuaries, or otherwise actively involved in the management of derivative, hedge, or swap funds. Now is that clear?

But, children, before we get to an exposition of what are truly the most amazing markets in modern finance, a number of anterior questions present themselves. If we are playing one of those walk-along-shoot-'em-up video games (and we might not be, but they are) we have to squish a few monsters such as image, rumour, and disinformation.

Level one – who are these people? And why should we care?

The market in which they work is not new, but its pre-eminence is relatively recent. And the body reflects the spirit. The creatures who inhabit this particular financial planet are in the main young or youngish, sometimes beautiful people. But despite the certainty of success, the unreconstructed late-1980s Ted Lapidus bull-market image – or perhaps because of it – they are people you would do well to actively avoid, right up to the point of paying good money not to have to sit next to them at dinner.

Unless, that is, you are prepared to make conversation about the strange universe that has brought them their money – and they are paid huge, huge wads of it. In 1993 one UK hedge fund manager, in his first year on the job, made more than $30 million. The money had to be spread around a few friends, but that is still good going for a start-up business. And this manager was by no means extraordinary – several principals of smaller, boutique-style operations made considerably more. It was difficult to find even a junior trader in one of the smaller UK offices with an income of less than $400,000 for 1993. In the United States, where there are more than 3,000 hedge funds, according to the Nashville-based research and advice organization International Advisory Group, people pay themselves even more. One manager raked in $1 billion in 1993. Now there is someone whose bets were well and truly hedged.

And then there is the considerable style of this success to consider – not only have they stolen the ball, but they're running with it, and have been doing so since the beginning of the 1990s. Everyone's running after them, but no-one – regulator, investor, or competing sectors of financial services – has been able to lay a hand on them. This is ball-stealing and, above all, ball concealment, transported to hitherto undreamed-of heights. They are phenomena, a quirk of market nature. Quite simply, in the 1990s, the business of managing derivative, swap or hedge funds (collectively referred to as the derivative industry and derivatives managers, at least for the moment) is undoubtedly the sexiest part of the financial services industry.

There have been, and will be, others. But so what? For now, derivatives managers are sitting on the magic carpet that is the moving average of where the market wants to be. As a consequence they have to deal with some of the strongest human emotions – awe, fear, jealousy, and the urge to destroy the crappy modern art with which they invariably decorate their reception halls. The feelings we have are the more powerful because, with the exception of the acrylic, papier mâché and frozen human embryo kinetic sculptures that are obviously just trash, these people are operating in a void. So we fear the unknown, the darkness visible that the derivatives managers have made their working environment. It is just over the wall of our own ignorance.

Level two – the wall

Welcome to Level Two on your quest to steal the secret of the Derivative Monster from its fiercely guarded lair. Your next mission is to hurdle The Wall.

It is worthy of reiteration. This is a wall that the derivatives managers have, quite consciously, constructed themselves. Its purpose is to prevent others from knowing what they do for a complex set of reasons – some legitimate, some capable of sinister construction (in that cynics would say that secrecy and complexity make impropriety difficult to detect). And they cannot allow this wall to fall, because if their business is understood – or the rest of the world thinks it understands, which is the same thing for many purposes – they will lose their position of maximum advantage, i.e. unfettered discretion and minimum surveillance.

Consider what happened when even a little light came through a chink in their wall of secrecy. Hedge fund manager George Soros (used as an example solely because he is well-known and respected and has an impeccable and justified reputation for the probity of his dealings) famously let it be known that one of his funds had realized a $1.5 billion profit by betting on a weakening British pound in September 1992. Rightly or wrongly (wrongly, as it happens) hedge fund managers were blamed for creating havoc in the currency markets, and for destroying Europe's somewhat pathetic attempts to achieve a single currency.

But that didn't really matter, especially to the isolationist tendency in the US. The ERM débâcle occurred in Europe, where they have those funny Monopoly-style currencies printed on coloured paper. But when the dollar began to move in a way that some of the US establishment didn't like, the role of people like George Soros began to seem important. Which led to a statement in June 1993 by House banking committee chairman Henry Gonzalez (D, Texas). Gonzalez said he would ask the Federal Reserve and the SEC to investigate the impact of Soros on the foreign exchange market.

'At a minimum it is in the best interest of the Federal Reserve and other central banks to fully understand Mr Soros' methodology [sic] for manipulating the foreign exchange market,' he said, since such institutions were 'competing head on with Mr Soros in an effort to manipulate the value of various currencies.'

Well what does this tell us, apart from raising questions about the literacy of Mr Henry Gonzalez? It tells me, at least, that he doesn't understand that the foreign exchange market is just too big to manipulate. This is not rigging the market in a few stocks with the help of some buddies, we are talking about grotesquely large, unknowable, untamable forces. In the context of the foreign exchanges the big, powerful Soros funds have all the meatiness of a leper in a wind tunnel.

Fuck with the markets? Perhaps these funds are just a little bit inadequate. OK, if you see a man throwing a sausage into the Mersey Tunnel or waving a pencil in Carnegie Hall and you call *that* intercourse, then fine. But otherwise, no. When it comes to fucking with the foreign exchanges size is all, and hedge fund managers like Soros just aren't big enough.

But Soros seems to have decided that he likes guru status (it makes financial sense to be a guru, as we shall see). And so he has to play the publicity game. But he is doing so rather badly. On the one hand there was a truly embarrassing piece of arse-kissing from *Business Week* in the summer of 1993, when Soros was quoted as saying how he liked to give to charitable causes, and the more money he made the more he could give away (at this point readers should turn to the inside back cover, where the publisher, one hopes, has thoughtfully provided sick bags). On the other hand, he has tried to offset the rage, anger, jealousy, etc, generated by his successful sterling play by announcing a loss of around $650 million on the yen-dollar rate in early 1994. He also testified before the congressional committee in April 1994 that hedge funds were a stabilizing force in the market, since they bet against the irrational investment decisions and erratic capital flows of the moronic multitudes.

Too little, George, too late. The powers that be have decided to try and regulate hedge funds and derivatives trading generally.

Edward Markey, chairman of the House Telecommunications and Finance sub-committee is on record as saying that 'the question is no longer whether regulatory or legislative changes will be made...but what form the changes should take.'

In May 1994 the US General Accounting Office issued a report stating (correctly) that the fragmented US regulatory structure is badly placed to deal with the fast-growing derivatives markets.

'The immediate need is for Congress to bring the currently unregulated OTC (over-the-counter) derivatives activities of securities firms under the purview of one or more of the existing federal financial regulators and to ensure that derivatives regulation is consistent and comprehensive across regulatory agencies.'

There are plenty of agencies to choose from – the Securities and Exchange Commission, the Securities and Futures Association, the Commodities and Futures Trading Commission, for a start. And those are just some of the relevant organizations in the US and the UK. Multiply that figure by the number of countries with companies trading in the international arena and you finish up with a lot of bureaucracy. So the regulators are on the case and will eventually cramp the derivative industry's style. Managers should make hay now, they've probably only got another twenty or thirty years before the authorities do something decisive and dynamic, like hold a seminar in Switzerland.

So what are the effects, intended or otherwise, of the wall of silence around derivatives fund managers?

The answer is quite simple. It's a straight trade-off between liberty and rumour. On their side of the wall, the derivatives managers can, for the moment, do pretty much what they want. On this side rage the forces of rumour, the almost uncontrollable alternative news medium.

But by no means all the effects of rumour are negative. There is at least one enormous benefit in keeping the rest of the world in the dark. It is the misguided notion that derivatives managers are savants or gurus. With it comes a rationalization of this belief – an exaggerated and unjustified estimate of their supposedly gargantuan financial muscle. Both have a dramatic and beneficial impact on the investment decision-making of derivative fund managers.

Let's deal with the guru factor first. When a fund manager achieves guru status he takes on the honorary status of an artist. His investment decisions become self-fulfilling prophecies – the financial equivalent of a performative statement in aesthetics.

It works this way. If an investor has the reputation for incredible smartness, that investor's track record and decision-making will be followed by his acolytes. Thus, when the decision to invest in, say, UK commercial property (viz Mr Soros' very public decision in 1993) is announced, there is a flurry of people following him. Similarly with another sector on which Soros made a call, like gold mining shares. And because, inevitably, the price of anything rises if lots of people decide to buy at once, the prophecy is self-fulfilling, at least in the short term. The investment itself may not have much merit if judged on prevailing considerations of financial soundness (whatever they are), but the very fact that a guru has made the call means that its price will rise. And of course success breeds success, the greater the number of people who abandon their own sense of judgment and assign it to the guru, the more money chasing the guru's call, the sharper the price increase, the greater the weight the guru's pronouncements carry, the greater the interest from other investors, and so it goes on. Eventually, a good investment becomes just that as and when the guru says it is.

So in a way it's just all too perfect that an industry stuffed full of gurus should invest in modern art. The derivatives guru says that an investment is a good one, and by the act of declaration makes it so. The modern artist takes some unusual artefact, and by saying it is art, transforms it into that very thing.

Level three – technical torture

Congratulations. You have had a quick look at life on either side of The Wall and have skipped over it. Now you must wander through the Technical Torture Chamber and come out the other side with your sanity intact. Few do so. Those who do end up rich. Those who don't end up writing about it.

But it's Thatcher's TINA, I'm afraid. There Is No Alternative. It really isn't possible to have an intelligent awareness of what's happening in these markets without learning a little of what they're supposed to be about.

So what are derivatives? They are contracts that derive their value from something else. The something else that determines the rights and liabilities between the two parties to the contract might be the notional return on $250,000, as affected by the three-month interbank rate, or it might be the price of cotton, copper or cocoa. The contract might bind both parties, or offer one party the option to exercise a right. Very broadly, there are two main types of derivative contract – futures contracts and options contracts.

Futures contracts are essentially bets on the future price of the underlying commodity or financial instrument in a number of months. Options offer the right to buy or sell the commodity or instrument at a certain price. Unlike futures contracts, which are a bargain for sale with a delayed delivery date, options contracts are hardly ever exercised. That's because there's little point in shuffling all the paper. For example, an option to buy shares at 100 when the price of that share has moved up to 120 is clearly worth 20. Why insist that someone buy a share in the market at 120, sell to you at 100, when you will then be obliged to sell it back into the market at 120 to realize your gain? Much better, surely, to receive a straight payment of 20 from the person with whom you have the contract and waive your right to take up the option. If the share moves the other way and falls to 80, you're hardly likely to exercise your option to buy at 100 when there's better value in the market. Options to sell are called puts, options to buy are known as calls.

That's that then. Simple enough. The derivatives market explained, the next challenge is to master the game of golf in twenty-five minutes.

It is of course more complicated than that. Aside from the technical details of trading in these contracts, the real challenge of understanding these markets is the way that managers put them together. These simple instruments can, when conjoined in a portfolio of forty or fifty contracts, some of which are options on options, options on futures, options with technical twiddly bits like floors, caps and all manner of juicy nonsenses, achieve bewilderingly complex effects.

An important point to be made here is the level of remuneration claimed by managers of derivatives portfolios. Just like crooked garage mechanics pointing at the innards of a car and claiming lots of work done to justify the size of the bill, so the complexity of the portfolio has been used to justify a charging structure of almost unparalleled greed. Derivatives managers, in addition to claiming the annual fees investors usually pay when their money is professionally managed, require a share of the profits. The normal rate is twenty per cent of net profits per annum.

The magic of working in the dark, on the other side of the wall, has created a lot of very rich people in derivatives management. Take, for example, the UK fund manager who earned vast sums in the first year of running his own company. He was perceived as having talent. So much so that he set up business with some $300 million under management. By the end of Year One he had $800 million under management, as the funds continued to roll in. His performance in 1993 was impressive (although subsequently, like the rest of the industry, it has been far from that). He achieved an excellent 50 per cent gain over the year – which means, taking just the $30 million, he would have realized a gain of $150 million, of which his company would have been entitled to 20 per cent, or $30 million.

It's a tough job, a difficult business, it needs clever people. But you have to wonder how much of the cleverness is marketing chutzpah.

Complex or not, expensive or not, the demand for derivatives exposure – a lot of it through the medium of derivative fund management – is increasing. Take the market in currency and interest rate derivatives (futures and options contracts) as an example. Between 1987 and 1992 the total market size more than doubled to over 450 million contracts per annum, according to statistics from Salomon Brothers. But these figures are difficult to compile and necessarily approximate. The actual size of the market is in fact much, much bigger. The Bank of England has more recent data on the number of contracts traded on London's derivatives markets per day. The average daily figure for financial derivatives more than trebled between 1992 and 1994.

To gain an idea what those contracts represent in potential liability, you must appreciate that an investor might lay out $150,000 on a contract to buy $1.5 million worth of bonds in six months' time (a bond futures contract). This means that the investor has ten times the amount of exposure to profit or loss than if the bonds had been bought for cash and held for three months. There are contracts which offer even greater multiples of exposure – up to fifty times the cost of a contract is not unheard of. Put a few of these contracts in harness together and you can achieve impressive effects: one prominent US manager is on record as having made a particularly aggressive interest rate bet, so that *every change of one hundredth of one per cent in a certain interest rate meant that he made or lost $4 million.*

To deal with that kind of play the derivatives markets have to have a lot of money in them. They have to be big, and indeed they are. Bigger, in fact, than the world's share markets. And the consensus of analytical opinion has it that they are destined to grow even more. By the way, all the figures quoted above refer only to the markets that the regulators know about. It does not include the over-the-counter market. OTC trades are effected purely on the basis of trust and recognition between players in an unregulated paradigm of capitalism. Estimates of the outstanding trades vary slightly, but a consensus figure for summer of 1994 was $3 trillion in daily outstanding contracts.

Level four – blind man's buff

This is a neat part of the game. You think you understand that very few people really know what's going on, and that once you're over the wall that keeps the financially unsophisticated out and have a passing acquaintance with what's being traded and where, then you're on the inside. Think again. There are new levels of the unknowable to penetrate.

Let's take as an example the case of the UK mutual fund company Save & Prosper and its attempts to deal with some of the competition for business coming from the derivatives management sector. Save & Prosper is the UK's seventh-biggest mutual fund outfit, part of Flemings, an international investment house with some $75 billion under management. S&P is a long-established player and gives every indication of being a well-run company with a sober management style. In the early 1990s it looked at a fund offered by one of its rivals which was offering a high rate of return on capital (10 per cent, subsequently reduced to 9 per cent, but still way ahead of any other yield in the market) with a guarantee that all the capital would be returned at the end of a set period. The fund pulled in $750 million within the first nine months of launch. S&P naturally looked long and hard at the product, tried to match it using its own technical department, and decided that it couldn't do so. S&P went on the record several times, saying that, despite its status as an expert player in the field with all its experience and its resources, *it couldn't work out what the competition was doing.*

Consider what an extraordinary statement that is in the modern competitive environment. What's really intriguing about derivatives management today is the fact that if the rest of the world doesn't understand it, it doesn't *have* to be fraudulent. This is purely because of the extraordinarily complex nature of the business.

If you had two mutual fund companies offering a product invested in, say, Taiwanese shares, where the average dividend payments on quoted shares are a matter of record, and you had one fund management company saying it couldn't understand how another produced the promised return for investors, you would have a straightforward coded allegation of fraud. Running a pool of company shares in the form of a fund is a relatively simple affair. A share is a share, and a pool of a hundred or so shares is just the same, but bigger, with some tricky administrative problems such as working out the average value of a share in the fund, collecting dividends, and so on. Basically, it's a job for a smart, computer-literate person with a modicum of financial knowledge.

But managed derivatives are different. The business is so arcane that when S&P says it doesn't understand how the competition does what it does, this is not necessarily a warning to other investors in the market. It may just mean simply that the company can't match its competitor's product because it hasn't got anyone brilliant enough to write a comparable computer trading program.

The closest example of how this works in the real world is chess. Although anyone who knows anything about chess also knows that at the rarefied level of major competition it is nothing to do with the real world and everything to do with monumental eccentricity. Sartorially speaking, things are a little duller than they used to be in the chess world. Some of the modern Grandmasters appear to have visited a hairdresser's at least once in their lives, serious skin problems are rare, and only a few players sport beards that look like refugees from some Ukranian stetl.

Intellectually, however, little has changed.

If you watch television coverage of a world chess championship – even if you have access to the analysis room, stuffed with Grandmasters, at the venue itself – you will be struck by two things. First, no matter how they try to make it sexy to a mass audience, chess doesn't lend itself to discussion by a large group of people. Second, you'll see that none of the experts really knows what's going on. Why? Perhaps because they're just sitting in a television studio or gossiping in the analysis room rather than concentrating on a prepared opening over the board? No. The other Grandmasters don't know what's going on in the game because the contenders themselves are so much better that they make the rest of the experts look like novices.

It's a little like the assault on Everest. The whole team can get up so far, then the advance party gets ahead with a couple of sherpas, and then, a few hundred feet from the summit, just one or two climbers continue. Shrouded in mist, the rest of their party, high as they are above sea level, cannot even see the two climbers at the summit. Their view, elevated though it may be, is as useful as that of the sailor spending his wages in a harbour bar. This, then, is the idea that the derivatives industry is asking us to buy – the curve of achievement is so steep at the very top end of what is essentially applied mathematical genius (with fractal theory being the latest fashion in this area) that the difference between being the fourth best and the fifth best in the world may mean that that fifth best just can't understand what the fourth is doing.

So the derivatives industry has arrogated to itself a new concept of investment Olympia. It is the land beyond the mist, attained only by those touched with investment genius. Even if the managers were inclined to divulge their trading secrets, there would be little point, since only fellow experts could so much as hope to mimic them. The rest of the world need only stand back and comment with awe as the gods of finance play with their bolts of lightning and their rolling thunder.

Small wonder that the derivatives manager is pathologically secretive about the way he trades. His secret is not *what,* but *the way* he trades. The value is the complex pattern of trades, the overall picture, not the individual fragment in the mosaic. It is not making a simple knight's move, but seeing the combination of moves, perhaps as many as eleven deep (accounting for millions of different potential positions if there are several pieces on the board). In mainstream finance, a single trade, the well-timed purchase of an individual stock, is as easy to understand as pushing a pawn. It is a purchase which stands or falls on its own merits. It either adds to the value of the portfolio or it doesn't. In derivatives trading, however, looking at an individual trade is virtually meaningless – while individual contracts will undoubtedly make or lose money, the argument is that each has a specific weighting in a computer-determined program that will produce optimum performance from a range of contracts. Indeed, most programs are designed so that it is virtually impossible for them all to be in profit at the same time. They provide checks and counter-balances, the one against the other, but are shaped into a complex mathematically structured pattern designed to obtain best value (the favourite market term is 'exploiting inefficiencies') in the various markets in which the derivative fund managers make their plays.

Probably the closest parallel with the trading patterns of derivatives management today is to be found in the bio-technology industry, which is basically trying to patent life itself. Bio-technology research companies are patenting complex cell forms which lead to innovations such as the goat that provides insulin-like secretions suitable for the treatment of human beings, or the tomato that stays fresh for months. These companies are not patenting a new scientific method from Mars. Just as the contracts which make up the complex trading programs are perfectly orthodox, so the complex cells to be patented are composed of orthodox, known entities. The genetic information is not new, nor even noted in a scientifically unconventional form. So what the bio-technology companies are trying to claim as their intellectual property is not the information itself, but the structure of the information, the radically different pattern of their genetically engineered cells.

This, then, is what the derivatives managers claim to have dis-covered – the financial equivalent of a seventeen-foot-tall, per-manently fresh, talking zucchini, which is also a cure for cancer. If that seems like quite a claim, think of what they are telling investors they are buying – most of the profit, less of the risk, from combining known elements in a different way. The managers say that to reveal the structure of their trading programs would be to give away the secret of the clever play that leads to the profitable score. So to make even their auditors fully aware of the trading methods of the fund would be to risk divulging trading secrets to the market.

Auditors are of course bound by a set of ethics that prohibit them from divulging such information. But derivatives managers appear to have an acute awareness of the way the real world of finance works. One axiom is that information, confidential or otherwise, that can be used to make a profit ultimately will be so used – and sooner rather than later. All of which is predicated on the somewhat unlikely assumption that everyone in the large and growing industry of derivatives management has worked out a way of making base metals precious. There are a lot of self-proclaimed geniuses and a lot of magic elixirs out there.

Level five – beat the market, part I

People who take themselves for financial sages will tell you that genius in finance is being right 51 per cent of the time. Welcome to Level Five – the part where the derivatives industry claims to be just that little bit better than the rest of the world, and is prepared to explain the broad principles of how it all comes about.

It is a beguiling combination of forthrightness and modesty that permits derivatives managers to (almost) claim they can beat the market. They say they have altered one of the few immutable laws of finance: there is no profit without risk. The subtlety lies in not claiming to be able to break that law and offer investment return without risk. The industry says only that it can bend it a little bit. Derivatives managers claim to offer a good opportunity for substantial return, while minimizing the risk of loss in a significant way.

When derivatives managers were turning in good performances in the early 1990s they told investors to examine not just the impressive gains, but rather the way in which the results were achieved. To promote the argument that these funds were genuinely low-risk vehicles the concept of volatility was paraded before an investing public. Volatility is, at best, a very crude indicator of risk. The logic is that the lower the price volatility, the lower the risk. In real English, this means the less the fund's price moves up and down in violent jolts, the less likely the investor is to have a heart attack.

What the derivatives managers are really saying, though they are too clever to be explicit, is that they are smarter than the markets. Broadly speaking, they attempt to prove this in two ways.

The members of the first group are known as 'trend followers'. They take a more or less orthodox view of the market in, say, orange juice futures or Spanish government bonds. Their tactic is then to follow the trend they have identified and buy contracts which will enhance their gain if they have made the right call. They, clearly, have less to hide from the market and their auditors. After all, their main concern is simply to get the best value contracts to back their judgment on whether copper or dollar interest rates will move up or down.

The second group claims to exploit systemic inefficiencies in pricing. These managers will not buy contracts on the basis of whether they think the underlying commodity – the entity from which the contract derives its value – will go up or down. They will look at things which they think have distorted the true value of a contract. For example, they may think that a whole market is undervalued in relation to another and buy in both to squeeze value from between the two – a classic arbitrage tactic. Or they may look at the tendency of the contract's price to move, i.e. its volatility.

If all that's unclear, remember this – a derivatives contract will make a lot of money for you if you either a) guess correctly where pork bellies are heading or b) you buy when pork belly prices are stable and they then start jumping around. Managers who explore avenue b) have no interest in the future price of pig meat, they simply look at the way the market prices the contracts and decide if that price is correctly judged.

And everything was fine until the derivative fund industry fell out of bed in the beginning of 1994, when suddenly those performance curves took a rapid, very nasty decline, making all those claims about limited downside risk look distinctly spurious. According to statistics compiled by Managed Account Reports, a New York-based derivatives performance monitoring firm, the 'average' derivative fund (a strange concept, as we shall see) produced a loss of 8.2 per cent in the first quarter of 1994 and continued to perform poorly through to early 1995.

Now of course it seems unfair to decry a whole investment sector just because, for a few months, it loses money (market jargon, for those who like their English castrated by a rusty teaspoon, is 'significant underperformance' or, even better, 'negative growth'). But you must remember two things.

First, that the derivatives industry has been claiming to be better than the rest of the financial world, living in a land of lower risk and virtually undiminished return. It's got a self-proclaimed reputation to live up to.

Second, the derivatives world has been secretive in the extreme. It has *asked* the rest of the world to keep its distance, and to judge derivative funds on their performance.

Level six – the hall of mirrors

Might it all be a trick? Complexity is one thing, but if no-one, not even the auditors, knows what is happening, might we not all be enjoying an enormous ride? To attain the higher levels of the derivatives world is not just a question of understanding, but ultimately one of faith. Look deep into the mirror, and decide whether what you see is real ...

There is another, much darker, formula which might describe these funds. It has nothing to do with financial genius (which, as J. K. Galbraith is fond of saying, always comes before the fall) and owes a lot to hearing the same tired old investment miracle story told again and again.

Consider the market behaviour surrounding the major investment hot spots in modern times. Taken individually, the components of this formula are innocent enough, but stir them together and the mixture is positively dastardly. The historical facts of the market's frenzy have of course differed. But the conceptual ingredients of the formula have remained more or less unaltered . . ..

Take a speculative cocktail shaker. Add four parts public ignorance to thirty-three parts greed. Toss in a little perceived genius – if you don't have any freshly ground perceived genius to hand, a little dried guru status will do. Season generously with mystique. Add apparent publicity-shyness to taste. Serve in opaque tumblers of awed, ill-informed media coverage.

It's a heady mixture – and an expensive one. Nevertheless, investors have consistently seemed to like it, as Chapter XI explains in more detail.

Anyway, derivatives managers are facing a crucial test right now. Just because they are playing the game of being gods of the investment world doesn't mean that the markets they invest in are somehow shoddy, or necessarily about to go into terminal decline. After all, there are still share, property and even junk bond markets. It is just possible that some of the derivatives managers really are investment geniuses, so smart that the competition can't even understand how smart they really are.

So let's look at the key sectors of this market in turn, with the aim of discerning how well the claims made for these products really stand up.

Level seven – the genius factor

Well, we've arrived. This is where it all happens. This is what has attracted billions from the general public and otherwise financially literate people who have signed up without really knowing how their money is being invested.

All the money has been pouring into derivatives funds. This is a generic term for funds that use derivative instruments. The most common sub-species are hedge funds, guaranteed funds, swap funds and funds of funds.

Funds of funds are based on the principle fundamental to funds themselves – that by spreading risk across a large range of assets you diminish risk. Common sense tells us that this must be so, if only in a relative way. If you buy a single share it will probably over- or under-perform the whole market. If you buy twenty shares, your cross-section of investments stands a better chance of mirroring the general market's performance.

Unfortunately, The Market in its turn stands a fair chance of doing something utterly insane at any given time, so we are left with a pretty strange conception of reducing risk. If risk reduction is the ability to accurately mimic something pretty dumb – say, the hopping of a rabbit across a road, or the meanderings of a drunk on the sidewalk – then spreading your assets is a pretty good way of doing it.

Derivative fund managers claim however to have a performance that does not move in line with the underlying markets in shares or bonds. Whoopee. What you get from the diversified assets in their portfolio is 'absolute' performance.

The notion of absolute performance is, unfortunately, completely unrelated to vodka martinis and the kind of performance you get after half a dozen belts of Absolut. The idea, if you can call it that, is that there should be no correlation between the pricing of a fund and, say, the Morgan Stanley index of world shares. In that sense, while other funds measure their performance in relation to an average value of a share market, the derivative fund's performance is not so measured. The absolute performance is supposed to provide steady gains – no matter what happens in the nasty, unstable little worlds whence derivative contracts come.

This is, as you have doubtless guessed, dangerous marketing nonsense of the highest order. The most important reasons are a) all performance is necessarily relative – there are good and bad derivative fund managers, the funds may be good or bad compared to other 'safe' investments such as deposits in a bank, the performance of these funds must also be judged relative to inflation, which is the ultimate benchmark of any investment, and b) isn't it just a bit too convenient to have 'absolute' performance? Isn't that like depriving investors – who have enough trouble making informed decisions anyway – of important criteria on which to judge an investment? And even if shares are riskier (an assertion which the latest statistics throw into considerable doubt) isn't it important to judge these funds against the most common form of risk investment? And finally, and perhaps most importantly, c) it's very unfair to ply the subconscious with vodka martinis.

Guaranteed funds have become popular in recent years because they sell well in a climate of fear. Promise investors their money back in five years, plus the possibility of a profit and they think they have a no-lose situation. Well, they do and they don't. What happens is that for every $100 invested, $80 or so, depending on interest rate levels, will be put into some kind of interest-bearing security that will compound up into $100 over the five-year term (there is another way, using zero-coupon bonds, but the principle is the same). The remaining $20 is then invested in a portfolio of derivative contracts which the managers crank up to gain maximum exposure to the markets. If they lose the $20, the investor just collects $100 at the end of the term.

This means that investors can lose out in two ways. First, they run the risk of losing spending power. If inflation runs at four per cent over the period of the guarantee, the Year Five $100 will be worth just $81.53 in Year One dollars. Second, they could do it themselves less expensively. They'd just have to invest in the right bond (not difficult to do – all you need is a calculator and a friend who is numerate), and with what's left over from your $100 you speculate yourself. Don't forget. Derivatives managers charge – handsomely – for this service.

There have been several cases of guaranteed funds failing, such as Dean Witter's Principal Guaranteed Fund III. Someone slipped up, and the fund fell 15 per cent from its initial value. At which point its speculative portfolio was liquidated and investors were offered the choice of waiting until 1995 to get their initial investment back, or settling for less when the fund ceased to trade (in 1992). But despite this and other cases, the regulators still approve, and the investors still buy.

Hedge funds are hot, but not quite the hottest part of the market.

The first really striking aspect of these vehicles is their name. Calling them 'hedge' funds is *Newspeak* on a par with the naming of the Orwellian Ministries of Truth and Love – or real-life governments' Ministries of Defence. But then the real world doesn't like honesty too much. There was considerable fuss, for example, over a splendidly named UK fund launched by venture capitalists and fund managers Johnson Fry. The vehicle, named The Vulture Fund, had an investment brief to buy up the homes of distressed sellers, Brits who had been forced out of their homes by high loan rates.

Hedge fund managers seek to exploit irrationalities in the market, and invest in a contrarian way to profit from them. The more aggressive managers will back their judgment with contracts that multiply profits and losses many times.

Others seek absolute performance. Enough said.

A number of signs indicate that the hedge fund sector has had its day. Hand in hand with the cruddy performance of these funds comes massive popular interest – alias Joe Kennedy's shoe-shine boy, the Biggest Fool.

Whether small investors are right (it happens sometimes) or wrong, the industry is growing. 'The number of US hedge funds appears to be growing annually ... media attention paid to the high rewards available to successful fund managers has motivated some individuals to start funds, and some prime brokerage houses have stimulated growth of the business through "how-to" seminars for "wanna-be" hedge fund managers,' said a research report from the International Advisory Group.

In other words, the investors may be fools, but the managers are at least smart enough to look at the charging structures reported in the media and they decide – quite rightly – to be a hedge fund manager.

When the market was booming it was effectively impossible for small investors to place money with a good hedge fund. 'Did you know that there is an informal insider network that often quickly fills the most attractive hedge funds?' asks IAG.

Well, yes, actually.

IAG recounts its own experience in trying to place a large sum of money with a fund with an impressive performance record that it had tracked.

'When we moved to make an initial contribution we were informed by our intermediary that the fund had closed. As it happens, we were let in but were probably the last investors for the foreseeable future – after only six months of operation! The fund was basically full. This kind of thing has happened fairly often.'

But that was in the fourth quarter of 1993, a long time ago. *Swap funds* were the next hot thing in the market. And managing one of these funds must be a dream job, if you are prepared to do that sort of thing. Consider the superabundance of benefits, versus the almost total lack of countervailing detriments.

First is the OPM factor – it's got to be other people's money that you speculate with. That's why derivatives funds in general have struck many people as being such a good idea.

Second is the charging structure, that fabulous twenty per cent of net profit after you've taken your charges. Let's be clear here. This kind of charge is levied purely and simply because the managers can get away with it. The rush to enter the derivatives fund arena may soon change all this. Because sooner or later someone is going to start offering investors a thing called value for money. Although there will probably be a lot of resistance to this, as many investors appear to believe only scandalous, sky-high, blood-leeching rip-off charges are compatible with management genius.

Third is the mystery factor. This is the wall behind the wall behind the wall. Quite simply, swaps make even other derivatives managers nervous of playing their game. This is not because of a large metaphysical sign marked 'eggheads only beyond this point'. Nope. Mainstream derivatives funds offer still-unexplored possibilities for turning ordinary people into blubbering wrecks with four-day-old potato salad where their brains used to be. What's genuinely alarming about the swaps market is that it's completely without boundaries. If you want you can swap your parcel of securitized floating-rate yen-denominated credit card debt for a fixed rate sterling income stream. Or, if you want to, you can swap it for Noddy's little red and yellow car that goes 'parp, parp'. It's up to the swaps player to define the market. For a deal to be good all that has to happen is that the parties concerned agree to it.

A typical swap trade might involve the obligation to pay fixed-rate German mark debt over three years (a concrete example of this might be a bond issued by a German car manufacturer which has been parcelled up and sold on). If you have this obligation, and you think German interest rates will fall, you will swap it for an obligation to pay at a floating rate over the same period. This is an interest rate swap. If you swap rights or obligations featuring different currencies, the trade is usually referred to as a currency swap.

Of course, it's much more complicated than that. The modern swaps market features trades of bundles of options and futures on interest rates (yes, you can have options on interest rate futures, if you like your ice cream double-double chocolate chunk with mocha topping) swapped against complex forward multi-currency agreements, etc, etc, etc.

So now, maybe, you're impressed? Scratch a swaps fund manager and you expect him to start haemorrhaging spread sheets, spilling reverse yield curves and deep-discounted cash flows on to the ground? This would be a mistake. Because the swaps market, like every other financial market, is a function of instinct. The dealers and traders have developed a somewhat strange mindset, so that for them a fixed-rate dollar debt instrument is something concrete and tangible. It has a behaviour pattern as predictable as, say a Siamese fighting fish. So when the capacity utilization figures for the US economy are published, they know which way the little blue fixed-interest-rate fish will react, just as they know how the green Swiss franc floater will behave. And then they instantly lay bets on which fish will win. Or if the frenzied shouting is done by white men as opposed to Asians, this is termed trade.

But ask a dollar interest rate trader what the contract in which he's trading 'ticks' is actually based on, and he's quite likely to have no idea. It cannot be overstated. This kind of trading, for all its synthesis of apparently complex information, is utterly instinctive. Yet for now, swaps specialists are left to themselves. They have the respect of an iconoclastic world.

Benefit number four is the definitively uncontrollable nature of the swaps market. A swap is a bet, a contract between two financially powerful parties. It has almost nothing to do with the real world, or the strange, warped kind of world that most regulators appear to live in.

The stance of the regulators on this point is a little like the prurient hypocrisy displayed by the more conservative elements of British society in the 1950s. The debate raged over whether homosexual acts between consenting men over the age of twenty-one should be legal. Some of the arguments against legalization were quite extraordinary. But a common theme was that simply condoning such conduct, even in private, would destroy the very fibre of British public morality. Eventually common sense and the elegant arguments of the jurist Herbert Hart prevailed. Homosexual sex had been happening for centuries and would continue to do so. In that case, why turn perfectly decent men into criminals and infringe their right to privacy and to choose their own sexual preferences? This may seem utterly trite now, but it was revolutionary then. So homosexual sex between men over twenty-one acting in private was legalized. And British society got no worse for it. In fact, it remains top of the international league table for sexual hypocrisy, followed very closely by the United States.

So what are you going to do to stop two perfectly respectable properly audited companies getting together in private to have a good time by rubbing bits of their balance sheets together? If they want to do it, they'll do it, and no chaperoning is going to stop them. Remember: money is power, money is sex.

Swaps are, sensibly enough, traded on the over-the-counter market. The OTC is a nice little euphemism for a loose group of institutions prepared to take each other on trust. The OTC is basically unregulated, although firms that trade on it like to be able to point to big lawyers' bills to show that they have gone through an elaborate system of study and implemented rigorous financial controls, that there will be precious few conflicts of interest, virtually no insider trading scams or managers trading their own accounts ahead of those of clients.

Right. We've heard it all before. Little insider scams are an integral, largely undetectable part of the market. They only come to light when the abuse is large-scale and systematic. When greed triumphs over even the most rudimentary common sense.

But for all the scare stories of billions of dollars of random, destabilizing, inherently bad capital liability, these markets have yet to prove a force for ill. That's because they are fundamentally not about the rest of the world. The swaps market has real meaning in one arena only – that of the swaps market.

Here is a classic example. In the spring of 1994 the market in Italian sovereign debt became more or less moribund. Nobody wanted to trade the bonds offered by the Italian government because the Italians had just elected Silvio Berlusconi to power, and – guess what? – nobody trusted him, and nobody had much of an idea about what kind of economic monetary and, above all, interest rate policy to expect. Confidence being a vital element in such markets, trade just about died out. Yet the swaps market in Italian bonds was buoyant. You could set off a liability in Italian bonds against whatever your counterparty wanted to take off its books. There was no problem in swap-trading Italian sovereign debt. How can this be? I asked one of the leading players in the swaps field.

'Because the swaps market is not the same thing as the underlying market. It is merely influenced by it,' he said.

In other words, what matters is the other party to the trade. If the party keeps its word to pay $1 million if an American football game is won by a spread of more than 17 points, you can set that off against $500,000 worth of liability on your bet that it will be raining in Seattle in ten days' time. The events in the real world do not matter to the validity of the contract. What matters is the confidence the parties have in each other, in their ability to honour their word.

So the fact that no-one actually wanted Italian debt didn't matter at all. The parties to the swap simply agreed to arrange their liabilities to one another by the workings of a moribund market. Remember the nobleman and the bet about which raindrop would be first to flow down the window pane? What mattered was the bet, the honour of the parties involved, and their willingness to pay. The fate of the raindrop, or whether anyone got wet, was supremely unimportant.

This kind of thing can produce large amounts of empty, ill-considered rage. Suddenly the moral universe is transported into the financial world. Surreal arguments about the morality of making money out of money are rehearsed in public. This is pure cant. To which, as it happens, the rebuttal is supplied by Kant.

Or rather, a great, but little-read philosopher who understood the application of Kant's concept of aesthetic indifference to the financial world.

Georg Simmel was quite a well known academic who published *Philosophie des Geldes (Philosophy of Money)* in 1900, since when it has remained largely ignored and unread. And this despite the fact that it is undeniably brilliant. It's just that if you read more than four pages at a time you will undoubtedly be reaching for the whiskey bottle, or the paracetamol, or possibly both. So take this next quote seriously – after mining it out of Simmel's text I had to lie down in a darkened room for a couple of hours.

Simmel argues that money has an existence in its own right, that it is more than just the representation of purchasing power. He draws a parallel between this sense of money's having its own identity and Kant's idea of aesthetic indifference.

'The connection between certain useful objects and the sense of pleasure has become so well established ... that the mere sight of these objects becomes pleasurable even in the absence of any utility. This explains what Kant calls "aesthetic indifference", the lack of concern about the real existence of an object so long as its "form", i.e. its visibility, is given.'

Simmel is drawing a parallel between Kant's treatment of representation and his own notion of money. Painting is more than merely a symbol, a representation (maybe a Cubist representation, but still a representation) of, say, flowers. What matters is the painting itself, which takes on its own value, a value far beyond its ability to convey an image or a message of flowers to the viewer. If this were not the case, Alan Bond, the 1980s auction buyer of Van Gogh's *Sunflowers*, got himself a really bad deal, since the flowers represented in the painting can be purchased for a lot less than $8 million. Actually, he got himself a bad deal anyway, but that was because the art market had been artificially inflated by the auction houses' injection of their own capital. They were lending buyers the funds to buy the objects they auctioned. Does that, by the way, sound very dissimilar from the junk bond market?

Anyway, the parallel with money is that it has its own version of aesthetic indifference. Money is more than just a token representing things that we can buy. It has its own identity, its own life. Simmel sees money as – wait for it – 'the reification of the general form of existence according to which things derive their significance from their relationship to each other'.

Don't reach for the whiskey yet, the good bit is coming up. The parallel continues, 'the more remote ... the utility of the object that first created an interest and a value ... the purer is the aesthetic satisfaction derived from the mere form and appearance of the object.'

Whoa! Simmel is a fan of abstract art. The greater the distance from representing reality, the purer the aesthetic satisfaction. So here is another level on which the connection between abstract art and the most technical forms of money-market trading have similar qualities. In both cases it isn't just a question of confidence ('this is art' – therefore it is/'this is binding a contract relating to Italian bonds' – therefore it is). There's an extra layer in each case – the distance of the artefact from the underlying reality.

Now, if the swap fund people have worked out for themselves that they are managing the financial equivalent of a Cubist nude (you know the kind of thing – a woman with three rectangular tits and a salad fork instead of a right leg), then I'm impressed, I really am. But you have to say it's unlikely. Nevertheless, it must be more than an eerie coincidence that their reception and office walls are festooned with modern art. It's surely instinctive – these people are drawn to it, because it appeals to something deep within them. All right, that something deep within them is the idea of making huge profits based on nothing but confidence and say-so. Maybe they really do understand about investing in art that isn't art until the artist says it is, and that there is a satisfying parallel with entering into obligations worth millions based on a non-existent bond market.

So what would the author of *Philosophy of Money* have made of these markets? There were no swap funds in Simmel's time, but it doesn't take much in the way of extrapolation to conclude that Georg would have loved them. He would have got his Durkheim-loving rocks off on an Italian bond swap which basically ignored the viability of Italian bonds. What was essential to the deal was the swap market in which the contract took place – a pure market of money in which the underlying reality of whether anyone actually wants sovereign debt from Italy is, at best, a distant refraction. For Simmel, this would surely be the purest form of money.

So when you read books like Michael Lewis' *Liar's Poker* that tell you the financial markets are shot through with bluff and counter-bluff, that the people who play those markets are addicted to risk, you shouldn't be surprised. But that is, at best, half the story. This analysis only explains the way the financial world works as a crude game played by dilettantes for their own amusement. Which, at one level, it is, whether the game is played with gambling dice or video screens.

Yet it is more than that. Money functions as an autonomous, perhaps rather frightening, language. It is a language of more than symbolism. There is a living, interactive code of metaphor implicit in money. Some of the ramifications of that are dealt with in 'Living With the Lunatic' at the end of this book. For the moment, suffice it to say that given the weird, surrealistic, metaphorical qualities of money, it's hardly surprising that both the markets and the people in them behave most of the time as if they were stark, raving mad.

CHAPTER VII

Ethical Investment – Render Unto Caesar That Which Is John Stuart Mill's

The death (almost) of greed, the origins of the ethical investment industry, some issues for 'ethical' consideration – (i) does our disapproval of the provider of a product taint the product? (ii) Whose morality? Moving moral goalposts and the profit motive (iii) Emerging markets and ethical investment – better turkey than murky. But does it work as an investment? And as an exercise in ethical purity? (i) It's fine if you don't care about the intentions of the people providing the product (even though the fund itself discriminates against investee companies on exactly this basis) (ii) The problem of inter-connectedness (iii) The primacy of the profit motive – the absurdity of imputing moral significance to a market's moving up or down. Ethical investing as pure evil – the perfect example of self-regarding harm

The death (almost) of greed

Welcome to that well-known pantomime, *Snow White and the Seven Deadly Sins*, playing now at a financial market near you. Unfortunately, the vestal virgin playing Snow White has been taken ill, and today her part will be played by Greed (miscasting, maybe, but Julia Roberts wasn't available). We've got to the bit where the wicked witch (played, naturally, by a Dead White European Male in drag) has fed Snow White the poisoned apple. She falls to the floor unconscious, and Lust enters stage right, wondering whether she's dead yet and it's therefore safe to check out her underwear. We already know that Lust is her father (and therefore a child abuser) but can he also be a necrophiliac? Lust turns to the audience, a gap-toothed smile etched across his goatish face. Is she dead, children, or isn't she? Oh yes she is. Oh no she isn't. Oh yes she is.

It could go on forever, except that we, as sophisticated market participants, know better. We know that greed, no matter how you dress it up in vacuous ideological nonsense, never dies. Greed is a study in morphism. It mutates, it transmogrifies, but it never disappears. Those who come to bury it are fools, those who come to praise it are contemptible. Greed is, simply, a fact of financial life. It's ugly, it's unpleasant, it's an extremely unattractive personality trait – one to be avoided as much as possible, or at least heavily disguised – but it's there, and it has to be dealt with, be you a player in the market, a commentator or an investor. Greed is the market's diamond tiara, fear its sapphire-studded necklace. Do one-legged ducks swim in circles? Did Rose Kennedy have a black dress? Is greed an integral part of the market?

Not relevant, not fair, and not necessarily, says one increasingly powerful group of investors and fund managers. These are people who have decided to employ their money in a way that they apparently consider to be ethical, moral, or beneficial to the environment. The ethical investment industry manifests itself in many ways, including shareholder pressure groups, corporate governance lobbyists, and, most importantly, mutual funds. The unifying factor is that all these mechanisms require that investments be put to some kind of test of their quotient of 'morality' or 'ecological soundness' before capital is committed or management decisions taken. Ethical investment (henceforth used as the generic term for both types of investment screening) is one of the fastest-growing areas of finance, with some $2.8 billion under management in mutual funds in the United States, and more than $1.1 billion in Europe.

The views of the investors and the managers must be listened to, if not because of their shining moral integrity, at least because of financial democracy and prudence. Simply put, it's just too much money to ignore, whatever name it's invested in. But to begin to understand the phenomenon which finds a popular market for God and greenness (actually, God and humanism and greenness, but that isn't alliterative) it is important to understand where ethical investment comes from.

The origins of the ethical investment industry

The origins of the ethical investment industry might, at first blush, suggest that greed is dead after all. Ethical investment began over a hundred years ago in the United States as a form of philanthropy by benign (or at least well-meaning – an important distinction in this area) businessmen and religious zealots. They wanted to do something more interesting (and safer, at the time) with their money than put it on deposit at the banks. The notion of investing in apparently harmless companies appealed to these souls. If they were to make money on the markets they wanted to do so from cheese manu-facturers, not breweries, from clothing companies, not tobacco baronetcies. The distinction between good and evil, the works of Satan and those of God, must have seemed clear enough then.

Unfortunately for immutable certainties, times change, and the waters of the fiery lake inexorably spread. Brewing and tobacco companies – despite their lack of capital backing from the ethically minded – have thrived and prospered and diversified, so that many brands of cheese have alcoholic half-sisters within the corporate group, and thousands of insurance policies are related to nicotine-stained cousins through the conglomerate family. And as for cheese ... Well, would you invest in something that exploits animals through the use of animal rennet? Or in a clothing company that sells garments made by minors and sweat-shop slave labour? But all that is history, which is, according to an ancient Chinese epigram, a dangerous pursuit, the past being so much less certain than the future.

To continue, then, our perilous journey through ethical investment history. Things remained pretty much flat in the US for decades. The amount of money in funds grew steadily, but much of that growth was attributable to the steady rise of the stock markets ahead of inflation. In Europe, the pattern was similar. But it happened later, and on a smaller scale. The industry really began to make its presence felt in the UK when an insurance company with a Quaker management tradition decided to market one of its investment funds as an ethical vehicle. The Quaker ethos had been putting investments through a screening process barring armaments manufacturers, etc, for years, so the launch of Friends Provident's Stewardship fund was ground-breaking only as a piece of clever marketing. It was not an investment innovation. At the time, the fund was pretty much on its own in the UK, but come 1989 – a watershed year for this financial sector – it found itself with twenty competitors. The story in Continental Europe reveals even more startling growth. From just five funds with $100 million under management in 1988, the Europeans saw funds multiply by seven and assets under management almost quintuple in the next five years. In the US there was a similar violent mushrooming in the late 1980s. Now how would you account for that?

Easy, says the ethical investment industry. Greed is dead, it really is. If you were a pathologist you'd write on the death certificate: 'Place – Just about every major market. Cause – Unsuccessful conscience-by-pass operation, a.k.a. hideous investor excess. Time – 19 October 1987'. That's right, the crash of 1987 took greed out of the game, and that's what accounts for the sudden growth of mutual funds a year or so later.

Bear in mind that it takes a considerable time to launch a mutual fund. The SEC, which must approve these things before they are sold to American investors, is not easy to convince of anything in a hurry, and the other regulatory bodies of major markets are no pushovers either (at least as regards something they already know about – show them an international banking scandal and just watch the instant game of pass-the-parcel, played to the merry accompaniment of the world's financial organs). So, runs the argument, these funds were launched in the late '80s – just as soon as practicable after the '87 crash. They simply catered for consumer demand, says the industry. And it was – and is – a perfectly sensible demand.

The more appealing form of this argument is beguilingly pragmatic. It goes like this. It's all a little bit more complicated than the facile crap you read in the Sunday newspapers, say the ethical investment advocates. The move to ethical investment is really nothing to do with this invented notion of conscience and caring in the 1990s, and its somehow seeping through to the markets, as though the world of finance were separated from real life by some thick but permeable moral membrane. No, you have to look at what investors were going through at the time, and the way they are. Of course investors aren't saints. Of course they got greedy during the market boom years. These things happen. But they also got badly overstretched, they got hurt, they got burned, and that made them think. And lo! Like Saul on the road to Damascus, they found after a period of moral blindness that there was something more than pure greed after all. There was a higher goal for their money than just setting it to chase more money. They wanted to put their capital to moral, ecological, ethical uses. Of course, they still wanted to have a fair return on their investment, but they wanted it deployed in a way that would do some good for the society in which they live, and that larger society which is Our World.

At which point it is time to draw breath. Readers are reminded that this book is written from the point of view that capitalism and the people who work in its financial markets are perhaps insane, but not criminally so. The mechanism of the market is mad, but it's workable and should be persevered with in the absence of anything better. The people who work in the markets are an extremely diverse lot. Some are greedy, some corrupt (but the same goes for academe, the media, politics, the law, just about any branch of any society). On the whole financial people are all right, although they can become a little demented and express themselves somewhat curiously if they've been working in the markets for too long. Many of them are extremely cultured and very intelligent. Perhaps best of all is the freedom to speak that so often comes as part of the package. You can have an argument (i.e. a discussion in which you disagree) about lots of things, including what they do for a living, without causing mortal, communication-destroying offence. If you want to see the other side of the coin, try disagreeing with, say, an art critic about anything remotely related to art. At the first hint of opposition – particularly if the conversation takes place at an 'Opening', or somewhere else that makes the critic feel territorial – you will be written off as a boor unworthy to be treading quails' eggs into the same carpet. Liberal arts, illiberal people.

So capitalism isn't intrinsically evil, and it's got plenty of really quite pleasant people working in its financial machinery. That said, the ethical part of the investment industry is the nastiest, most harmful piece of ill-thought-through hypocrisy across the entire spectrum of financial markets. Ethical investment is an abomination, a vile, cancerous, morally corrosive malignancy. At its worst it's a shabbier piece of shysterism and moral duplicity than selling old ladies cruddy insurance policies. At its best it's just enormously, subversively damaging to thousands of suckers. Oh yes, and as an idea it completely collapses in on itself when subjected to even rudimentary analysis of the way the markets work. To be clear – it's totally fucking stupid. In short, ethical investment is not a good thing.

Some issues for 'ethical' consideration – (i) does our disapproval of the provider of a product taint the product?

You don't need to be a champion Kremlinologist or a giant among cryptographers to guess what the worst case might be. What follows is a true story, though it would be nicer if I were making it up.

It is the late 1980s and I am visiting a friend who designs financial software systems (you see already the kind of ritzy, Hollywood starlet-drenched lives financial journalists lead). He is working on a contract for a minor investment house in an area where the City of London peters out into the urban wastelands of the east. A voice issues from the back of a bank of screens.

'We've got to get the bastard punters in somehow.'

My friend takes me over to the owner of the voice and introduces me as a financial reporter for a national newspaper. He is senior investment director of the firm, one which has recently bought shares in the company I work for. The beneficial owner of those shares, it has just been discovered, is the lovely Robert Maxwell, currently in the final (or should that be terminal?) phase of his expand-or-die campaign. We allude briefly to Maxwell and agree to disagree. The investment director thinks Maxwell will keep expanding, I think he will fail – though dying seems like too extravagant a gesture. The director is an open, yet uncompromising character ('couldn't give a flying fuck in a hurricane what people think of me,' is how he describes himself) and we chat amiably enough. I ask what his stratagem is for hauling in the 'punters'. Well, he explains, in the post-crash gloom people are not just running scared, but they're looking for someone to blame. The societal group chosen for the sacrificial bonfire is 'yuppies' (now an archaic term. Even then an empty phrase meaning merely 'someone who earns more than me whom I don't like.') And to help people feel morally superior to yuppies, he is assisting in the launch of an ethical fund. Sleeves rolled up, he has two packets of Marlboro and a bottle of Beck's by his side as comforters to help him in the production of this financial conveyance of superior public morality. And, although I don't know whether he skins puppies or tortures little boys for pleasure, he has also committed another sin, namely the heinous crime of being South African and white. So in terms of socially undesirable traits, the maker of the vehicle has more or less the full set.

This raises two issues.

The substantive question is whether the fact that we disapprove of the maker of a product in some way taints that product. So what if this is a cynical, nasty guy with a complete set of *Guns and Ammo* magazine and a penchant for early Donny Osmond? Cheese is cheese. A door is a door. If they feed the family and keep the draught out, they do what you want them to do. Isn't that what matters, rather than the marketing intention of the dairy farmer or the carpenter? Maybe, maybe not. More of that later.

(ii) Whose morality? Moving moral goalposts and the profit motive

Issue number two concerns the incessant fluctuation of contemporary mores. Or, in the demotic, moving moral goalposts. The inevitable change in the fashionable view of any topic has been touched on earlier. What's interesting from an investment point of view is the way that the ethical investment industry has adapted to those changes, and has corralled as much as possible into the realm of the ethically legitimate − and therefore investable. South Africa provides one example of this, and the vogue for emerging markets another.

Thanks to the disassembling of the mechanics (if not necessarily the mentality) of the despotic and abhorrent system of apartheid, it's now OK to be a South African white. Unless, that is, you give credence to the crypto-fascist school of racism and divisiveness which substitutes mind-numbing social mantra for measured thought. All whites are racist, all men are rapists, five nines are forty-five ... Anyway, Mandela and de Klerk won the Nobel Peace Prize, international trade sanctions were lifted, and the ethical investment industry pronounced another area fit to receive its support. And so the funds flooded in.

Or not. Not ahead of the first free elections they didn't. Why? Because of that other not unimportant motive for investing − greed, or the profit motive when it's washed its face and put on its Sunday coat.

Here I steal a quote from *International Fund Investment*, the *Inter-*

national Herald Tribune's mutual fund magazine. In a piece on ethical investing in Europe Peter Silvester, investment director for Friends Provident, says, 'Ask someone if they prefer to invest ethically as opposed to randomly and almost everybody says "yes". *But the instinct to seek out a good return overrides the instinct to invest responsibly.* We've demonstrated, however, that you don't have to give up one to get the other, that ethically screened funds can actually out-perform funds which have no restrictions on their investments.'

Let me make it clear this passage is not to be regarded in the same light as that spoken by the anonymous South African. The quote, with my own italics, has the hallmarks of being made by a decent, well-intentioned man. It contains the three vital elements in considering ethical investment – a) it's a potent marketing force b) the investments in fact do quite well compared to 'non-ethical' vehicles and c) there is a fundamental tension between the dictates of conscience and profit, and *ultimately the profit motive wins.*

You might say that this is the conclusion of a cynic, that a knock-out victory for profit doesn't always have to be the case. This would be wrong. Aside from the testimony of people who have spent their lives in the investment industry that this is in fact the case, there is a powerful argument based on competition in the market. This argument is ventilated in more detail later. Its conclusion is that it is possible to invest ethically, but you have to exclude profit (which is greed with a haircut, don't forget) from the picture.

(iii) Emerging markets and ethical investment – better turkey than murky

Anyone doubting the primacy of profit in ethical investing should take a look at the undignified scramble of ethical funds to invest in emerging markets. Authorship of the phrase 'emerging markets' is claimed by a number of people. One story goes that it was invented by a manager who was having difficulty in persuading western institutions in the late 1960s to invest in the economies of what economic aid organizations like UNESCO and the World Bank still like to refer to as lesser developed countries. Seeing that this phrase was conjuring up images of badly irrigated paddy fields, dirt track roads, Cambodian whorehouses and Bombay opium dens, the manager changed the words from 'lesser developed country' to 'emerging market'. The emerging markets epithet undoubtedly has a much more positive ring to it. The institutions bought.

Thanks to the outstanding performance of emerging market funds in 1993 the pioneers of the emerging market industry became a small band of financial super-heroes. People everywhere wanted to emulate their success, and above all to reproduce the investment performances of their funds. But if we begin to strip away the layers of euphemism, we see that what we're investing in is an emerging market, which is a lesser developed country, which is a country which has a different concept of human rights (as the premier of Malaysia pointedly explained to the United Nations . . .), which is a country that tolerates what the west would call slave labour and the coerced labour of young children for pitifully small wages. There's a hint of polemicism here, but only a hint. When you hear an economist talk about low wage costs in Thailand, Vietnam or Peru, that's what's being cited as an economic 'good'. And a lot of fund investors are perfectly happy with their doubled returns in a single year. So be it. (A brief tangent – when you hear an economist talk about anything, you know you're in the wrong place – unless you're being paid an exceptionally large amount of money to stay there.)

But when the ethical investment industry starts poking its profit-seeking little nose into emerging markets, in the hope of offering investors the opportunity to get in there and exploit human misery and *feel good about it*, it's time to throw up. Preferably in an economy-sized, Prince Charles approved, neoclassical toughened plastic vomitorium. If you haven't got one of those, a very big bucket will do.

What is missing here, surely, is some form of cognition, even if it makes you uncomfortable. For example, I eat meat. I love it. I give thanks for the duck or the cow that died so ignobly every time a tender little bit of one finds its way on to my plate. How do I justify it? I talk a good game about hierarchy of suffering, and the primacy of the human animal. But I know I would have to be very, very hungry to get out there and slaughter my own lamb chops. I'm also very fond of haggis, the great chieftain o' the pudding race, but if I had to rip out the heart, lungs and liver of a sheep, boil them up with cereal and seasoning and stuff them into a sheep's stomach I'd probably settle for the spinach rissoles. It's because of weak people like me that butchers make a living. I am a carnivorous coward, but keep the meat coming – medium rare, nice and pink.

The one point in my favour, I hope, is that I don't try and delude myself that I'm doing *good* to the sheep when I'm eating its minced vital organs. Is that roast chicken a voiceless victim of speciesism? Too right it is. Pass the chestnut stuffing. There are arguments about preserving the species, good husbandry, etc. Forget those. They're for farmers trying to avoid being blown up by animal rights lunatics. I'm a coward with money that I'm prepared to exchange for fleshy nutrition. *Credo in multas carnes.*

So what is the ethical investment industry doing when it repositions itself to take advantage of the boom in emerging markets? Is it trying to offer a paternalistic version of capital investment, seeking to encourage enlightened working practices (you know, the investment equivalent of free-range hens, which are allowed to scuttle around a bit before they're slaughtered)? Or is it simply telling its investors what they want to hear about the light perspiration workplaces (as opposed to sweat shops) in which they invest, and making sure that they too can make money from the advantageous economic climate like other investors? Which is stronger, the urge to do good, or the will to profit?

To refer back briefly to Mr Silvester's dictum. The worst case for ethical investment is when its marketing edge is being used by people who care for nothing except marketing edge – manifestly the policy of our South African marketeer (a jolly little word, with its self-aggrandizing cavalier overtones – one of many wonderful contributions the language of marketing has made to modern idiom). While the investment itself might be sound enough, is it really all right to sell someone something which is a piece of considered obfuscation? Something which appeals to the conscience and simultaneously hoodwinks it? At least when naive clients are sold some fifth-rate insurance policy they have a chance of discovering that they've bought an apocryphal piece of shit. Whereas an investment that might bring in a reasonable return will leave well-meaning clients in the moral darkness, thinking they're actually doing something to fight oppression, alcoholism, whatever, by sitting back and getting rich. The answer is as clear as the division between finance and morality itself. Financially, go for the ethical fund every time. Morally, better turkey than murky.

But does it work as an investment?

So much for the marketing motives of the ethical investment industry. What about the substantive issue of whether the product itself works? The question of efficacy breaks down into two separate areas – financial return, and the feasibility of creating a portfolio of companies that is genuinely pure and untainted according to classical ethical criteria (to reiterate – eco-friendly, no-drink, no-smoke, no-arms, no nasty politics).

The financial point is quickly dealt with. It's far from clear that the extra layer of ethical screening that shares undergo before being bought by a fund provides investment benefits. But it's equally debatable that investing in a more limited universe of shares hurts investors' returns. An independent survey of UK pension fund performance carried out by an actuarial firm, The Wyatt Company, as quoted in *International Fund Investment,* ranked the Friends Provident Stewardship Fund 15th out of 74 UK pooled pension funds over twelve months ending in spring 1993. Those results are good, but that's probably because of the management company and the particular time period. More general statistics from Micropal indicate that results vary, according to the period of years you choose as a basis of comparison. How interesting, you're thinking. The most definite conclusion is that these funds move broadly in line with the markets in which they are invested. Sometimes they will, as a group, do a little better than the average fund, sometimes a little worse. The conclusion? Financially, these funds present no problem.

And as an exercise in ethical purity?

Finding an ethically pure share, however, is not so clear-cut. You can argue that, even if the managers are greedy, this has no bearing on the efficacy of a product made from objectively pure ingredients. All right, the goalposts have shifted, but a screening committee of well-intentioned (or even cynical, but smart) people can do its best to offer investors a stake in companies that don't manufacture, say, armaments, drink, or tobacco products, and don't have factories in countries with politically 'unacceptable' regimes. In other words, the product is what counts. A piece of cheese is acceptable if made with non-animal rennet. It doesn't matter if the moron turning the handle of the churn is a chain-smoking alcoholic who bites the heads off hamsters when he's in party mood. The cheese is still sound.

This argument is a baby seal that deserves the light-ginger-soda-and-ice treatment (in other words, it's going to get a Canadian Club on the rocks). There are three objections to it (considerably fewer than the many there are to the Canadian Club quip, but short of arming yourself with a cattle prod, this is one of the few sure ways of getting into a real conversation in eco-friendly locations like Vancouver). Anyway, there are two major objections and one minor piece of heckling to deal with. The important arguments concern the inter-connectedness of things in the market and the complete amorality of the market as a mechanism – the argument that money knows nothing except itself. Let's start with the third, the quibble.

(i) It's fine if you don't care about the intentions of the people providing the product (even though the fund itself discriminates against investee companies on exactly this basis)

It's really no more than a little piece of logic concerning the intentions of the people providing the fund. If you say that their cynicism, their moral probity or otherwise, doesn't matter, fine. But if you apply that logic to the companies making the products in which the fund invests, you find a fund with a self-defeating purpose. Because the fund looks beyond the materials from which a coat is made (guess what – fur is out, synthetic fibres are in) to a different plane. The ethical screening process typically takes account of the moral quality of the producers of that product – the companies' working practices on safety and hours, their nondiscriminatory employment policies, etc. To be logically consistent – i.e. not guilty of a vast, gaping hypocrisy – the purveyors of the funds should be as clean as the companies they invest in. Not all of them are. Hardly surprising really, is it? That a fair chunk of the financial services industry should discover a conscience just at the time it became convenient to sell shares that way is, well, stretching credibility. But does it really matter? I think so, but maybe I've got my foreskin pulled right over my head. Maybe I'm staring into the inscrutable depths of my own urethra on this one. It's entirely possible. Being wrong, that is.

(ii) The problem of inter-connectedness

A more important problem for these funds is that they just don't stand up to their self-imposed ethical criteria as soon as you begin to look closely at them. This is because of the inter-connectedness of things within a market. Let's take a social parallel to illustrate why the idea of investing in a 'pure' company is pathetic, self-deluding, unworkable nonsense.

Imagine creating an 'elite' social set. You are inviting guests to a reception at the White House or Buckingham Palace. You select ambassadors, the intelligentsia, the stupid and the rich, the great and the good of medicine, law, finance, the theatre, the media. Even, if you're not too choosy, Hollywood film stars. On the way to the party the guests have to step over a drunk slumped on the ground. This drunk has no social graces, no job, no home.

And yet?

And yet he lives, at least exists, in the same societal framework. The drunk will be no more than five, at the outside seven, personal relationships away, not just from several of the invitees, but from the President or the Queen. This is no exaggeration. It is a purely social version of pyramid selling. Four or five layers in and you've mopped up half a nation. So even the most unfortunate of the down-at-heel will be surprisingly close to the constitutional head of state.

All right, the President is hardly likely to throw down a half-finished cocktail and dash across the White House lawn to hand over a discreet wad of green on the strength of a call from a friend of a friend of a friend of a friend of a friend of the drunk outside. But the point is that they are connected, that they are basically the same animal, and that they each have a social radius which brings them closer together. Moreover, by playing their respective roles (and being a drunk is a role – forget that conscience-salving garbage about underclasses, as though these people aren't somehow in our comfortable, monied world) the President and the drunk form part of the same society.

The relationship is much tighter and more tangible in the markets. There are fewer entities in a market than in a society – by a factor of hundreds of thousands. And there are palpable, usually traceable, indicators of a relationship. Instead of a handshake or a nod there is a transfer of money that signifies commerce and transaction. In fact, no company is more than three trading relationships, at the very outside four, away from another. This assertion has a number of important ramifications. Before exploring them it's only reasonable to adduce some evidence to back up the putative connection.

International Fund Investment offers some specific stocks for examination. 'A number of ethical funds have bought shares in German companies such as Veba AG, an electrical utility, GEA, which produces cooling and warming systems, and Gerresheimer Glas AG, which manufactures glass products. French companies popular with ethical funds include Compagnie Générale des Eaux, which deals with water distribution and treatment, SITA, the waste management and recycling concern, and pharmaceutical giant Rhône-Poulenc.

'Natural cosmetics maker Body Shop International PLC and life-science research concern Amersham International PLC are among the popular ethically-screened U.K. companies. Moreover, US concerns such as New World Power Corp., which sells electric power generated from renewable sources, and Thermo Fibertek Inc., which manufactures equipment and accessories for the paper recycling industry, are to be found in many European ethical fund portfolios.'

Ethically screened they may be, but they consort with whores and urchins. With some of them it isn't even necessary to look beyond one relationship. Rhône-Poulenc, for example, is part-owned by the French government. Not much wrong with that, except for the French government's lousy record on nuclear safety (old, increasingly unsafe plants, many sited near major population centres) and its interesting attitude to international law, ecology and human rights. It's not difficult to find evidence of all three. Remember when the French secret service blew up the Greenpeace ship in a New Zealand harbour and managed to kill one of the crew?

Gerresheimer Glas AG provides a less obvious example. It calls to mind an argument I once had with an investment director at the London stockbroker Buckmaster & Moore. He told me about a fund (not his own firm's) that refused to invest in a glass company because – I am not making this up, really – it supplied some of the bottles it made to the UK Ministry of Defence. In other words, the fund wouldn't invest in the glass company because soldiers drank from some of its bottles. Other funds did invest in the company, however. Presumably all the funds would have been happy to invest in the sand company that provided raw materials for several glass companies, one of which made money from supplying soldiers. It's a completely arbitrary question of drawing a line in the moral, er, sand. And to draw arbitrary lines and attempt to imbue them with some kind of value or moral worth is the height of vanity. The next question is who supplies sand to Gerresheimer. You don't have to go very far before you reach a kind of financial lowest common denominator, the basic building blocks of commerce, the need for capital, the requirement for trade, which guides all businesses.

Inevitably important in this kind of enquiry is a company's bankers. How well greased by the communal lip is the cup of banking? It's not a question of saying that bankers are the lowest of the low. The simple fact is that all these companies are drawing their funding from the same, mixed-up, less than perfectly pure source. It's called capitalism, it's called money – an entity that knows nothing except itself.

The Germans, incidentally, have no mutual funds that are labelled 'ethical'. This, according to the investment arms of the big banks like Deutsche and Dresdner, is because of logic. If you have a fund that is deemed 'ethical' it follows that other funds are less ethical or possibly even unethical. So the clean German mind and the newly shined and polished Teutonic conscience (the Germans think very seriously about moral issues) quite rightly cuts the activity of investment right out of the messiness of moral judgment.

The Californians look at it in a different way. The practice of subjecting companies to a green audit is increasingly common on the west coast. Standards of 'greenness' are being developed, in a similar way to universally accepted financial reporting standards, and companies are subjected to a test of their greenness. Investors may of course disagree with the idea of what is ecologically sound, but the idea is clear. Instead of looking to make a profit, the investor can reap a harvest of green points. Now that makes sense of the tension between morality and the profit motive.

(iii) The primacy of the profit motive – the absurdity of imputing moral significance to a market's moving up or down

And, to reiterate, the profit motive will always win. Whatever perniciousness Margaret Thatcher had in mind in the late 1980s when she railed against South African trade sanctions, there was at least a tiny kernel of truth in all the dissimulation. Financially, trade sanctions against the South Africans were useless. At the time, Lady Thatcher pretended she was concerned about creating more unemployment among South Africa's blacks. Perhaps her real fear was that withdrawal of British capital would have meant instant replacement by Japanese or Swiss money. What actually happened was that a number of British companies officially pulled out of South Africa. Some of the British capital was replaced by finance from other countries, but many British companies rerouted their profitable capital investments through subsidiaries, offshore companies and trusts. The only important financial effect of trade sanctions was to provide lucrative work for lawyers and accountants. The profit motive is like water finding a level – if there's a pocket of profit to be filled, it will be filled.

None of which is to say that politically trade sanctions were not an important and useful thing. They created an international awareness of disapproval and a climate of isolation, even if the financial hurt they occasioned was minimal or non-existent. As a political gesture, sanctions were almost as effective as not playing sport with South Africa. As a financial weapon, sanctions are on a rough par with a low-calibre water pistol. How many successful campaigns of trade sanctions have there been? The Iraqis soon found partners before the west got its hobnail boots on in the Gulf War. How many starving Serbs are there in internationally frowned-upon Serbia (an impossible question to answer – but those who are hungry are certainly not going without because of international scruples about taking Serbian money).

The financial point ultimately is this. It is idiotic to try and find a morally sound investment. Maybe it's possible to scoop a handful of clear water from the stagnant pool of capitalism, but what good is that if the pool is dammed by a vast log of mildewed, mossy green? What do you do? Shut your eyes, drink the water and pretend the rest is pure too? Do you step over the drunk, relegate him to a 'subclass', not part of your world, and imagine that the presidential party is full of genuinely lovely people (all of whom have stepped over the same drunk)? It's easy to see why Marxism had its appeal. Its dogma did not permit such sloppy, self-indulgent thinking. Unfortunately Marxism, as manifested in this century, looks even madder than capitalism.

So the search for an untainted company is the casuistic, arbitrary drawing of lines. It is priggish, incoherent, dysfunctional and snobbish. And the really good bit is that its nature as ineffectual sophistry isn't even the most serious objection to ethical investment. The conclusive argument revolves around the way markets work.

Essentially, ethical investment propagates a moralistic fallacy. The fallacy stems from a failure to take account of the maddening but simple nature of the markets. Managers and investors have perhaps been deceived, or have deceived themselves, by living in an era where The Market has taken on the status of a demigod, a provider of certainty. All those clever people, they can't be wrong. Can they? They must know the difference between right and wrong. So The Market, the philosopher's touchstone, the importer of clarity in an obscure world, has naturally been seen as capable of taking on a moral quality. To reiterate: for the children of the '80s and '90s, orphaned in so many ways, The Market has been like some kind of parent.

But just because Mummy says it is so, doesn't really make it all right. It is an absurdity to impute some kind of moral message to the functioning of a market. Markets go up and down. That's it. This is not reductivism, this is a bald statement of all there is. Markets react to external stimuli and adjust their prices on amoral, price-related criteria. What is the moral quality of a market index? You might as well argue about the morality of a litmus paper turning pink or blue, about the ethical import of the fluctuations of a thermometer, or the rights and obligations of an elevator stopping at one floor as opposed to another.

Consider the following cases. Olof Palme, the former socialist prime minister of Sweden, is assassinated in the streets of Stockholm. The Swedish share market adds a little. A ferry boat between Belgium and Britain rolls over at sea, hundreds of people die. A stock called Channel Tunnel is instantly marked up sharply. John F. Kennedy is shot dead. Wall Street shares rise.

The question presents itself: what are these people in the markets doing? Are they immoral in reacting to these terrible pieces of news the way they do? In the cases of the dead politicians there was simply a dispassionate judgment as to the impact the dead man's successor would be likely to have on the business climate. In each case, the markets did the only thing they could have done – which was to go up or down. In each case it was clear that, however horrible the events of the day, those events had to be assimilated and given a financial meaning. And there are only three possibilities – up, down, or stasis.

To confuse the amorality of the market with the immorality of the world – the seamless, super-charged hyper-judgmental world we live in – is very easily and depressingly frequently done. Now there comes a point, naturally, when the things that happen outside the market impinge on the consciences of those who work inside it. Imagine working the Jerusalem floor around 2,000 years ago when news come through of Herod's edict that all male children born during a certain period must be slaughtered. What's your reaction? Sell shares in Baby Gap on the strength of an anticipated weakening in consumer demand, or organize some resistance? It needs to be an extraordinary case for that kind of action – which is radical civil unrest, perhaps leading to war – to be appropriate. The John F. Kennedy assassination, for example, did not require the brokers and dealers to resign *en masse* and form vigilante groups to track down the killer(s) – although a few death squads for today's conspiracy theorists might be a good idea. Should the brokers have resigned out of conscience, left their families to feed themselves and gone off to do something to help right the terrible wrong? Of course not. They just did their job, which is, in large measure, second-guessing where the market will go next.

The move to mark up Channel Tunnel shares on the back of tragedy had a similar apparent financial logic. The sick joke is that there was a widespread misapprehension that the stock bought was of a company which owned and would operate the rail link between Britain and mainland Europe.

Positioning oneself to make money from tragedy doesn't sound good, but it's becoming less popular than it was. For example, the death of Mexican presidential candidate Luis Donaldo Colosio in spring 1994 had the vulpine financial analysts circling the chart thermals. The day after his death the Mexican stock market was closed, and the first reaction was that on the back of political uncertainty the Mexican market would suffer. I was at an investment conference in Zurich that day, and heard two analysts say how unfortunate the man's death was, but what an excellent opportunity it afforded to buy into bigger stocks like Telmex, the Mexican telephone company. But when the market opened on the Friday, the markets had already performed their task of assimilation of risk, of discounting the event and guessing what the consensus view would be – and then making that view expensive. Telmex actually rose that day.

But whether a stock rises or not doesn't make any difference whatever to the moral universe. The market can be interpreted as a grisly kind of X-ray picture of real life. It doesn't know about emotion, sentiment, or good or bad taste, let alone the bewilderingly complex notion of right and wrong. It only reveals the financial skeleton beneath the dramas and the emotions – whether, in the light of events, there will be more buyers than sellers.

The mechanism of the market is amoral. The decision to adopt a market system and to live in a society which cherishes that system to a point beyond even beatification (we are talking outright deification here) has a complex set of social, political and moral ramifications. But the beast itself is no more than that – a simple, mindless beast. What you do with Barney the Dinosaur is your own choice. But once you bring him home and decide to live with him, you have to decide how to behave. Will you be kind, or will you take my advice? My advice, by the way, is a series of massive electric shocks applied through testicular electrodes – but then I've seen one Barney video too many.

So where does all that indignant rage come from? Where, you may be asking yourself, do I get the sheer cheek to use words like 'abomination' about this ethical investment industry which is kept alive and well by a few cynics and lots of well-meaning people? The short answer is that ethical investing is well-meaning, but it isn't benign. It is, in fact, a kind of moral lobotomy. Admittedly, it's the kind of ethical short-circuit that only the feeble-minded are likely to be seduced by, but it's a pernicious form of brainwashing nevertheless. Why? Because the poor, dumb bastards who invest in these funds really believe that they're actually doing some good in the world. If only that were the case, what a fine and noble thing late twentieth-century capitalism would be. We would have achieved a state a little beyond Oscar Wilde's dream in his essay *The Decay of Lying*, where the only work done would be the pleasurable business of maintaining the machine that nourishes and provides. Because in late twentieth-century capitalism we appear to have a phenomenon that permits us to do good in the world while sitting around on our fat arses getting rich! Perhaps it's not quite so noble as Wilde's vision, in that instead of creating beautiful things we're probably going to bridge parties and looking at works of art in the deluded notion that it will help us one day to have a single worthwhile thought pass through our entirely hollow heads.

Ethical investing is in fact the financial version of the therapeutic fallacy, the idea that simply being in the presence of great art magically makes you a better person. Happily enough, this is rubbish. You can plant a cretin in front of a hundred Poussins, a thousand Canalettos, a million Rodin sculptures, and the cretin will remain an unenlightened cretin. There is no overlap between art and the observer if the observer simply treats the art as wallpaper, if the observer doesn't know how to, or hasn't the sensitivity or wit to begin to, see what's going on. So it is with ethical investing. You can't just sit there passively and pretend that you're contributing to the moral balance of the universe by collecting investment reports from your fund manager.

Ethical investing as pure evil – the perfect example of self-regarding harm

You could argue that this is a perfectly reasonable activity in the shallow, almost valueless world we live in. You might say that the choice between good and evil, the ultimate question and most important decision in life, according to writers like Anthony Burgess, is more difficult to make today than ever before. Mainly because we are so seduced and manipulated by clever images and false realities – yeah, blame it on the media, like everything else. But ethical investing is a purely bad thing. It might not do much outward apparent harm in the world, but it is a perfect example of John Stuart Mill's concept of self-regarding harm. As such, it is a private vice, and permissible. But the danger lies in the fact that this kind of investing tries to tell us we are doing something when we are not.

There really is a simple, palpable point to be made here. If you want to make a difference, you've got to *do* something – go spend an hour in a soup kitchen, give a beggar some money, agitate for political reform, stand for election for something where you might make some tiny, tiny difference. Whatever. But don't be conned into thinking that investment has any moral value. Finance is a world where an interest rate change is viewed as a plus or a minus – in the same way that thousands dying in a Bangladeshi flood or a Rwandan war is. But don't forget, the latter events are always less financially important than a change in base rates. Investment? Ethical? Give me a fucking break.

CHAPTER VIII

Credit and Charge Cards – A Plastic Passion

The credit card that flies below personal radar. Plastic as part of daily life and a way of escaping from Sting in a rain forest. How Japanese fund managers invest in Minnesotan farmers. Sustaining the passion – (i) corporate cards and the modern marriage – obey, love and honour major credit cards. A tangent – plastic and other forms of holiday money compared. Why you should make sure that you do leave home without a traveller's cheque. Sustaining the passion – (ii) affinity marketing as a facilitator of shallow ostentation, or the promotion of self-deluding dick-headedness. Affinity cards as financial tranquilliser.

The credit card that flies below personal radar

There is a new range of ultra-exclusive credit card. To own one (or rather possess one, since the card owns you) you have to be rich beyond the dreams of mortal men. Sultan of Brunei, Schmoonei. Croesus, eat your heart out. You have to be bigger than a medium-sized bank to have one of these tiny, condensed nuggets of pure, outrageous spending power (actually, you merely need an annual income of a quarter of a million dollars, but 'the spend', as they say, is completely unrestricted). There is one trait that betrays the awesomeness of this unholy sceptre of raw consumption, this plastic, magnetic-stripped version of the adrenal gland – its colour. Unremarkable in every other way, it is the only hue and shade that such an implement could be – stealth-bomber brown.

So what if stealth bombers are really black? This piece of plastic is as soft and deadly as a velvet-wrapped atom bomb. The Insignia card, a new product from the Eurocard/MasterCard group, can devastate a million-dollar line of credit in seconds. A credit card – any credit card – can wipe out the personal finances of ordinary people before they even know it. And their not knowing is really the whole point, the chill beauty of the concept. The central idea of credit cards is to get people to spend money without even knowing that they're doing so. Extirpation of the consciousness, excitation of the appetite. Like a stealth bomber, that innocuous-looking little bit of plastic doesn't register on the consumer's personal radar screen. The only time you really know it's there is when the payload is dropped. Come the dread moment when the accounting for Littleboy is finally done and the fatal statement of account drops on to the mat – that's when you realize that you've spent far, far more than you thought, and maybe it's time to sell the car. If you shut your eyes you can experience that bright, intensely painful flash and see the twisting column of smoke forming itself into a fat cinereous mushroom in the place where your bank account used to be.

'The store,' said one Los Angeles boutique owner commenting on his acute choice of minimalist decor to a *Business Week* journalist, 'forces people to cleanse their mind and do the major damage to their credit cards that we appreciate so much.'

Here is a person who understands. Put a consumer in a darkened cell with a credit card and the first attempted means of escape will be aggressive wipe-through motions on the bars of the window. Although you have to question whether the store owner got it the right way round. Just who is damaging whom here? To say the consumer damages the credit card is like saying the alcoholic damages his daily two bottles of whiskey.

You might equate the force-feeding of credit to the unwitting populations of western democracies with other sinister practices. Cigarette companies distribute free cigarettes to the peoples of Africa, because once they're hooked they're a captive customer base. And once they're chemically compelled to buy the product, the shipments get progressively more expensive. Heroin dealers do much the same thing.

It's fun to draw the parallel, but is it really fair? Is it fair to treat credit as some kind of addictive drug that is massively corrosive to the bank balance and the faculty of reason? Is it right to argue that the providers of credit cards have the same Olympian moral authority as a street-corner crack dealer? Perhaps not quite, perhaps not entirely. But since when has life been fair? Ask a rich person, ask an Insignia card holder.

In any event, there is clearly something more important than just business going on here. Consider the growth of consumer credit (this is a neat marketing term, meaning personal debt), which is startling in the extreme. It has become a huge, huge business in a remarkably short space of time. The rapidity of the card industry's development has been phenomenal, of an order that indicates credit does strike some elemental chord or play to some innate weakness in us all. We have succumbed to some strange plastic passion.

Plastic as part of daily life and a way of escaping from Sting in a rain forest

MasterCard, a big player on the world stage whose intersecting red and yellow circles are inescapable on this planet, affords as good an example as any of the state of the credit business today.

MasterCard International Incorporated is a payment services franchise. The idea is that the card issuer takes a cut of any payments for goods or services made using its cards. Retailers are willing to give up a percentage of the money they take because – guess what? – they have discovered it significantly increases their turnover. In fact, MasterCard doesn't issue cards itself. It has a card processing system that it allows member banks to use – for a fee. So the banks issue the cards, take their cut, and pay a percentage of that on to MasterCard in exchange for being able to use its central processing system and to offer their customers the ability to spend in any store that displays the yellow and red circles, or to take money from any automatic cash dispenser which displays that logo.

At the end of 1993, almost 22,000 banks and other financial institutions had signed up for the MasterCard franchise, of which 12,681 were in the US, and 7,691 were in Europe. There were more than 227.9 million bits of MasterCard plastic in circulation – that represented an increase of more than twenty per cent on the year before. Users of MasterCard plastic found it accepted in four million locations in Asia and the Pacific region, three million locations in Europe, three million locations in the US, and 1.3 million locations in Latin America (have credit card, will travel). The gross dollar volume of the MasterCard business for 1993 was over $320 billion.

Bear in mind, if reading all those figures hasn't left you feeling entirely sick, that this is an organization that accounts for less than half the market in pure 'credit' cards (credit cards can be roughly defined as things which offer you the option of paying later). If you look at the credit and charge card market (charge cards offer a short stay of execution, but require payment in full at the end of every month), MasterCard accounts for considerably less than half the market, since it is competing not just with Visa (mainly credit cards), but American Express and Diners Club for charge card business. So this is big, really very big, business. These are numbers that really mean something. The figures themselves may be arid and sterile bits of mathematics that reveal a far lower volume of money changing hands than is the case on the capital markets operated by the banks, but consider the fact that these figures are generated by ordinary people like us. We are not talking about silly numbers transferred across international borders on the foreign exchanges, but numbers that have meaning as the agglomeration of millions of separate wipe-throughs and Personal Identification Number entries, of tired signatures at the end of long meals in over-priced restaurants. This is the honeycomb created by the collective economic swarming of millions of human beings. Credit cards and their symbols are everywhere, almost literally everywhere ...

Imagine yourself stranded in a rain forest. You are all alone (it could be worse, you could have been with Sting, watching him find soulmates – if you could do it without throwing up too violently – among the Noble Savages whom he apparently thinks have just walked out of a tract by Rousseau). As it is, you are having to do other nauseating things like commune with nature and discover that your soul really is wrapped in cling film after all. Just think of the pure joy you experience when you hear those rescue helicopter blades, pure and thickly disruptive, like a really good rock guitar riff. You look up and wave frantically, the pilot waves back. You are stupid with joy. And then you notice the MasterCard, Visa and American Express logos on the side of chopper – and you know you are home. You have already eaten your Visa card, but have been dutifully saving the American Express for a rainy day. So they lower the winch down, complete with one of those little wipe-through mobile validation machines. You oblige and tap in your Personal Identification Number, and your credit is good! They winch down the harness and you sit back and watch the meter tick as you are whisked to civilization and cold beer. All you have to do is go through one more simple credit transaction and then you can sleep.

Yeah, well, it hasn't quite reached that stage yet. But the growth of credit card use and the ubiquity of its marketing symbols in the vista of the street life of developed economies is truly remarkable. Incidentally, credit card usage has found an almost perfect inverse correlate (using a logarithmic scale, naturally) in the diminishing acreage of the world's rain forest. As yet, no-one has worked out the connection. But when you read some witty, lightweight little piece on this very subject in *The Economist*, remember you read it here first.

How Japanese fund managers invest in Minnesotan farmers

The next bit is particularly tough to really comprehend. Until the late 1950s, these cards that we take as much for granted as the chairs we sit in, these humdrum bits of plastic in (almost) everyone's wallet, these staffs of modern consumer life – *didn't even exist.*

The credit industry has changed so much and is now so huge and so all-pervasive that the early years seem as quaint and as removed from contemporary reality as a Norman Rockwell print. The first testing of authentic credit cards occurred in 1958 in the Californian town of Fresno. The Bank of America mailed 60,000 unsolicited bits of plastic to its customers. This was test marketing in a very crude form. The logic apparently was that if the consumers didn't like it – well, it would be a small, insubstantial failure in a small, insubstantial town.

There was an initial lull, followed by a spate of defaults. Consumers used the cards and then failed to make payments. And who can blame them for not taking plastic seriously? It didn't look like real money, i.e. dollar bills, that they were spending. But eventually the card business became popular – and profitable – for Bank of America. By the late 1960s the bank had more than a million card holders and was making a profit of over $12 million from the operation.

Naturally, there were imitators. The MasterCard network sprang up from a Citibank operation started shortly afterwards, and in Europe a Swedish banker named Wallenburg began a Eurocard operation as an alternative to the rapidly expanding American Express card.

So now we have what in financial terms might be called a mature market. Given the level of growth and the limited number of people there are to sell to, perhaps it is a mature market that is still expanding, but it has all the sophistication of any modern capital market. There are large numbers of specialist service providers, and the right to receive the income stream from credit card holders is often bundled up into a securities package and sold as a kind of junk bond on the international market. Thus a Minnesotan farmer might have a credit card issued by his local bank, which has contracted out management of his account, the sending of regular statements, chasers for payment, etc, to a specialist back-office firm in Texas. Meanwhile, the right to receive the interest he pays on his line of credit has been purchased by the manager of a Japanese Tokkin (a kind of mutual fund) who likes the currency risk of the yen against the dollar and wants dollar floating-rate debt as part of his fund's portfolio. Industry analysts in mid-1994 put the amount of credit-backed securities floated on the market at a minimum of $22 billion.

Now this is a statement of confidence in our plastic passion. Although the international capital markets appear to be a long way from the profession of social and psychological scientist, they are offering us their verdict on what happens next in the only way they know how. They are prepared to trade, to develop a complex market based on their expectations that the use of instant credit in card form will continue, and will continue to be profitable for those running the industry. In other words, the Japanese fund manager thinks the Minnesotan farmer will keep using his credit card, and keep paying the bills.

The interesting question for the social and economic historian is what happened to consumers' attitudes to debt – because the evolution of this enormous market with all its tricksy little capital market trimmings could not have occurred if people hadn't borrowed the money.

Joseph Nocera in *A Piece of the Action* explains some of the history of American consumer attitudes. 'On the one hand there is no aspect of personal finance more likely to inspire anxiety and even fear ... On the other hand, among the reasons finance companies prospered was because they saw this refusal by banks to make personal loans as a yawning void, which they rushed to fill. Despite the denunciations, despite the free-floating anxiety, Americans have always borrowed money to buy things – if not from a bank, then from *somebody*.'

Consumer debt has risen steadily in both the US and the UK over the past twenty years – both in nominal terms and as a percentage of household income.

As the credit card industry has boomed so the language that describes it has flowered. Or perhaps that should be mushroomed. In any event, credit cards and their caustic critics – notably J. K. Galbraith – have offered us a term for the thoughtless spending that having an instant credit line engenders. The flat, mechanistic phrase 'marginal propensity to consume' has forced its way into modern vocabulary like some brigand robot. So much for the economists' nomenclature. As is usually the case in economic studies, it offers us nothing except a new piece of algebra for the meaningless mosaic of economic academe. The almost entirely worthless language of economics tells us that if you increase people's ability to borrow (widen the margin of potential) they buy more (increased propensity to consume).

On the assumption that no-one's life is irrevocably changed by this dazzling line of analysis, let's proceed to some more interesting questions. How are the credit providers, the feeders of our plastic passion, going to sustain their expansion, i.e. keep us consuming more and more? And what social effects will their marketing moves have?

Sustaining the passion – (i) corporate cards and the modern marriage – obey, love and honour major credit cards

There have been two major developments in the last few years. One of them is a reasonably neutral way of expanding the market, the other has somewhat sinister implications for those of us foolish enough to believe that consciousness – actually being aware and awake – is a good and increasingly rare thing, and individuals should accept responsibility for their own actions (or at least actions taken when one is not exercising the inalienable right to drink- and drug-induced automatism).

The problem facing the industry is how to sustain the impressive growth both in dollars spent and numbers of individuals holding plastic. Those very encouraging figures for the card companies (MasterCard added twenty per cent to its customer base in 1993, don't forget) are also discouraging, because it provides the credit card industry with a glorious past that is difficult to live with. The way forward in the past few years has been to expand in the corporate sector, with the corporate card.

The phrase 'corporate card' can be applied to two distinct credit products. The first is the big corporate client which enrolls key members of its staff on the card and pays the bills itself. This is supposed to offer the corporation's finance department an accurate means of checking what its employees are really spending their money on. But this is not, of course, a real benefit for two reasons.

First, the controls applied by the credit processors for accepting retailers are less than stringent. Just about every whorehouse in Bangkok will take plastic, for example, and the closest the accounts department is going to come to finding out that one of its senior executives has been indulging in life-threatening activities on the company credit card is a three-word identifier on the statement. It will specify something like 'management consultancy services'.

Second, if you give otherwise sane human beings a credit card and inform them that they will not be responsible for picking up the tab you are creating instant consumer dementia. You can explain that there is no real difference – other than cash flow – between having to pay and reclaiming from the corporation and having to be accountable. In both cases only justifiable expenses can be allowed. That's the theory. The practical effect is that otherwise sober male executives in their fifties take their corporate credit cards as a mandate to behave badly. Very badly. In fact, they behave like Bel Air schoolgirls getting their revenge for Daddy's failure to upgrade their Porsches for this year's birthday by taking Daddy's credit card for a walk down Rodeo Drive. The executive with a corporate credit card behaves like the non-earning wife (or husband) with a card that draws on a joint account. Here the marriage vows have been subtly reworked. The working spouse does the loving and the obeying, the spending spouse just takes out a major credit card and makes sure that the store does the honouring. We are talking, at best, severely dislocated notions of responsibility. And quite often we are talking about a dastardly form of consumerist inter-personal warfare – revenge spending.

Which is why this kind of corporate card has had a beneficial impact on credit turnover. It is also why lots of corporations are deciding that handing out plastic to their employees is a little too much like distributing solvent and plastic bags to eight-year-olds. It is a practice they are deciding to stop before it all gets too messy.

There is another avenue of corporate card activity that has seen a huge surge in popularity. This is the corporation-linked card. The benefit from the credit card companies' viewpoint is that while the number of consumers may not rise very greatly, the number of cards will. In other words, the corporate credit card is sold to an individual who already has a card or two or three. This is good for two reasons. First, issuing a card generates revenue in itself. Second, the corporate card offers some kind of inducement to consume. The idea is that the more you spend on the corporate card, the larger the discount you get when you decide to buy some of the corporation's products. The discount is inevitably tiny in relation to the consumption required. Spend $2 million and you get a free middle-of-the-range Chevrolet is the usual formula.

But people do spend. US consumers have snapped up cards issued by airlines so as to get points for free flights every time they buy a pair of socks. You can obtain credit cards that help you get cheaper cars, cheaper insurance, cheaper just about anything you want in the way of goods and services. The communications corporation, AT&T, even went so far as to produce a credit card that offered cheaper credit. It has been a huge success, although a much-resented one in the industry. Because, after all, everyone knows it makes better business sense to offer an expensive product (i.e. credit) with bullshit add-ons than to cut the margins on the product itself. That makes for competition, which makes life more difficult for everyone except the consumer. But the immutable rule is that if profit is there to be made it will be made, and AT&T's incursion into the market in the early 1990s was merely symptomatic of the fact that credit was seen as a good, profitable business with a nice fat margin to trim.

A tangent – plastic and other forms of holiday money compared. Why you should make sure that you *do* leave home without a traveller's cheque

Before moving on to the second, and altogether more worrying marketing thrust of the credit industry, a word must be said in favour of plastic. As financial products for the traveller, credit cards are an absolute essential. They are secure, offering a minimal risk to the owner if they are lost or stolen, once the card issuer has been notified. As a means of exchanging money they are much, much better than paying rip-off tourist rates over the counter at a bank. In addition, the thousands of cash machines that accept plastic cards do not go to lunch just as you reach the front of the queue. They are not surly, and they frequently offer you a choice of four languages in which to effect your transaction. They might provide you with local currency at inter-bank rates (although some take a fancy spread for doing the deal), and the exchange will typically take several days to be debited to your account. And as an extra, many cards have an automatic insurance contract attached to every purchase you make. This can help with all kinds of nasty legal problems.

Compare credit cards with traveller's cheques, and you really begin to see what a good deal they offer. TCs are superior in one respect only – they have better security, in that you are supposed to produce ID and sign each one before obtaining cash. But the downside of TCs compared to credit cards is huge. In addition to wiping the floor with TCs in that counter exchange rates on TCs are genuinely predatory, credit card currency exchange transactions are interest-free loans in the consumers' favour (this is the grace period between the bank in Bergen, whose ATM the card holder uses, reporting and converting the transaction. There will then be a further delay before a bill is sent to the card holder.) With TCs it's the other way round – you pay all the money up front and the supplier of the cheques sits on the cash and earns interest while you travel. Now perhaps we can make sense of those really nasty American Express commercials where famous people offer you advice on what to do if you get home from a trip and there's a cheque left. 'Why not save it for a rainy day?' is the suggestion. Well, here's why not. You're already giving the issuer of the cheque an interest-free loan. If you 'save it for a rainy day', all you're doing is extending the term of that loan indefinitely. Really. Who do they think we are?

Sustaining the passion – (ii) affinity marketing as a facilitator of shallow ostentation, or the promotion of self-deluding dickheadedness. Affinity cards as financial tranquillizer

Anyway, back to our plastic passion. The second prong of the credit card offensive is known as affinity marketing. This strategy to sustain consumer appetites is both clever and dangerous. At least it is dangerous and harmful, as far as the individual is concerned. Because the idea of affinity marketing is stealth bombing of consumer consciousness gone mad. It is subversion with a capital V (that's right – you don't even notice the upper casing until you're halfway through the word). It really is poison in the sleeping king's ear, and it works like this.

You are issued with a card that shows your *affinity* to some group, association or cause. When the card is issued the association or group with which you have your affinity receives a small up-front payment, and subsequently a tiny percentage, usually around half of one per cent, of all the money spent by you, the user of the card.

The card will have a pretty design indicating what your affinity is. This facilitates much flourishing of wallets over lunch tables. For example, in the UK there are affinity cards for people who like to flaunt their membership of the Porsche or Jaguar owners' clubs. There is a Royal Yachting Association card, an Institute of Directors card, a card for alumni of Cambridge University. There is a card for the World Wildlife Fund and even a card for the Labour party – today's version of what the 'card-carrying Communist' used to be. There is also a Rolling Stones card, a fact that might be shocking to those elderly and confused enough to think of the Stones as symbols of anything other than growing old in a gym. The era of rock rebellion was already long over years and years ago, certainly by the time Roger Daltrey, lead singer of The Who, was peddling American Express cards in television commercials. (The Who, incidentally, is a group that has to its, er, credit the classic of zimmer-frame rock 'Don't Get Fooled Again'.)

By the way, we're launching our own 'Fool and His Money' affinity card, coming soon to a smart lunch table Electronic Fund Transfer Point Of Sale outlet near you. Why don't you sign up now, show the world you're part of the exclusive set foolish enough to shell out hard-earned money to buy this book? Make a statement, and subscribe. All monies go to the best (the very best) possible cause.

When you get back to the real world, however, you might want to argue that there's nothing much wrong with all this affinity business. All you're doing is giving money, automatically, to a good cause.

To an extent, maybe. As a prop for the irredeemably vain, it works. If the shallow ostentation of flaunting one's Cambridge background every time one feels the need to impress the quality of one's academic credentials on someone one is hoping to be getting involved with, as they misleadingly say, intimately, is OK, there's clearly very little wrong with this kind of modern consumerism. As a cheap way of showing off, it's absolutely fine. Having a card proclaiming your membership of the Jaguar Owners' Club is, after all, a far less expensive way of gaining a little hollow social status than buying one of the wretched things and then having to drive around in it.

But if the consumer who whips out his pretty little panda card thinks that he's saving wildlife through a minute donation to the World Wildlife Fund, that consumer is a self-deceiving dickhead. All right, there's some financial benefit. If multiplied by the millions of the mass market, the benefit may be substantial. Agreed. But the perniciousness of this kind of marketing does not work on the macro, mass market level. It works in a very profound and subtle way to subvert the idea of individual consciousness, and the meaning of a single act.

The whole cleverness of credit cards is that they obliterate awareness. You spend without being aware that you are really spending. You are 'cleansed' of the difficulty of parting with money. It's a truism that it's a lot more difficult to peel off many notes from a wad of bank notes than it is to squiggle a signature on some funny-looking docket and forget that in some dark tomorrow the bill will arrive on your doorstep. So what these affinity cards do to the individual is devalue any positive notion of what the individual might do to, say, clean up the world.

Here's the central dilemma. If your aim is to improve the environment, is it better to sign off on a credit card voucher for $150-worth of champagne (which will send a grand 75 cents to Friends of the Earth) or is it better to spend three minutes putting back trash that's spilled from its can, or maybe even five minutes writing a letter to the town hall asking for better rubbish disposal facilities?

Affinity cards with a 'feel-good' factor invade the spirit with a big dose of passivity. It's so easy to imagine that you're actually doing something by using credit cards — which are as close as the financial world has yet come to inventing Stematil, Valium, Prozac, or whatever the hot new tranquillizing drug for unhappy housewives is these days. Just as the credit card takes the pain (and the consciousness) out of the act of purchasing, the affinity card takes the giving out of charity.

In terms of credit transactions as stealth bombing, affinity cards do the best job of all. Their payload is a kind of neutron bomb — the kind that leaves the buildings intact, but destroys all human life. They insidiously make you passive, take control of your consciousness by fooling your conscience, and yet they still encourage you to spend. Like quality cocaine, they are a fun habit to have if you have lots of money and enjoy misspending it. And the effect of credit is similar to cocaine's — a quick high followed by a continuing numbness. It's addictive, it's dangerous, and, as passion goes, peculiarly plastic.

CHAPTER IX

Lawyers – The Best Money Lawyers Can Buy

'The poor have to labour in the majestic equality of the law, which forbids the rich as well as the poor to sleep under bridges, to beg in the streets, and to steal bread' – Anatole France, *The Red Lily*

'A lawyer with his briefcase can steal more than a hundred men with guns' – Mario Puzo, *The Godfather*

Tough career choice I of the late twentieth century – abattoir superintendent or litigation lawyer? Tough choice II (clients only need apply) – death or bankruptcy? Lawyers as Mafia-indoctrinated nuns. A homily – lavatorial hierarchy as snobbery in its purest form. The dawn of client awareness and the jackal v. commercial chambermaid theory of legal practice. Legal 'creativity'. Lawyers as spittoons. Why Roman lawyers are best.

Tough career choice I of the late twentieth century – abattoir superintendent or litigation lawyer?

'I want the best money lawyers can buy.'

It sounds all right, at first, doesn't it? Perhaps we have chanced upon some stray aphorism that escaped unrecorded from Oscar Wilde's Tite Street drawing room. Maybe it's a neat little gloss on Engels' acute but infelicitously expressed observation that equality before the law is a bourgeois sham. In any event, it hits you with the force of a clever, acidic little inversion of a humdrum cliché. Its rhetorical impact leaves us surprised, blinking at an abruptly revealed truth. *I want the best money lawyers can buy.* There must be something in it, mustn't there?

Well, there is. But not very much. Far from Oscar's forked-lightning tongue, it has the shallowness of a second-rate Mel Brooks one-liner (it may even have featured in one of his movies, but it's really not worth the effort of researching). It offers us no more than the empty tricksiness of an Elvis Costello lyric – because lawyers don't buy you anything at all in literal, monetary terms. In the world of money what they do is this: they cost you. They cost you a great deal for the pleasure of doing your deals, making sure that those telephone trades are legally enforceable, and generally being an expensive piece of muscle.

Criminal lawyers, on the other hand, offer you hope. The hope they offer is that of liberty, in exchange for which the usual price is complete destitution and despair of a different kind. Lawyers in general, and criminal lawyers in particular, offer a superb service in exchange for vast amounts of money. The service they offer is the means to get at someone in the nastiest way legally possible. There are easily available ways that are even nastier, such as offering small sums to drug-crazed adolescents to shoot people or burn their houses down. But you have to balance the massive satisfaction this might entail (especially if your victim happens to be a big-billing lawyer) against the difficulty and danger of dealing with an Uzi-toting monster looking for the ultimate high. The ultimate high is always the next, and your life certainly isn't going to get in the way.

No, there's nothing else for it. Unless you have a highly developed street awareness and can call upon a rat-like cunning in dealing with dangerous psychopaths, you are pretty much forced into the lair of the legal rodent itself. That is assuming that you are a normal, healthy person who occasionally wishes to cause distress, anxiety and fear to some of your fellow human beings. Or maybe you want to do that to most of your fellow creatures, most of the time. In which case it's a tough career choice between abattoir superintendent, or, if the line of sociopaths at the office door is too long, litigation lawyer.

Anyway, to deal with your lawyer's actions, your victim had better have a great deal of money. The more the better, in fact. Because only the super-rich can hope to escape unscathed from the bitter embrace of the modern lawyer.

Tough choice II (clients only need apply) – death or bankruptcy?

Examples abound. Bill and Hillary Clinton claimed that they were under severe financial pressure from defending themselves against the various allegations concerning their dealings in the Whitewater affair. Mike Tyson, once a multi-millionaire, has apparently been reduced to poverty by the legal costs of defending the rape charge he still denies. And consider Denis Levine, the high profile merchant banker and insider dealer. According to James B. Stewart's excellent book, *Den of Thieves*, the prosecuting attorneys for the SEC and the New York District Attorney's office regarded it as a major victory that they were able to have Levine's ill-gotten assets frozen at an early stage in their prosecution.

'The freeze gave the SEC its principal leverage with Levine, handicapping his efforts to lead a normal life and even making it difficult for him to pay his lawyers' fees,' writes Stewart. When Levine's lawyers attacked the restraining order, Judge Richard Owen 'upheld the freeze on Levine's assets. The SEC had won its first major battle.'

You see, Engels had a point. Equality before the law *is* a bourgeois sham. As some British judge or other put it (exactly which is a matter of controversy), the law courts of England are open to all men, like the doors of the Ritz Hotel.

In more or less real life it works like this. If IBM or some other infinitely powerful corporation decides to sue you, you will almost certainly lose. If the corporation wants to prove that two plus two equals five, it hires an expert accountant to argue the case as a witness in its favour in court. It hires the very best (i.e. cruellest and nastiest) legal minds to slice apart the testimony given by you or your experts – if you have the resources to find them and pay their expenses. And so you lose and have to pay whatever the court decides is fair compensation to Mr Big, and then there are the court costs, the attendant bankruptcy, the break-up of your marriage, loss of family life, the descent into drug-dependency, alcoholism, swigging hair lacquer in the street, perhaps even not telling Jehovah's Witnesses to fuck off and die when they next try and ram eternal happiness down your throat. What you need is the best lawyers money can buy, or you're dead.

But the choice between death and bankruptcy is really the criminal lawyer's contribution to modern society. The law of money, corporate legal work and civil litigation (which, considering the nit-picking hostility between litigants, ranks right up there with civil war and friendly fire as an Oxymoron of Our Times), are generally less distressing, although – and this is difficult to believe – more expensive.

Lawyers as Mafia-indoctrinated nuns

There is an anomaly here. While, naturally enough, the principal guiding force, the unfailing identifier of the modern attorney, is unalloyed avarice, there is something else in play. The legal profession is not purely a function of money in the way that, for all its pretensions, banking is. While bankers seek to validate their unbounded appetite for profit by claiming they are following in the hallowed footsteps of the great pioneers of capitalism, lawyers have an equally specious claim – that of objectivity.

This gives us a clue as to one of the most important functions of the law – a neat way of cloaking social policy in the dark shroud of pseudo-objectivity. Law, said the distinguished and much-vilified US judge Robert H. Bork, is 'vulnerable to the winds of intellectual or moral fashion, which it then validates as the commands of our most basic concept'. Anyone with a real eagerness to see how language can become meaningless – except as an instrument of social policy – in the minds and mouths of lawyers, should read Herbert Hart's *Concept of Law*, in which he deftly illustrates how a rule forbidding cars to enter a public park can be sensibly interpreted as permitting exactly that (if the car is erected on a plinth as a monument to a dead war hero, and therefore does not transgress the social purposes behind the rule, such as avoidance of noise, pollution, danger to children, etc.). Failing that, attend an Irish matrimonial court, where the advocate mouthing the words 'illegal conversation' is in fact referring to something known (but not referred to in Irish law courts) as adultery.

But lawyers have a professional tradition, a *modus operandi* above and beyond (or beneath) this. Functioning in tandem with the pure greed universal in the profession, lawyers have a working tradition that has evolved over the centuries, from the days of the advocate offering to argue the ignorant shepherd's case before the king, through the era of Blackstone's commentaries, through organized pleading, the organic growth of the common law, and the establishment of business specialist practices with their rows of copperplate-scribbling clerks, through at last to today's slick, word-processed, client-customized documentation and advice. Yes, lawyers are sustained by a fine and noble tradition – that of systematic cruelty and exploitation.

You must understand that big legal firms operate as a weird kind of hybrid between a closed-order nunnery and a Mafia extortion racket. Whatever the Mother Superior says is so, is so. Except that Mother Superior doesn't speak. To discover the rule you have to be a kind of financial anthropologist, watch behaviour patterns, and deduce the social norms of good practice. You could, for example, wear brown suits to work. Or you might choose to urinate in the partners' lavatory on the grounds that it is just the same as the lavatory marked 'Gentlemen' but four storeys closer. You might not even be rebuked for such conduct, but it would be noted. And by it you would damage your chances of elevating yourself from legal novitiate to a higher place in the order (with the ultimate goal of becoming partner and achieving Heaven on earth). Only hugely successful extortion – guiding a succession of new clients toward the rotating knives in the billing office, ramping the bills of existing clients sky-high and then persuading them to pay – only that kind of performance can save you from the consequences of committing an error of the brown-suit variety.

Of course, you can always screw up big time. One friend of mine, an incipient alcoholic of variable temperament (which, eerily enough, describes most of my acquaintances), managed to dance naked in front of the entire tax and commercial department at the Christmas party of the large London law firm that employs him as a senior litigation lawyer. Joe – astute fellow that he is – thought that his memorable karaoke rendition of 'Let's Face the Music and Dance' (perhaps it should have been 'Should I Stay or Should I Go?') might have affected his chances of partnership. But, incredibly, he did not give up hope for several months before realizing that his best bet was to leave the convent and settle for obscurity in the provinces. Now that is a triumph of conviction over rational sense to give your average Jesuit a quiet hard-on. (All names, by the way, including those of the songs, have been changed to protect the guilty – also to stop the litigious bastard suing.)

A homily – lavatorial hierarchy as snobbery in its purest form

And now here's a toilet tale, which is what I'm sure you've been waiting for. It is not a scatalogical joke, but a homily. In its own quiet, sad way, this is a New York story, because New York is the attitude capital of the world, and this is all about attitude. It so happens the scene is set in London, at a law firm where the partners even had attitude about the lavatories. It is not unlike the firm at which I qualified as a lawyer myself (Oh yes! I am not without sin, but then, I'm not casting the first stone either), and provides an interesting case study into the mores of legal practice.

This firm was and is one of the biggest in the UK, an international outfit with offices in several European countries, the US and Asia. It has, in the mid-1980s, some sixty partners, a handful of whom – say, five – are women. Yet in its headquarter offices in the City of London it segregates its cold and unaccommodating lavatory space along these lines – Ladies, Gentlemen, Partners, Secretaries, Partners' Secretaries. The assumption is of course that all partners are men, that all secretaries are women, and that there is a qualitative difference between the urine passed by ordinary secretaries and those who have the privilege of working for partners. Maybe it made the partners' secretaries feel good. Maybe it was a clever ruse on behalf of the partnership (including female partners, who presumably relieved themselves most of the time by freelancing as secretaries). This insane paradigm of hierarchical nonsense actually existed until the middle of the 1980s. And the crowning irony is that there was no substantive difference between the quality of the facilities provided in any of the lavatories, for both men and women. Even the toilet paper was identical – Stalinist-scratchy, i.e. painful but good for the Communist soul. I know. Subconsciously preparing for a career as a fearless investigative journalist, I waited until everyone had gone home one night and checked for myself. Given that the facilities were identical, the act of classifying them differently was to have a hierarchy just for the sake of it – snobbery in its purest form.

This might seem rather petty to you, but the names on the lavatories were instrumental in deciding that, after qualification, I had to get out. Which I did, stealing as much whiskey as possible from the partners' dining room before I left. I mean – would you want to work for people like that?

The dawn of client awareness and the jackal v. commercial chambermaid theory of legal practice

Yet my personal story of a world of mind-boggling pettiness, mean-mindedness and unremitting selfishness is unremarkable in the extreme. Much more worthy of note is the fact that times are changing for the legal profession. The outside world has pretty much sussed the noble practice of law. Once upon a time the real business of law was as remote and unintelligible to the layman as the deliberately arcane language of a commercial lease, a franchise contract, or a 'simple' property transfer. But notwithstanding the best efforts of lawyers to resist the advent of the twentieth century, membership of the profession is not entirely restricted to white, privately educated males.

An honourable – or rather egregious – exception to this is the English and Welsh Bar. This is the side of the profession which deals with advocacy. It is still, despite recent half-hearted reforms, essentially a restricted practice. The right to wear anachronistic Georgian wigs and argue cases in the highest courts essentially belongs to advocates. And by offering an attractive career structure which involves not paying newly qualified lawyers at all for the first year, entry to the profession of advocacy is effectively means-tested. The ability to practice requires acceptance by a set of practising lawyers – which offers an excellent means of informal, unreviewable control of those who are admitted. There are in fact quite a few women and some members of racial minorities practising as advocates, but the members of the English bar are far too clever to offer the world hard evidence of the need for reform. When such reform is thrust upon it, the profession of advocacy shows its steel. Lord Mackay, the Lord Chancellor, came to office with the best of reforming ambitions which have so far gone largely unrealized.

The quality, the genuine cleverness, of these advocates should not be underestimated. Nor should be the public esteem in which they are held. Take the case of Robert Alexander. When he was a practising senior advocate, Alexander was virtually beatified in British society. His earnings of reportedly more than £1 million per year and the sheer enormity of the rate at which he billed himself out (one can only speculate, but a bottom-of-the-range BMW for a day's work would probably be only a mild overestimate) were viewed as matters of simple wonderment. There he was, this genius of commercial law, Chairman of the Bar Council, a sign that meritocracy wasn't just a piece of collective whimsy. Alexander *deserved* it all for his wit and his wisdom. He was a great man. Until he left the law and became chairman of National Westminster Bank. Whereupon he was seen – quite rightly – as an apologist for a not-very-well-run bank. Overnight, he became a man with nothing interesting to say.

But the lawyers who concern us here are the corporate lawyers, the money lawyers. And it is an undeniable fact that people from a wider variety of social backgrounds have infiltrated the non-advocate branch of the law. These lawyers, who undertake work for big financial clients, like banks, insurers and property companies, have, partly as a consequence of their social diversity, lost much of their tradition with its implicit secrecy. A vital component of the ritual of humiliation and exploitation is that after being humiliated, you get to do the humiliating – it's the same principle on which the British run their world-famous centres of excellence in sodomy and torture, otherwise known as the private schooling system. So once a lawyer has spent years bending over and shutting up about it, when the time comes to do the exploiting he expects to find victims as willing as he was.

But they aren't, and, essentially, the gaffe has been blown. One dinner-party story too many has been told of the firms who consider that their bills aren't exorbitant enough unless at least half their clients complain. Lawyers are seen as peripheral and parasitic in a way that is quite new. There are pay telephone lines for people who like lawyer jokes (*Q. What do you call two thousand lawyers drowning in a shipwreck? A. A start. Q. What's the difference between a cockerel and a lawyer? A. The cockerel clucks defiant, a lawyer fucks de client. Q. What's black and brown and looks good on a lawyer? A. A doberman, etc, etc.*)

Nowadays, people know that the meter is ticking as soon as they walk through the door of a lawyer's office. Their lawyer friends have told them. They know that lawyers don't know the law, they just know how to find out what they don't know (nothing wrong with that, but it does go against many a popular illusion of legal omniscience, or at least competence). They know that lawyers – unless they are engaged in the theatre of the courtroom – consider themselves to be on the fringes of the action. Always there, always paid, but never quite actively involved.

Which leads us to a choice of interpretation. Do we regard lawyers as the jackals of capitalism, the margin feeders, the cowardly attack dogs who prey only on the weak and the vulnerable? Or do we see them in a slightly more benign light? As a species of commercial chambermaid who comes in and clears up the mess once a couple of banks have rolled in the hay together. The lawyers in their dark uniforms who make sure that the 'bible' (a lawyer's term – used without a trace of irony) of documents is in perfect order, that every stray semi-colon in a fifty-thousand-word syndicated loan agreement has been excised, that all the necessary registration forms are properly filled out, filed in the appropriate places with the requisite number of copies. What's the major difference – apart from the small matters of literacy and (usually) social background – between doing that detailed, dull work, and folding lavatory paper into a neat little pointy shape or leaving a chocolate on the neatly puffed-up pillow?

Here's one. The chambermaid leaves a little note that has its letter *is* dotted with little hearts and the loops of its *gs* embellished by smiling faces. The note says 'thanks for letting me serve you' or something equally insincere. Mind you, the shock tactic of truth – 'What a slob! And what were you doing with those towels and that strawberry yogurt?' – *that* kind of cheery little message probably wouldn't elicit the hoped-for, respectably sized tip left in the envelope. The lawyer, on the other hand, sends you a deliberately incomprehensible data dump of everything that everyone and anyone in that lawyer's office has done, thought about doing, or generally wondered about on your file. If the receptionist rests a cup of coffee on your manila folder you'll be charged for it. It will be buried away in there along with the photocopying (a major profit centre in modern law offices) and those meals you had with your adviser that you might have thought would be charged against the general office account. And then, when the legal imagination has been exhausted, there is the trick of adding in a neat little catch-all 'general disbursements' as a means of rounding up the bill to the nearest ten thousand. And all this comes at you with the unrelenting mild certainty of a monk singing plainsong. The bill is a little like this sentence in that it is deliberately written with as little punctuation as possible to sweep the unfortunate reader along like some quiescent small furry animal frozen in the headlights of a legal pantechnicon that is remorselessly rolling your way. Including sundry disbursements and value added tax, at seventeen and a half per cent.

That's the other end of the universe from a note in rounded, girlish script exhorting you to have a nice day. Have a nice day is what you don't do when lawyers send their bills. But then, if you're a bank who's been having a bit of rumpy-pumpy with a promiscuous insurance company, you probably made quite a mess of the bedroom.

Corporate management, on the whole, is still undecided as to which view it takes of the legal profession. Apart, of course, from the view that, to be absolutely fair to the legal profession, they're complete bastards.

The common tactic in dealing with lawyers is to play the market a little, spread the work among a few firms and let price competition work its magic. With a large element of its mystique gone, the corporate sector of legal practice has never been quite so truly subservient to the industry it has always notionally served as now. As corporations fight to pare down legal bills, the corporate departments of the law firms are desperate to hold on to business because a) it sustains an edge over competing legal firms and, at least as important, b) it sustains an edge over other departments within the firm.

The war at home in most legal firms is usually even more bitterly fought than the battle with the competition. The prevailing orthodoxy, developed over the last few decades, of exciting merger and acquisition work, management buy-outs, refinancings, company flotations and so on, has it that the corporate departments of all large law firms are the real engines of the business. The tradition of suffering in silence may be one thing, but once the dues have been paid and partnership attained expectations are high. Mother Superior in the corporate department had better bring home a great deal of bacon or, vows of silence notwithstanding, there will be mutterings at vespers.

So why do we have lawyers and what do they really do? Reams of garbage have been written on both topics. Here's my brief (sic) contribution.

Lawyers are an undesirable by-product of peace in developed economies. They are the quartermasters in the hot wars of trade, and especially finance. When trade was about merchant princes in Venice doing raw deals on the basis of sheer goodwill and trust, there was little need for much documentation. Lawyers serve some purpose in a sophisticated capitalist system, but after a point they simply add to what economists like to call the transaction costs of a society. After a certain point – vague, but clearly passed in a country such as the US – they cease to be a positive force. Instead of helping society run in an orderly way through litigation, they merely help it to be litigious.

'There is some evidence that the number of lawyers in a country is in inverse proportion to its growth rate,' writes Hamish McRae in his book, *The World In 2020*. McRae cites academic research from the University of Texas and says that this provides evidence for his broad, perhaps not entirely surprising, conclusion that 'too many lawyers, so it would seem, actually destroy wealth.'

Another aspect of elegant legal superfluity in our supposedly civilized world is the entity called international law which is taught at universities, but whose very existence is still in doubt. Wait for the day that the US government can sue for illegal restraint of trade by the Japanese and you will wait a very long time indeed. There are good jurisprudential reasons for this – mainly the Benthamite notion that law is essentially rules enforced by sanctions, with no Rousseau-esque moral gloss of consent or anything of David Hume's notion of collective self-interest.

Legal 'creativity'

Some lawyers, in their sad, arid little way, claim to be creative. Creativity – apart from the judicial practice of interpreting words purely to fit personal prejudice – typically consists of charming little tricks like 'needlizing' documents. The technique of needlizing a document came about through a combination of dullness and greed – this is an unusual pairing in finance, since naked greed is usually exciting to watch. But then a cynic might argue (but not too strongly if he didn't want to get his threadbare ass sued) that pedantry and avarice are the twin hallmarks of successful modern commercial lawyers of this sort.

Take as an example the acquisition of a piece of a small company. There are many, many bits of paper to be made pretty and wrapped up together in a 'bible' – the acquisition agreement itself, a shareholder's agreement, various comfort letters, board minutes, any special resolutions of the company convened at extraordinary general meetings, registration forms, and so on. Naturally, each firm develops its own standard way of doing these things, and will churn out almost identical documentation for each broadly similar transaction. Which is where the needlizing comes in. If the other side's lawyers have seen the same 150-page acquisition agreement twenty times, isn't it just possible that they might not notice an extra clause or two on page 121 the twenty-first time they see the acquisition document? Those two clauses – the needles in the haystack – might represent a complete negation of the safety clauses for minority shareholders that have been built in as standards in that type of agreement. If the other side isn't extremely vigilant the needles will get through. That means the other side's clients might sue if the needles are ever used. It also means that the other side pay lawyers to read through things they have seen hundreds of times before. And all at the bargain-basement rate of several hundred dollars an hour (the price of a Beemer every sixty minutes is the exception rather than the rule, even in the weird Noddy Land that is legal practice). So the other side finds the needles and sends back an amended draft, with needles of its own. And so it goes on, a very expensive game of Pig-In-The-Middle with the client's bank account playing Porky. This combination of the juvenile and the mercenary is what passes for one aspect of legal creativity.

They are also trying to grow their businesses through the creative expansion of the concept of economic loss. The idea is to persuade shareholders that if a company's stock has performed worse than shares of similar companies for two consecutive quarters then the management of that company is incompetent. The shareholders, argue the lawyers, should sue for economic loss in contract or tort (sometimes it's a fine line between the two). And if the shareholders all band together to start a 'class action' the lawyers can make a good fee. And to make sure they have access to all the necessary information, some law firms have bought tiny holdings in all quoted companies. That way they have right of access to meetings and all the privileges of more substantial shareholders. They can also start an action themselves and invite fellow shareholders to join in.

This trend has a direct impact on stock market behaviour. If a company's management knows an action is being prepared, it will do things like sell off divisions of the company to bolster the share price over the short term. The division might be vital to the long-term interest of the company, but the advent of the lawyers makes the quick fix essential.

In this way, lawyers can have a direct and dramatic impact on The Market. They are also perfectly placed to do insider deals. Imagine: you as a lawyer know you are in a position to force a company's management to jack up its share price. Do you buy a call option, anonymously, through one of those offshore companies you know so much about, thereby making a profit of five, ten, perhaps fifteen times your orginal outlay? No, no, of course you don't. You're a lawyer, after all ...

Lawyers as spittoons

Lawyers are also useful as repositories. Apart from their increasingly important role as the butt of hate-filled jokes, the collective spittoon for universal, if mild, contempt, there is another repositorial function. It is staggeringly hypocritical, given that most of their clients see them as half-vagabond, half-prostitute, but lawyers are the repository of trust and respectability. A cynic might say, the beast, that lawyers' clients pay them to investigate or sanctify their business processes. And after scrupulous enquiry, due deliberation and presentation of their bill, the lawyers will usually lend their 'good name' to whatever it is the client wants.

Two quick examples that might raise an eyebrow.

In the orgy of greed, back-biting and criminality that was known as the takeover boom of the 1980s, a senior stockbroker at a leading UK firm was accused of impropriety. The brokerage's solution was to call in a firm of lawyers that had not been involved in other legal work and to ask it to investigate. The result, amazingly enough, was that the broker in question was exonerated of misconduct. Correctly no doubt. The fact that the legal firm was paid to adjudicate, thereby making the lawyer both financial supplicant and judge, is not relevant.

Again, lawyers are useful before any impropriety has been committed. If, for example, a securities firm wishes to trade on a completely unregulated market, it is most convenient to invite a legal firm in to devise a whole system of information flows and financial reporting, to construct Chinese Walls and ensure that a system for dealing with potential conflicts of interest are put in place. The firm can then – so a cynic might say – announce that it has spent a great deal of money on putting such a structure in place, and promptly get on with the business of subverting it. It's good business for the lawyers, who are in the golden hole position of offering advice which is not followed (and not even the most fertile litigation brain has yet worked out a way to sue on that basis). And it's a convenient way of purchasing market confidence for the trader.

Why Roman lawyers are best

In examining the law, it's difficult not to have sympathy with the demented academics who claim that Roman law is the only true law. Instead of having to bother with the practicalities of day-to-day life, of seeing this strange industry and the people who work in it as the servant-parasites of commerce and trade, it's much more pleasant to look at pure concepts and see how they apply to Justinian notions of interlocking will in contract and strict liability in tort. Forget judicial foible, needlizing and all its time-costed wickednesses, give me Paul, Ulpian and the other great jurists of the glossist tradition.

Of course, my predilections have nothing to do with any liking for Roman law concepts or its study. Nor do I prefer these lawyers over the present-day legal community for their charm, their wit, nor the precision or clarity of their writing. No, no. The clinching factor in favour of Roman lawyers is that all of them are dead.

CHAPTER X

Financial Journalists – Et in Arcania Ego (especially Ego)

'[The fourth estate] – the great engine – she never sleeps. She has her ambassadors in every quarter of the world – her courtiers upon every road. Her officers march along with armies, and her envoys walk into statesmen's cabinets. They are ubiquitous.' – William Makepeace Thackeray, *Henry Esmond*

Ulysses revisited – why what financial journalists offer the world is every bit as useful as myrrh-scented traffic lights in rural Calabria. Factual reporting and the Hall of Mirrors. Objectivity – alias truth as a fashion accessory. Things designed to impair journalistic objectivity – freebies and public relations people. Professional ethics and expenses – the night I was chairman of British Steel. What you get – our best shot. When it goes wrong – the conch-shell theory of insider trading. Good reporting – and curiosity.

Ulysses revisited – why what financial journalists offer the world is every bit as useful as myrrh-scented traffic lights in rural Calabria

Buck Mulligan would have made an excellent journalist. As he skips into the pages of James Joyce's *Ulysses* he hums lightly to himself *'Introibo ad altare Dei'* – I shall enter upon God's altar. And as he makes this light-eyed little promise to himself, what is he doing? Apart from abandoning the classical accusative in favour of the Church's ablative, he is merely performing the mundane, marginally narcissistic little ritual of shaving. But he offers us a version of himself as a kind of Liffey-based Melchizedek, a man about to part the curtains of the tabernacle behind which lie the mysteries of the world.

The idea of journalist as conduit, a priest-figure linking the ordinary world to the smaller, secret, Olympian universe of power, is not new. In his introduction to *The Faber Book of Reportage,* John Carey, Professor of English at Oxford, assesses reportage (the quintessence of 'factual' reporting – of which more later) in its modern context.

'Reportage supplies modern man with a constant and reassuring sense of events going on beyond his immediate horizon ... Reportage provides modern man, too, with a release from his trivial routines, and a habitual daily illusion of communication with a reality greater than himself. In all these ways religion suggests itself as the likeliest substitute for reportage, at any rate in the West.'

Of course it requires chrome-plated self-confidence to put yourself forward as the interpreter of secrets for the masses, the guide to an arcane world of 'greater reality'. In fact, to do the job of journalist well, you need such impregnable insouciance about the world and your place in it that you see no tension whatever between humming a ditty about entry into the realm of the divine and scraping at your ugly mug in scummy water. Step forward Mr Milligan, your computer screen and your expense account await you.

Already we see that flaws — notably the fault of *hubris* — are built into the journalist's job description. Again, the idea of punishing those with the arrogance to seek after the higher, secret knowledge that is supposedly the journalist's goal, is not new. Far from it. Carlo Ginzburg, an Italian academic, points out in his essay *The High and the Low. The Theme of Forbidden Knowledge in the Sixteenth and Seventeenth Centuries* (from his collection of essays *Myths, Emblems, Clues*) that the Christian world has been warned against the folly of seeking after higher things ever since a largely mistranslated letter from Saint Paul urged the Romans not to despise Jews. The mistake, according to Ginzburg, was in confusing a verb used with moral significance (*sapere* — to be wise) for a construction with intellectual force (to know). The result was that at the close of the fifteenth century, Niccolo Malermi, in one of the earliest translations of the Bible into Italian, wrote 'Do not seek to know high things.' In other words, *Paul's Epistle to the Romans: 11.20* was seized upon by clerics and the ruling classes as a convenient instrument of social control.

So the clergy and the power barons — broadly equivalent to the first two estates of France's *ancien régime* — were happy to chastise the uppity members of the third estate who arrogantly sought to enter their territory and discover their secrets. But of course if they keep coming it's difficult to oppose by brute force. Sometimes deflection is the better course.

When Thomas Babington Macaulay identified journalists as the fourth estate he was merely imbuing physicality with spirit. 'The gallery in which the reporters sit has become a fourth estate of the realm,' he wrote in 1828. He was publicizing an already existing platform, close to power but not offering the exercise of it, to which journalists could assign themselves. In practical terms, this fourth category means that, while still remaining part of the unwashed masses, journalists get to meet captains of industry, ministers of state, the denizens of power and pomp, the great and the good. They are wined and dined, taken on 'freebies' ranging from a trip to the races, to weekend holidays for two, to round-the-world flights, and generally live above their means. While their salaries are hardly third estate, journalists, especially financial journalists, like to bleat about them constantly. Their entirely synthetic social milieu, a product of their elevated professional acquaintances and the schoolmarm ethic of attempting (in theory at least) to tell the truth, makes them claim that they are vastly underpaid. *Especially* financial journalists. The fact that their good opinion is solicited by people who earn five, six or (pick a figure between two and one hundred) times as much as they do convinces them that they are drastically and cruelly exploited by their employers. Everyone who dwells in the elevated and secret world of Arcadia – or perhaps that should be Arcania – has a Big Ego and earns Big Money to match. Apart from journalists. As casual visitors, they just have the Big Ego.

A by-product of this situation is the Achilles' heel of journalists, the freebie. The freebie is, basically, a bribe. Its purpose is to affect and impair the judgment of the journalists. The freebie appeals to the journalists' false sense of grievance about their supposed lack of material comfort by offering them anything from a free drink to a round-the-world trip. If, as the American humorist P. J. O'Rourke suggested, the ultimate performance car is a hire car (actually, it's a stolen car, but let's move quickly on), then the ultimate meal is that which is bought by someone else. This is, literally, a question of personal taste, but I find food purchased by the French taxpayer is particularly delicious. Freebies, the spurious notion of having something for nothing, and the limitless supplies of false praise that are heaped on journalists' heads by the suppliers of freebies are all deeply deleterious to the practice of journalism. They are also, for those of us who are hair-trigger, pump-action, high-calibre, general-purpose gluttons, soaks and lechers, a great deal of fun. Of freebies and their effect on news judgment, more later.

But whatever their numerous faults, foibles and vanities, financial journalists are the most important gateway to the arena of money for the rest of the world. They are the media through which we must travel if we wish to acquire knowledge, higher or otherwise, of the mysterious commodity of money.

This question then presents itself. Are they, on the whole, doing a good job? The standard way of tackling the issue would be to construct a crude dichotomy between factual reporting and representation of opinion. As we shall see, the borderline between the two is wholly subjective, but for now, let's take the orthodox route.

Opinion necessarily requires an 'interesting' view of events. An opinion columnist who merely recycled established ideas on the Gaza strip, systemic tension within the European Union, or the future of the Latin American bond market in a climate of rising US interest rates, would quickly be out of a job. So the columnist must offer exciting, sexy opinions. And – here's the rub – not let a cutesy view of the world so override what's actually going on in it that the column reveals itself as well-argued rubbish. Polemic must have some semblance of realism, otherwise it isn't polemic at all. So even the most tendentious opinion columns must be anchored in fact, or they will be labelled agitprop or bad fiction. The art of doing this is to offer a wry view of the world and then disagree with yourself. The language used must refer to real events, appear to be rooted in common sense and intelligent awareness of the world, but it must not commit itself to one view or the other. In other words, to be really successful as an opinion columnist, the writer must not express an opinion.

However, different writers have different ideas of success. William Safire of the *New York Times* and Bernard Levin of *The Times* in London express their views unequivocally, and have been pretty much unequivocally wrong and unequivocally right about lots of things. Sarah Hogg's views, on the other hand, were much more difficult to discern when she was the economics editor of *The Independent* in the late 1980s. The view of her underlings at the time was that she was angling for a place in Arcania. Her comment pieces were seen as rather public memoranda for the benefit of 'David' – alias Lord Young, the then UK Minister for Trade whose inability to get results made him look increasingly confused and generally embarrassing. Whatever her motives, Ms Hogg succeeded in getting a good seat in the UK establishment – as the personal adviser to John Major. After jumping the Major ship (or was she, as some suggest, pushed?), there was a juicy little life peerage as she completed the transition from commentator to commented-upon. One can only surmise that the Tory estimation of the Hogg contribution to British political and economic life is equivalent, at least in terms of gong-count, to that of her fellow baroness, Margaret Thatcher. The award, of the Happy New Year 1995 vintage, was made despite recurrent criticisms levelled at Major that he fudged and equivocated, not-withstanding the excellence of his advice. Reduced to writing (with a few judicious excisions and the occasional extra verbal twirl) his utterances might well have been treated not as bad politics but good journalism.

Ah yes, journalism. One thing that journalists of the Hogg school would (quite rightly) never allow themselves to be drawn into is the dangerous business of signalling to readers or viewers which way the markets are going next. Economists and financial specialists on the whole know the markets well enough to diagnose more than a tinge of irrationality in them. But they sometimes cannot avoid involvement in this exercise in futility if the mainstream, generalist hacks who usually have overall control of TV, radio and newspaper concerns, decide that the market is a hot story. The dilemma of the financial journalist is how to explain to the executive editor or programme controller a) that he (the boss is still, usually, a he) is a dick-for-brains because b) the markets are almost completely unpredictable. Correction. The dilemma is how to explain that the markets are unpredictable without arguing themselves out of a job as expert commentators and forecasters. The result is that titles such as *Newsweek* will occasionally find themselves so excited by the ruinous depression of a bear market or the euphoric highs of a bull run, that the market story will appear as the cover story. The usual format is a collage of screaming traders in an open outcry pit, plus a cartoon of a snorting bull or rampaging bear. The result is the perfect allegory of a myrrh-scented Calabrian traffic light.

To elucidate. Southern Italy has a huge and enduring appeal to many people, but respect for the orthodoxies of the law is not one of its more prominent qualities. Forget all the heavy stuff about the Mafia and parallel systems of government, let's concentrate on traffic lights. If you approach a crossroads in Calabria and the light is on green, what should you do? Go? Only if you're prepared to risk your life. Because the person driving on the intersecting road will see a red light and break it. It's natural. Road safety by-laws are a pathetic, puny part of an official system that is held pretty much in contempt anyway. Not to break the red light would be an embarrassment. In one of the world's most unreconstructedly macho spots it would be a challenge to your manhood — even if you're a woman. So if you see a green light, you have to slow down, because you can be pretty much sure that anyone coming to the red will break it. Thus order, albeit a topsy-turvy order, reasserts itself. Red means go, green means stop.

Subject the moral of this tale to financial analysis and you have what is known in the markets as a leading negative indicator. You have advance warning given by something that indicates a positive and the markets subsequently do something negative. A well-known example of this is the index of optimism among analysts. If they are optimistic about the future of the market, the market generally falls (one possible explanation for this is that they are optimistic because they have invested all their clients' money, but that means there is no new cash coming in — no Bigger Fool to be found).

The concept of leading and lagging indicators belongs primarily to the chartist. The chartist looks at graphs and ratios of market liquidity, bond yields against interest rates, all manner of data, in fact. The idea is to try to find the perfect indicator that will tell you when the markets are about to fall or rise. And, according to one chartist at the headquarters of Fidelity, the world's biggest fund group, the timing of market cover stories is a pretty reliable guide as to the future direction of shares, bonds, or whatever. The principle is that if the cover depicts a bear and screams a depressing headline like 'All Floors Down to 200' it's time to buy. If there's an upbeat headline and a picture of a spunky-looking bull, sell quickly. The same usually goes for companies. For example, in July 1994 *Newsweek* ran a cover story on Bill Gates and his company Microsoft. Let's hope the media have it right this time — but the instinct has to be to sell, sell, sell!

In other words, the journalists who are supposed to bring prized and previously secret information back down to the rest of the world consistently get it wrong. What they offer the world is a leading negative indicator for market moves. And this despite their status as conduits to the higher realms, priests who descend from the divine grove reeking of incense and myrrh. So the next time you're driving in rural Calabria, rub some ointment on a traffic light and you'll have created something every bit as useful as a market prediction by a financial journalist.

Factual reporting and the Hall of Mirrors

So much for the opinion side of the equation. What about 'factual' reporting, the business of bringing enlightenment to the world?

The whole question of what 'factual' reporting might be necessarily turns on the nature of a fact. As definitions go, this may seem disappointingly empty, but in media terms a fact is a fact, in particular a newsworthy fact, only if a journalist says so.

Consider the case of Madame Edith Cresson, former prime minister of France. Her appointment caused some mirth even in a country where, shall we say, a politician's private life is, incredibly enough, genuinely private. Suffice it to say that her accession to office produced one of the great headlines in any language, which ran in the French paper *Libération*. This organ – in bold type on page one – informed its readers, deadpan, that '*Cresson est Mitterandienne au fond de son être*'. Which translates, very crudely, as 'Cresson is Mitterand's to the very depth of her being'. The rest of the coverage, as it had to be if the government were not to close the paper's offices down there and then, was totally straight.

But the real news story came about when a UK Sunday paper, the *Observer*, ran a page-one article pointing out that Cresson had stated in a book of interviews with powerful women that one Englishman in four was homosexual. While there may be some truth in this, the *Observer* saw it as a foolish enough comment to merit coverage. The television, radio and daily papers traditionally feed off any halfway-interesting story from the Sunday press when the newshold is difficult to fill at the beginning of the week. They saw the story and positively waded in. It had just enough of the right ingredients – an opportunity to mock Europe, to beat up on a powerful woman, to throw crap at the French – to run prominently in most of the UK media. And the furore did not go unnoticed across the Channel. The French press reported, in its fiercely chauvinstic way, the chauvinism of the English. And that French reaction in its turn became the subject of comment in British papers.

At this point we must draw a line and look at what is being paraded as news. If we take Cresson's opinion on the sexuality of the English male as the French view of the English (which it isn't, but no matter), the UK press reporting of it was the English view of the French view of the English. The French newspapers' outraged coverage of the belittling of their prime minister (something they themselves were to do far better than the English press could ever have done) is the French view of the English view of the French view of the English. And when the French media comment drew the attention of the British we had — wait for it — the English view of the French view of the English view of the French view of the English.

Now journalism isn't quite all done with pure image, but sometimes examination of journalistic method does make it seem as though we are strolling through a Hall of Mirrors that magnifies and distorts out of all proportion. Let's not forget that the basic 'fact' at the heart of this little media tempest was a stray comment made several years before in a book whose literary merit was perhaps not of the highest (the fact that the author owned the publishing house no doubt helped the editors skip the odd infelicity).

The truth (which suddenly seems like such a dangerous word) is that as far as the media are concerned, fact is a function of news judgment. The news, as one senior editor of an international newspaper is extremely fond of repeating, is where the newspaperman is. In other words, news, the facts that a journalist decides to be relevant, is no more than the function of journalistic opinion. Similarly, the difference between opinion and factual reporting is that, in the opinion of the journalists, one set of opinions is fact and the other set of opinions is, er, opinion.

By which time you are no doubt craving a little honesty, sincerity and plain dealing. Your common sense must tell you that all this stuff about opinion and fact is really just pure sophistry. We know that some things are true and others are false. Life is complex, truth or truths are difficult to understand and tremendously difficult to report, but to call the whole thing opinion is at the same time sadly simplistic and cheaply pedantic. Your instincts tell you there is a difference between right and wrong, myth and reality, and good news reporting offers us simple, palpable truths. Facts, not opinion. Facts based on professionalism and objectivity.

Objectivity – alias truth as a fashion accessory

Well, there is something in that line. News reporting is certainly predicated on professionalism, and those engaged in it like to allude to a thing called objectivity. There are, for example, newspapers that call themselves *The Truth* (Australia), *Pravda* (Russia – pravda, for those who don't know, is the Russian word for truth) and *The Independent*.

Aren't these titles genuinely embarrassing, perhaps on a par with the Catholic Truth Society or the Protestant Truth Society (somebody's got to be wrong)?

The Truth? Whose truth? Protestant, Catholic or Shinto? In Russian or English? These first two papers have, on occasion, offered representations of reality that have little correspondence with the truth. How many downmarket dailies like the Australian paper have never exaggerated a story here, maybe distorted one or two little things there, to make the tale more fun for the readers? Very few – because they know that the truth, or at least the honest untainted reporting of what is believed to be true – is incredibly boring. And *Pravda* is *Pravda*, a title associated for the entire duration of the Communist Party's spell in power with lies.

Now deliberate lying was and never has been part of *The Independent's* noble, whiter-than-white journalistic brief. Scrupulousness in thought word and deed characterized the early days of the paper (a copy editor was fired, for example, for using the neologism 'gobsmacked' in a headline – although in later years the word subsequently appeared regularly in the paper). True enough, it did not back any of the UK political parties, its stories did not have the subversive slant of, say, a Rupert Murdoch organ covering media regulation. But how could it be said to be 'independent' when the journalists filling its pages were predominantly white, more-or-less liberal, middle-class males, with pretty views on social issues but a healthy interest in making money? In a society that has a significant percentage of racial minorities, where women outnumber men, the self-styled independence of the newspaper did not extend to hiring a representative proportion of blacks and Asians and other minorities — which is the status to which the women were relegated.

Listen, there's nothing wrong with being a white European male — even one that isn't dead. I am one. I love it. I am mad with the sheer phallocentric joy of living, and, in my own crude and obvious way, oppressing. White European males are good. I like them. I play sports with them. I drink with them. I have deep, meaningful conversations with them. We understand each other. We are friends. But let's not have any of this shit about hijacking concepts like independence and nailing it to the mast of well-meaning (if ultimately self-interested) liberalism. Just shut up and pass the beer.

The concept of independence is to be seen in its proper light in *Paper Dreams,* a book by Stephen Glover, one of the founders of *The Independent.* Glover tells us that the name was chosen because market research into the project showed a favourable response from potential readers. The connotations of the name — young, modern, 'quite left-wing, but not unbalanced' — excited the advertising agency doing the research. The agency felt that the name would attract a readership that would appeal to advertisers. Indeed, the paper, which many believed to have some kind of handle on the truth, became a British fashion accessory in the late 1980s. The earnest readers just bought it on its own, whereas those concerned with style points would be seen on the London Underground with both *The Independent* (well-meaning white male liberalism, semiotic subtext 'truth') and the very downmarket daily the *Sun* (semi-naked women, difficult to believe stories, semiotic subtext 'lies'). This was a cool thing to do. It showed media-sensitivity and a taste for eclecticism. It was the British middle classes' equivalent of having 'LOVE' and 'HATE' tattooed across the knuckles.

Things designed to impair journalistic objectivity — freebies and public relations people

An important part of the attempt to produce 'objective' news standards was *The Independent*'s rule that journalists should not accept freebies. In the UK this was a marvellous departure into previously uncharted areas of purity. In the US, it's the standard. A journalist taking one drink too many from a press officer (or flack) is flirting with unemployment. Apart from causing acute pain to the freebie-pampered Brits, this edict produced one marvellous, completely counter-productive result in the early days of the paper. An international food and drink conglomerate was offering financial hacks a magnificent freebie – a flight on Concorde to the company's factories in the US and Canada, several days in luxury hotels, and the fun of engaging in the feeding frenzy while there would be other animals from different organs at the trough. The collective freebie generates a very dangerous form of showmanship. Just as some journalists like to show off by asking the most aggressive questions at a press conference, others like to show how good they are at wallowing in the freebie swill. The benefit from the company's point of view is 'familiarization'. The company doesn't try to pretend it has a hot news story, and so the management can then relax a little and get to know the journalists as – and this is a very technical use of the phrase – human beings. The idea is to subtly infiltrate the barriers of professional scepticism and help the reporters see the management as people.

Or possibly not see the management at all. It's always an enjoyable discussion, that early morning 3.35 a.m. gathering round the detritus of sustained consumption of unremitting ferocity by twenty or so media vultures. Those with frail constitutions and those with a real life to lead in the morning have gone to bed. Your hosts – nice people who work for insurance companies or banks – are long asleep. The stragglers meanwhile are working on turning their livers into 45-pound medicine balls of dead pig marinaded in alcohol. Some have already succeeded. The look of the the bar, whichever bar, is always the same. You gaze about you and realize that a giant packet of potato chips has mated with a carton of Marlboro cigarettes. The mother creature's water – strangely like stale beer – has broken, and, yet again, you find yourself sitting in the afterbirth.

'So.' You look slowly about you as you say this, waiting for the drowsy, pink-eyed attention of your colleagues.

'What do you reckon?' You press the can to your lips and pause for effect. 'The big question is, surely, this. Is our objectivity being impaired?'

If you're lucky, they don't throw things at you.

But the press relations rationale of this kind of freebie is that when a real story breaks, perhaps the hack will visualize a person at the other end of the microphone or call line, rather than a besuited lying bastard who is trying to prevent the hack from carrying out his duty to inform the public. Although corporate management doesn't see much immediate return for its spending on these junkets (they like to think they can buy their way into print and onto the screen) this kind of press manipulation is generally very successful.

But back to the Allied Lyons freebie, on which the newly launched *Independent* took a very dignified line. It was important for reasons of status and show that it be seen to participate, but the paper decided that it would pay for the trip. A cheque for several thousand pounds was duly written with the intention of preserving the lucky hack's news judgment and objectivity. The result was the exact reverse of what was intended. The hack in question — a delightfully seedy, enthusiastic smoker and champion drinker of the old school — stayed sober while his colleagues re-enacted the days of Tiberius and Caligula along the narrow aisles of Concorde. Our Hero, meanwhile, was looking anything but the half-pugilist, half-sybarite of well-earned reputation. He sipped mineral water, asked earnest questions and wrote lots of extremely dull stories to justify his expensive presence. Back in London, the advent of each piece of excruciatingly boring copy was greeted with mounting merriment. The hack was filing five times per day, and each and every piece of drivel was sent straight to the spike (this used to be literally a spike, on which stories that didn't make the newspaper were impaled. Nowadays it's a part of a computer system that gets erased every working day.) None of the other journalists on the freebie bothered to file anything, since wandering round a factory floor in Halifax, Nova Scotia (the bits of the trip where the somewhat nervous hosts tried to sober their guests up) just wasn't interesting. But the *Independent* hack's laptop never stopped whirring — by paying for the journalist to go the newspaper had completely wrecked his news judgment, or what passes for objectivity. Freebies are dangerous things.

And so, by the way, are press relations people. Some journalists think that it is a standard term of press officers' contracts that they have to sleep with the journalist as and when the journalist requires. Not quite as high a percentage of press officers as journalists think this, a statistical quirk that has been known to cause problems, not to mention a few chilblains, in early morning four-star-hotel corridors around the world. Apart from sleeping with the journalists, press officers are, apparently, there to answer questions and find people in the company who can talk knowledgeably on various topics (i.e. formulate almost complete sentences without falling off their chairs at the thought of being quoted).

There are two specialist branches of the calling. The first is the PR person whose job title is 'economist'. Economists perform an important practical function in investment houses and banks. The problem is that no-one actually knows what it is. But they are at any rate available to be quoted on general economic matters in articles that nobody (at least nobody remotely sane) bothers to read. Economists may have a clause in their contracts specifying that they are to obtain 'coverage' for their employers. They can expect to get bonuses if they do so.

The other specialist type of PR person is French. French PR people have the perfect job, because it seems that most of them have managed to eliminate answering journalists' queries from their job descriptions. Anglo-Saxon journalists typically wonder what it is that press officers are supposed to do. Understanding how doing absolute zilch, bugger all, sweet zero can be called a professional activity is a task of a profundity and complexity to make Confucius weep.

Professional ethics and expenses – the night I was chairman of British Steel

Another method of preserving professional standards very common to financial journalists is the completely meaningless expense claim. This wily stratagem consists of an expense claim in which the journalist refuses to name the people with whom he has dined or had lunch. The reasons for submitting such claims is, officially, confidentiality. You see, journalists pride themselves on protecting their sources. And the reason for this, naturally, is that it helps them to build up a relationship of confidence and trust, while respecting the professional reputation, liberty and possibly even the life of their sources.

But total confidentiality is, it must be said, a very useful thing if you want to make things up. When challenged on the accuracy of a story, the journalist holds up that holier-than-thou hand, points behind the veil of secrecy and whispers pious words like confidentiality. And what chance does a member of the accounts department stand against a journalist's professional integrity? A very senior member of the *Sunday Times* editorial staff once bought me a supper at Chez Laurent in Paris that included a $120 lobster salad (and this was just the starter). When asked back in the office to justify the obscene expense of this meal he valiantly refused to reveal the identity of his source — me. But when pressed in private by his editor, he hinted that I might have been the chairman of British Steel. Although I don't think I was, not even for part of the evening.

The fact that I have never met a journalist who didn't fiddle expenses (apart from all my past, present and future colleagues, of course) is a mere detail of history. The important point is that they are professional, and bring us truths about — yes — the quality and integrity of the people who manage our money and run the world's economy.

What you get — our best shot

So instead of objective truths conjured out of the sky by priestly savants, our representation of journalism is necessarily a little closer to the best efforts of the collective subjectivity of a flawed, but occasionally (i.e. when sober) earnest crew of men and women. Unfortunately, those best efforts, even when they are made without trying to put some twist or spin on a story to please a favoured contact in Arcania, are not always very good.

For a start, there's the execrable style of mainstream financial journalism. Here's my hypothetical worst-ever opening sentence: *BoinCo, the highly leveraged Chieftain tank to Tampax conglomerate, faces troubled times, analysts said yesterday.*

That one has just about everything. It has all the grace of an 18-ton truck, badly overloaded with dependent clauses. And to compound the counterfeit authority of this rolling period, it has lots of jargon. Journalists love jargon for the same reason lawyers and engineers do. It's not just a convenient shorthand, it's a way of covering up ignorance and stopping others asking inconvenient questions.

What's wrong with 'heavily borrowed'? Nothing. It's just that leveraged is a more technical word that makes the journalist look more knowledgeable. And 'Chieftain tank to Tampax'? What are we to make of this kind of garbage, a favourite of financial writers? They are striving for the effect of colour and depth by rummaging around in the product range of a corporation, plucking out two disparate things and putting them in apposition to one another. Somebody should tell them that eclecticism is yet another nasty, contagious disease of the late twentieth century. 'Troubled times' is a straight cliché, a device that is in many cases indispensable, but to be avoided in opening sentences. And then, that great catch-all, cop-out phrase, 'analysts said'. Does that mean 'the consensus view among analysts who spoke on condition of anonymity'? No, it means 'this is what we think, but we are going to pretend that someone else said it'.

It's easy enough, of course, to destroy your own little model, complete with designer flaws. But just look at the financial press. Pick up a paper today. It's full of lazy, shallow writing. Watch financial reports on television for devoted repetition of ill-understood market clichés. Or then again you might do something useful and productive, like play pinball.

When it goes wrong – the conch-shell theory of insider trading

Entertainment, of course, is not necessarily what consumers of the financial media are looking for. What many of them want is inside information, a glimpse of life on the mountain top. Unfortunately, you just don't get that with the media. First, newspapers are useful for synthesis and news analysis, but are hopeless at conveying detailed investment advice such as stock tipping in sophisticated, febrile electronic markets. Maybe pay-television might do the trick. Fork out a few dollars, slot in your card to the decoder and you get the Guru of the Month giving that morning's investment conference.

But newspapers cannot compete in this area – if they try, the result is all too often disastrous. If you don't believe that, read the *Wall Street Journal*. Read it, but think carefully before acting on anything that comes close to investment advice in its columns. The paper is still living down the ignominy of having one of its staff writers jailed after involvement in an insider dealing ring that revolved round a widely followed investment column. Exactly why it was followed so assiduously is something of a mystery – even though share markets are far from efficient, news travels. Perhaps it was something to do with the authority of print (if it's there in black and white, it must be true) or maybe it was the mystique of Deep Throat, that very strange and unusual icon of dark and secret knowledge that readers want to believe in. In any event, the medium seemed to lend the message credibility. It is this effect that William Golding illustrated so well in *Lord of the Flies*. When the speaker holds the conch shell to his lips, the others must pay attention. The conch shell offers form, dignity. It, rather than the speaker, commands respect and attention.

Too much respect and attention, according to some former employees of Continental Illinois, the US bank that failed in the 1980s. According to some theories, the run on deposits and the crisis of confidence in the bank was started by inaccurate reporting from one news agency that spiralled and snowballed (if you like gyrating snowballs) as one agency after another called to hear the denials that anything was wrong. The story is very much of the 'when did you stop beating your wife?' variety. The more you splutter and cough your innocence, the more savage the scrutiny. And eventually your credibility goes. No smoke without fire, etc.

Again, there is the story told by a colleague of his days as financial radio broadcaster, when, just for fun, he set a false rumour in motion. He says he said, crassly and bluntly, to a broker contact: 'What's this I hear about an offer being made for X?' X was a catering company that had not previously been the subject of such rumours. The next day its shares were up twenty per cent. Or so the hack says. He also says he didn't buy any shares himself, nor did any of his friends or family. He just wanted to see what would happen. Apparently.

Good reporting – and curiosity

Anyway, the question of what constitutes good reporting remains at best only partially answered. Some journalists do find out things. They actually go out and make discoveries. They are few in number, and invariably win Pulitzer prizes (although one Pulitzer prize was recently awarded for a series of child deprivation stories centred on the unhappinesses of a non-existent child. Hurray for contact confidentiality and protecting your source.) But finding things out is rare, since it involves hard work and, occasionally, considerable personal danger. Better to settle for the vast majority of financial reporting, which is really looking at a non-secret event, such as the publication of a company's annual report, and analysing it all.

I know good reporting does exist, since I was once lectured on this subject for three-quarters of an hour at a media wedding. Two BBC television editors were getting married, and for some eerie reason perhaps not unrelated to a distinct aura of general self-congratulation, I kept expecting someone to toss a hand grenade in our midst. This didn't occur, but after the first twenty minutes of my conversation with a very senior news journalist at one of the British commercial channels I couldn't understand why not.

His views on good reporting made sense. Yes, of course it's subjectivity and of course all journalism is selective, he said. The art is to make sensible selections and offer some kind of 'balanced' view. Beyond that, the good journalist will try to take the story just a little beyond the headline of the press release. A good reporter will try to take us behind that simple reporting of fact and give us a hint at the dynamic that might have brought the story about. And how does the journalist acquire this sensitivity, this perfect news sense? I was told that this came about from having a keen interest in the world at large, from being a generalist able to understand the specialist. Which was splendid, except that the man I was talking to had just droned on about his own job for the best part of an hour without taking the slightest interest in the wedding around him or (unbelievable, but true) in delicious, lovely media-darling *me*. *I* was the person with whom he was supposed to be having a conversation, but who was really just supplying questions. This man is known for his obsession with his job, so his complete lack of anything approaching journalistic curiosity must be ascribed to his monomaniacal conviction that he had the most interesting job in the world. *Et in Arcania Ego (especially Ego).*

CHAPTER XI

Living With the Lunatic

The market as adopted idiot child. What to do – Financial advice, Part I (including a tour d'horizon of choice financial lunacies from the seventeenth century through to the present). Financial advice, Part II – How to exploit the inadequacy of number as a relational metaphor, explained two ways. (i) Method number one – briefly, with jokes. Oral sex made boring, or indexation made interesting, the choice is yours. (ii) Method number two – at length, without jokes. Absurdism, the lunatic, and what it all really means (maybe). Regulation and control. The Market – Our final choice.

The market as adopted idiot child

So – where do we go from here? In the name of sophistication and the pursuit of intellectual certainty the developed countries of the world have adopted a market ethic which is crude in the extreme and has all the brain power of a freshly scrambled egg. Market forces have swarmed over entire economies, adding and subtracting trillions to the financial worth of nations as the traders play with their currencies. The bankers and financiers who run the rest of the system are properly concerned with the profit it generates and little – usually nothing – else. Mutual funds have brought millions to the markets, but offer little in the way of professional competence and nothing in the way of consumer enlightenment. So-called ethical investment is cynical marketing poison, and credit cards are dangerous, consciousness-erasing drugs, a kind of super dope with a magnetic stripe. Governments have accepted their proper place in the order of things, which is on the sidelines. And journalists are on the sidelines of the sidelines, hooked up to a drip-feed of cheap bribes and false praise.

But don't worry if this black analysis of modern market economies depresses you. The situation is actually worse than that.

Think of the market ethic as some adopted idiot child, an awful adolescent cretin that has just been released from the local lunatic asylum. The cretin – alternately shouting and laughing, screaming and crying – has been doing strange things since our step-parents, Maggie and Ron, dragged him in from the street and gave him a permanent home. He roams through the house, through every aspect of our lives, breathing heavily and generally being inescapable. And what about those things he does? We just don't know what he'll get up to next. Will we find him trying to eat Maggie's underwear with a power drill and a garden fork? Will he be smearing the sofa with Vaseline and dried flowers? Or will he just be humming Barbra Streisand's Greatest Hits (if The Market likes it, it can't be bad. Can it?) and attempting to copulate with the pool table again?

The question, then, is ineluctable. What do we do? How do we treat this lunatic? Do we live with him or throw him out? And if we live with him, *what do we do*?

For the moment, let's assume that we live with him. It is a reasonable assumption to make. To throw the market system out of developed western economies would require the kind of bloody social revolution that would have had Trotsky calling for tea, sandwiches and quiet, reconciliatory chats. Clearly, the practical question is what to do with the wild child that is the market ethic.

What to do – Financial advice, Part I (including a *tour d'horizon* of choice financial lunacies from the seventeenth century through to the present)

The thing to avoid at all costs when living with the lunatic is following him. History is pebble-dashed with the guts of those who perished in great financial catastrophes. The details vary, but the essence of each story is that these individuals simply followed the lunatic around the house until they fell through the inevitable trapdoor.

Take, for example, the great Tulipomania of seventeenth-century Holland. Tulips are a kind of lily that first came to western Europe in the mid-sixteenth century. Fashion being as arbitrary as it is (just like a financial market, in fact) the growing and possession of tulips became a matter of considerable interest in the trading centres of Holland. So much so, that by the 1630s, a vigorous and apparently ever-burgeoning market in tulip bulbs had evolved.

Charles Mackay, in his book *Extraordinary Popular Delusions and the Madness of Crowds*, describes how the people of Holland 'one after another ... rushed to the tulip-marts, like flies round a honey pot. Everyone imagined that the passion for tulips would last for ever, and that the wealthy from every part of the world would send to Holland, and pay whatever prices were asked for them. The riches of Europe would be concentrated on the shores of the Zuyder Zee, and poverty banished from the favoured clime of Holland.'

People mortgaged their houses, sold treasures, to participate in the tulip market. More and more moved to join in the benefits of the ever-escalating price of tulip bulbs. Until the crash came in 1637. No-one knows quite why the selling began – but then no-one ever does – and suddenly panic set in. In a few days the price of tulip bulbs had disintegrated to something close to the levels (adjusted for inflation) that you would expect to pay today for what is, after all, just a flower. There was bankruptcy, misery, poverty and degradation. And all through following the vagaries of the market, the manic meanderings of the lunatic.

Tulips would today be bracketed (if they were to have any investment value at all – which they don't) as a 'collectible' and appear among the more exotic investment features in one of those dangerous magazines that lead the weak-minded into believing it's easy to make money by investing. It seems incredible now that people should have mortgaged their houses to buy flowers. Nowadays we require a slightly more cosmetically appealing vehicle as a repository for our discarded rational judgment. Banking scams fit the bill perfectly.

One of the earliest and best-known banking scams, in a long tradition of banking fraud that bankers like to keep quiet about, is the collapse of the Banque Royale in eighteenth-century France. John Law, a brigand Scot, began a banking practice in 1716, and soon estabished what became known as the Banque Royale. This institution was heralded as the instrument by which the debt-ridden kingdom of the young Louis XV would be saved from complete financial collapse. All the Scot's scheme did, as Simon Schama elegantly points out in *Citizens*, his history of France during and before its 1789 revolution, was to hasten it.

The scheme was the prototype of many later scams based on incomplete, inaccurate or deliberately misleading information. Law's ploy was to offer investors a share in a fabulous speculative adventure – the mining of gold in Louisiana. The fact that there wasn't the slightest indication of any gold deposits did not stop shares in the Compagnie d'Occident being a massive success. Demand reached incredible heights, as did the price of the stock – until one of the major investors decided that he would rather have gold than paper, and encashed his shares. Again there was a crash. Again yesterday's millionaires became today's paupers.

The South Sea Bubble, which rose to prominence in the 1720s, followed an almost exactly similar pattern. Predicated on the ludicrous assumption that Spain would allow British ships to bring to Europe the wealth of a continent it had claimed for itself, the South Sea Company generated mass speculative frenzy, created and instantly destroyed fortunes, and broke the lives of many investors and some of its creators.

It would be pleasant to report that with the improvement in communications, scams based on ignorance and disinformation died away. Unfortunately, this is not the case. Vast areas of Florida swampland were eagerly bought by an ill-informed American public in the 1920s. Real-estate investors were buying blind, and were consequently robbed blind.

Share investors took on board wrong information of a different sort. In the days before the Great Crash of 1929 (this was, incidentally, heralded unforgettably by one of *Variety* magazine's many great headlines – 'Wall Street Lays an Egg'), the public's confidence was constantly boosted by wise sayings from the Good and the Great.

J. K. Galbraith in *A Short History of Financial Euphoria* laments that even highly intelligent people appeared to have surrendered their rationality in favour of greed. He cites as an example Irving Fisher, a Yale academic who pronounced, just days before the crash, that 'stock prices have achieved what looks like a permanently high plateau'.

'Heavily involved in the market himself,' writes Galbraith, '[Fisher] too surrendered to the basic speculative impulse, which is to believe whatever best serves the good fortune you are experiencing.'

But Fisher, expert though he was, was still on the outside of what was essentially a rigged and manipulated market. When, after the Crash, the activities of those who hadn't committed suicide were investigated, a number of controls were instigated. Margin calls –

essentially provisions to make sure that investors had to put up some money for their speculative bets – were instituted. The Securities and Exchange Acts came into being, and the Securities and Exchange Commission was set up to regulate the business of investment.

But those controls weren't sufficient to prevent the massive market rigging, insider dealing and fraud that occurred in the junk bond market and the associated takeover frenzy in the 1980s that we touched upon in Chapter IV.

Nor was it sufficient to dampen the speculative ardour for stocks that led to the crash of October 1987. Galbraith attributes this to a kind of collective amnesia that occurs when investors stay near markets for too long. He argues that the financial memory lasts for around twenty years – which is as good a measure as any. Galbraith derides the idea that the 1987 crash was caused by the US government budget deficit (it had been around for some time, and is still with us – in a vastly expanded form – today).

The madness goes on and on. The countries of eastern Europe with their naive investors are particularly fertile ground for utter financial insanity. Consider the case of the Russian investment company MMM. The company promised all the superficial benefits of capitalism, i.e. easy money. Floated on the Moscow Commodity and Raw Materials Exchange in February 1994, the price of its shares multiplied by a factor of fifty within six months. The company mounted an aggressive advertising campaign, featuring ordinary folk buying on a Tuesday and selling for a fat profit on a Thursday. Cheap slogans abounded (*Niet Problem* was a typical line). MMM succeeded in attracting billions of roubles with its promise to buy back its shares for more than investors paid. So ten million investors committed their money despite the fact that company never at any stage revealed what investments it was making. Eventually, a fine July day dawned when the company, which had been a sponsor of the 1994 soccer World Cup, failed to keep its promise to buy back its shares at a higher price than investors had paid. The company's network of 60 Moscow offices and 76 offices in 49 other countries eventually folded, and Russian individual investors had their first hard lesson.

Commentators could draw little comfort from the débâcle, other than that the saga might shake up an astoundingly lax Russian regulatory system. And there is some distance to travel before Russian regulation matches even the dismal standards of the western world. Bear in mind that, huge though the holes in the BCCI balance sheet now appear, at least the bank wasn't making transparently ludicrous claims as to what returns it could provide.

But the question remains whether legislation is desirable or feasible.

Commenting on the US authorities' failure to introduce any further regulation or legislation after the 1987 crash, Galbraith writes: 'The recurrent and sadly erroneous belief that effortless enrichment is an entitlement associated with what is thought to be exceptional financial perspicacity and wisdom is not something that yields to legislative remedy.'

He is right that new laws won't save idiots from themselves. How many people do you know who think they are dumber than they actually are? People mostly believe themselves to be far smarter than they really are. The clever ones are those with just a small gap between their self-image and reality. Naturally enough, then, those who follow the fashions of the market are always going to attribute intelligence to the lunatic and those describing his random movements. As they don't know what they are doing themselves it is vital for their own self-esteem to believe themselves clever enough to be following in the footsteps of some market guru, some extra-smart fund manager. People want to believe in gurus and perfect markets. It makes life easier.

But Galbraith is wrong in lamenting the lack of control and legislation. What is needed is less and different control of the market, not more. But of social and political controls, more later.

Financial advice, Part II – How to exploit the inadequacy of number as a relational metaphor, explained two ways

(i) Method number one – briefly, with jokes. Oral sex made boring, or indexation made interesting, the choice is yours

As an exercise in writing technique, there is no contest between making oral sex boring and indexation interesting. The former is easy, the latter difficult almost to the point of impossibility.

If you don't believe the part about boring oral sex, pick up an airport novel. Their pages are typically packed with the low terminology of pulp sex – engorged manhoods, clutching tunnels, salty rivulets, etc. Reading them you discover lots of challengingly painful, not to say difficult to believe, passages of anatomical detail, but the effect is usually about as erotic as watching your mother press sausagemeat into a turkey's bottom. Some of these writers couldn't hold an intelligent reader's attention if they were offering straight reportage of the end of the world (right – obviously not, because there wouldn't be any readers to read the text – but you know what I mean).

So in the wrong hands, so to speak, oral sex can be pretty dull. However, making indexation interesting (indexation being the numerical track we keep on the whereabouts of the market lunatic) is tough. It is the south face of the literary Eiger, and all you have for gear is a spare T-shirt, your sister's ballet shoes and a Quentin Tarantino attitude that tells you no matter how improbable things become you're going to write yourself into and then out of that tight corner.

The thesis is that market indices are just numbers that measure, but rather imperfectly describe, market activity. Numbers, like theories of physics that describe the universe, are really a species of relational metaphor. Now the task in hand is to substantiate this in an interesting way ...

The inadequacy of number as a descriptive tool is well illustrated by that common piece of locker-room jargon, the Blow Job Probability Index. The BJPI, which is, as you might imagine, an indicator of the likelihood of a mouth playing hostess to a penis, can be used as an index of the state of a relationship.

So a man and a woman meet at a drinks party. On a scale of one to a hundred, score zero on the BJPI. Then they date, maybe go to dinner. Living as we do in an era where the foreplay, let alone the love, comes after the sex, let's assume there's a fifty per cent likelihood of intercourse. But what about fellatio or cunnilingus? (Always a key question, that one.) It depends enormously on the cultural background and sexual tastes of the parties concerned. Let's say the BJPI stands at 20 on first bedding.

Then the relationship blooms, they see each other regularly, and the BJPI climbs steadily. The BJPI, in fact, comes into play every time they go for a drive and he's at the wheel. Then they get engaged. Time to do two things. One, re-base the BJPI, which is now at screamingly high levels all the time, twenty-four hours a day. Two, he should see if he can't find a miniature crash helmet for his willy.

And then they get married, at which point we begin to see the BJPI behave in a way that traders following a market index would call, in all innocence, choppy. Yep. Sideways trading – and we all know 'sideways' is the fully invested person's euphemism for downwards. Soon the BJPI is trickling along the baseline again. True, there are occasional, event-oriented blips where the BJPI rockets up toward the 100 mark on occasions such as birthdays, anniversaries and the aftermath of major rows. Overall, though, the BJPI finds a new base and trudges along it.

Now one thing at least is clear. The BJPI is a completely useless way of measuring the overall state of a relationship. It doesn't take account of whether the couple has had children, whether they are temporarily living apart for work-related reasons, whether they are in love and happy together. It doesn't even tell you whether they have lots of different kinds of sex. All in all, a stupid, ridiculous way to measure the strength of a relationship.

Yet that's how markets are measured. Perhaps 250 share prices are amalgamated into a single figure, and you ask how the market is, and the answer is 'up five'. That tells you nothing about the other 1,000 companies listed on the exchange, nothing about the wellbeing of individual companies and industrial sectors within the index. Basically, it tells you next to Sweet Fanny Adams, zip, bugger all about the market. It measures, but does not adequately describe.

The next step, given that numbers are poor relational metaphors, is to extrapolate further meaning from the nature of indices as metaphors. These are metaphors that are creatures of the mind put to a practical use. This has a bearing on a long-standing argument about whether things such as psychological barriers exist. They do, and it's hardly surprising.

It so happens that academic statistical research shows that market indices rarely close on the exact level of a round number, alias a psychologically significant barrier, such as 1200 or 16,000. The indices fight shy of such closings, like a horse wary of jumping a fence, and then they vault over them. So in some tiny way it is possible to predict the meanderings of the lunatic, as tracked by a market index – at least when the market index is near a round-numbered 'barrier'.

The challenge to investment professionals is to to take that theory on board and devise a trading programme that can take advantage of it. As yet, none exists that takes acount of an index as a form of metaphor.

(ii) Method number two – at length, without jokes

What follows is an extended treatment of this idea of index as metaphor. There are no jokes. Readers who have had enough of the theory are advised to avoid this passage and turn to 'Absurdism, the lunatic, and what it all really means (maybe).'

Market Indices: Breaking the Real Psychological Barrier

How far is it from New York to Boston? Should the answer to that question come back as 'Five hours', most people would believe that they had been effectively and appropriately answered. Yet the mutual satisfaction of interrogator and respondent is an epistemological nonsense: their understanding is based upon a set of assumptions that permits a question which appears to be about distance to be satisfactorily responded to in terms of time.

The shared assumptions underpinning that simple exchange are myriad. It can be safely stated that both parties assume a voyage is to be made, that the voyage will be by automobile, that weather conditions are normal, that the driver will use large freeways as opposed to picturesque country routes, that speed limits will be exceeded no more than is usual.

It is my contention that these shared assumptions facilitate communication, that the assumptions themselves are metaphors, which are in turn based upon numerical metaphors, and that the metaphorical nature of numbers is yet to be appreciated by the financial markets they describe through the medium of indices.

Briefly, if the question 'How far is it from New York to Boston?' can be satisfactorily answered by the statement 'Five hours', so the question 'What's the market doing today?' can be satisfactorily answered 'Up twenty'. In both cases, the question and answer are phrased in language which is metaphorical at its tersest and most compressed.

Indexation and Number

The essence of indexation is the attribution of a numerical value to an entity which financial analysts variously describe as a 'benchmark' or 'barometer' or 'indicator'. The precise basis on which the number is calculated is the subject of intense debate within the financial industry. The appearance of each new index generates further argument, usually as to the perceived worth of the index. The arguments almost invariably centre on the method of calculation that leads to the final number. The number itself is generally accepted as an absolute, a measure imbued with some kind of scientific objectivity.

It is contended that the word 'measure' is itself a form of metaphor, and itself subjective. It is also contended that scientific objectivity suits certain scientists' purposes, but has no worthwhile philosophical basis.

Number and Metaphor

In his book *Physics as Metaphor*, Dr Roger Jones argues persuasively that the notion of objectivity is a false god, a comfortable icon that scientists are pleased to worship. His conclusion is that physics can be an aid in understanding the world about us and, indeed, 'life' if we cease to pretend it is external and objective and embrace its subjectivity.

The proposition put to readers here is considerably more modest. Namely, that numbers are metaphors, and, as expressed through the medium of an index which purports to be a measure, they are necessarily subjective. It is further contended that using a subjective approach we can begin to analyse and understand the way markets and indices interact.

Numbers are difficult to define. Natural numbers, or integers, seem easy enough. But let's take the case of the apparently easiest number of all: one. We see one man. But what if he has just one leg? Or has lost an eye? There is still one man, although society has developed special words for the disabled (or 'differently abled' in politically correct jargon). And what if he is very short? Society again has developed special words for very short people. Or if his growth is not stunted, but he is sixteen, technically adult, but quite small?

Immediately we realize we are describing someone by a series of qualities – height, age, the requisite number of limbs. The number of men depends upon their having the qualities defined as appropriate to men. If we see three men, one of whom is half average height, the unkind observer might say he saw two men and a dwarf. This example shows us two things: that numbers can be broken down into sets, and that deciding which list of traits should characterize the set needed to make up a 'man' is an essentially subjective decision. The observer decides what is important, and this constitutes the definition of one man. Thus the simplest number of all – one – is really dependent on subjective assessments of what constitutes the concept of 'oneness' as applied to a man.

Description and Measurement

The notion of number as metaphor may not seem relevant to the 'real' world, where we use numbers to measure things – the circumference of the earth, the distance to the Moon, the width of an electron, with superb accuracy. Man has landed on the Moon, after all, so how relevant is the subjective, metaphorical nature of numbers, and, by implication, measurement?

The answer is that it's very important indeed. The argument that measurement is really no more than subjective confirmation of 'objective' data, such as the length, breadth and depth of a table, is in no way refuted by the operational efficacy of the numerical metaphor.

The *raison d'être* is the narrowness of contemporary financial thought. The flight from theory has given us financial principles of at best qualified application, as my critique of the efficient market hypothesis below will demonstrate. Nevertheless, the wise polymath knows what data are relevant. For the purposes of this essay, such matters as Werner Heisenberg's Uncertainty Principle remain unchallenged. The theory is, in hugely truncated form, that all data gathering is subjective, and must be understood from the point of view of the observer; given that the observed world is the subject of scientific data gathering, the unobserved world cannot be measured or described and is meaningless to the empirical scientist.

All that is metaphysics, as is the notion that the physical world can never fully coincide with the idea of a unit of measurement. A foot ruler has measuring gradations which, however fine, have some physical mass, and therefore do not correspond exactly to the perfect, ideal foot – this is the old Platonic concept of reality as idea and the physical world as just an imperfect attempt at realizing that idea, the truth.

Where the notion of measurement fails is in its ability to describe the things to which it applies. Newtonian physics was good enough to get man to the Moon. But Einstein's theory of the universe is generally accepted to describe the universe more satisfactorily. In other words, we can measure accurately, but measurement does not describe what we measure. Part of the reason for this is that scientific theory, like number theory, is metaphorical; it is based on subjective intuition, of principles which go in directions predetermined by their underlying assumptions.

And making those assumptions is an intuitive act: Copernicus' theory of a solar system which had the earth revolving round the sun, rather than vice versa, was based on his empathetic genius. His was an outstanding feat of intuition; to refute the Ptolemaic theory of the solar system, he had to make an intellectual leap of 93 million miles, to stand in a putative sun and see the earth from outside itself. Similarly, Einstein imagined the theory of relativity. He dreamed it, and then woke up and wrote down the insights of his subconscious.

Dr Jones tellingly compares scientific theory to a set of railroad tracks – we know how to get to Chicago from New York. The principles allow us to predict with certainty how long it will take, when we have to change trains etc. But (as a parallel to failing to tell us about the country in between the two cities) the railroad system (like scientific theory) will not tell us how to get to the small town thirty miles from Chicago, with no rail service.

Measurement works on the same level as the nineteenth-century politician Metternich's delightfully cynical definition of truth. Truth, he once stated, is that which is confidently asserted and plausibly maintained. That kind of breathtaking disregard for the truth as a quality with intrinsic value would have made Machiavelli blush. Yet he would no doubt have admired the beauty of the statement. What it tells us is that for politicians, as for economists and the creators of indices, what matters is not the substantive content of the data with which they operate, but that it is accepted as data – that it is *operationally* true. Thus Metternich's operational definition of truth holds good for the circumstances in which he requires it to function – the apparent veracity and efficacy of words as used in the black art of statecraft. Henry Kissinger, incidentally, reportedly made frequent use of the following line when debating policy: 'And this proposition has the added merit of being true.' In other words, instead of just being operationally true, the proposition might 'really' have been true – but this would merely be an added bonus.

The financial parallel with operational truth is clear. An index, expressed as a number, will not tell us how certain sectors or individual companies have done (the market is up twenty, that's all). And the individual pricing of companies will not tell us how the company itself is doing as a business, merely how the market perceives that business, and how this translates into a price. Thus a corporation within an index and the indices within the market are victims of the reductive nature of numbers as metaphor, numbers which measure accurately enough, but do not describe what is really going on.

The Primacy of Metaphor

Our reliance on numbers to do something which they are not suited to do – namely to describe as well as measure – has a number of key ramifications. The most important and obvious effect is on market index behaviour. I contend that indices as metaphor have a special value of their own, whether attributed to them consciously or otherwise by the market.

In his paper on psychological barriers in asset prices and the efficient market hypothesis, published in 1990, R. Glen Donaldson contended that international data revealed a hesitancy on the part of traders to push popularly tracked indices across a -oo 'resistance level' (e.g. 1500, 1600, 1700 etc). He argued that this information was not rationally relevant to the pricing of the individual companies.

Put at its crudest, his data revealed impressive evidence that the indices' closing prices fought shy of a -oo point, with lots of closings just short of the point. Then, once the -oo had been crossed, the markets would move ahead fast. The image – if readers will excuse the use of metaphor – is very much that of the horse which shies away from a fence and then finally finds the courage to jump over it. In statistical language, it is shown that the distributive frequency of index closings is sharply lower on -oo points, when, if -oo points are to be ignored according to the efficient market hypothesis, the distribution should be random – and ultimately evenly spread, if an infinite number of examples are taken.

So what we have here is empirical evidence suggesting that the markets do in fact take account of -oo closings, that there is such a thing as a psychological barrier.

Beyond this point, empiricism – which of course can never exist, according to Heisenberg – offers us very blunt tools of analysis. If, however, we accept the notion of number and index as metaphor, we can go further. We can take the idea of metaphor as a worthwhile, prime concept in itself, and ask what the markets should do with it.

Metaphorical Analysis: Practical and Theoretical Effects

If we are to accept metaphor as a prime tool of analysis a number of consequences flow from this assumption. First, it ought to be expected that the markets pay attention to 'psychological barriers', if only for the reason that metaphors are creatures of the mind. Everyday life is littered with examples of how individuals, singly and collectively, are influenced by the powerful symbolism of numerical metaphor. How far away is Boston? The answer 'five hours' tells us it is a trip that can be made in a day. Whereas the sixteen hours to Chicago puts the journey into a different category of strenuous expedition.

This use of numerical metaphor as a kind of differential symbol is sometimes more conscious. Classic examples are to be seen in every department store, where one of the oldest marketing ploys is still considered effective: a coat sells at $199.95, rather than $200. Why? Because the consumer is being asked to consider the object as being in the $100 price range – albeit right at the top of that range – as opposed to being in the $200 category and so, perhaps, automatically excluded as unaffordable. By pricing the coat at $199.95 the consumer's points of comparison are different, and he is not being asked to jump the $200 pricing level – a kind of psychological barrier. Merchandisers at least seem to understand the importance of psychology in asset-pricing theory. What counts is not the five-cent price reduction, but the number as differential symbol, or relational metaphor.

Already we have a significant problem with 'perfect market' notions of the market as an efficient arbiter of asset prices: such theories don't take account of the way we, as human beings, use numbers to measure and describe, to symbolize and simplify. Proponents of the perfect market have drunk too deeply at the wells of econometrics – they would do well to learn from store merchandisers, or at least to do a little more shopping.

A second important consequence is that we need not look for a correlation between the movement of the index (the numerical metaphor) and the economic reality of the commercial fortunes of the companies in the index. If metaphor is prime, the numerical value of the index has an importance because of its place within the continuum of the metaphor. In other words, the attitude of the markets should be expected to be like the fairy tale of the emperor's clothes with a twist: the emperor really is wearing clothes (i.e. there really is a psychological barrier) until the people decide that he's naked (once a barrier is passed it is no longer psychologically significant).

The point is that there really is something important attached to a -oo psychological barrier figure. Until, that is, the figure is passed. Then, the common mistake is to assume that because the barrier was passed it could not have been psychologically important at the time – that the emperor was always naked. But the truth is that, because of the primacy of the index as metaphor, there really was a psychological barrier, until it was broken. In other words, in metaphor, psychology is all.

Computer trading programs take account of index levels, but not psychological barriers. They recognize the existence of resistance points, but the programming is based on consolidating gains and closing out losses. For the program designers the challenge is there: find the psychological barriers, and program some fuzzy logic into the system. Office management systems use fuzzy logic in budgeting for extra personnel cover on Mondays. Why Mondays? There is of course no special reason for staff to fall sick on Mondays (weekend hangovers discounted), other than the simple fact that individuals often feel less inclined to go into work at the start of the week. If office management systems can identify the work-shy, why can't trading programs look at closing prices and second-guess psychological barriers?

At present, the approach to market psychology reeks of embarrassment. The entire corpus of perfect market theory has a psychological underpinning of fear. Financial 'scientists' had a feeling that the piecemeal approach to market sentiment – rumour, guru comment, gut feeling – was too imprecise to work with. As such, modern financial thought is a slave to crude empiricism which clearly fails to account for phenomena such as psychological barriers.

So while much of the work done on pricing theory is valid and worthwhile, unless and until it is understood that markets really do depend on psychology – of the individual traders and of the market as a collective entity – market models are never going to correspond more than approximately to what happens in real life. To finish with, naturally enough, a metaphor: perfect market theories and trading programs offer us walnut dashboards and hand-embroidered steering-wheel covers for a car whose wheels will fall off at the first corner.

Absurdism, the lunatic, and what it all really means (maybe)

So much for the very limited financial predictability of market behaviour. The really important issues raised by dealing with the lunatic are non-financial and non-numerical. They are consequently less easy to contain and define. But two of the most important social and legal aspects of dealing with the lunatic reduce to two questions. First, should we throw him out and take in another lodger? Second, if the answer to question one is no, what is the best way to deal with the lunatic's strange behaviour?

The answer to the first question is, after a very brief period of hesitation, no. We should keep the lunatic.

Making that response was made considerably easier for me by the brisk walk I took on a visit to Russia in 1994, in Volgograd to write a paper for a European business school.

The people in the street were dressed well enough. They looked properly nourished, even if their smiles were dotted with cheap gold.

The stores had food in them that was inexpensively priced for a westerner, but prohibitive for a Russian without dollars to exchange at more than 2,000 roubles to the greenback. A consignment of bananas had hit town and, extraordinarily for a city sited on such a fertile plane, they were cheaper than onions. Housewives hawked radishes grown in their gardens. Everything was for sale. This was the beginning of a capitalist market, Russian-style. People complained that the produce was too expensive. Yet they got by on a combination of street cunning, barter, and – yes – hardship.

But the real aura that Volgograd exudes after its years of Communist control and central planning is one of bewilderment – and naivety. How many people must have wasted their money on MMM, believing a criminal myth to be capitalism?

There are more symbols of interregnum – the abandonment of one system and the inability to embrace another. Just as impressive as the relics of Communist idol-worship, like the giant statute of Lenin that still glowers over the canal connecting the Volga and the Don, are the unintended monuments. They are dotted along the twenty miles or so of river bank to which the city of Volgograd clings in a thin, six-block strip. These are the monuments of obsolescence. Abandoned cranes, empty foundries, smokeless factory chimneys, they remind you of some giant toy set left out in the garden to rot, slowly, into the ground. So little of this industrial capacity is used any more. The cerebral cortex of Communism, the central planning of factory production – and the planning of the workers' lives – has gone. And so the Russians are left, blinking in the sun of capitalism, confused by their sudden freedom. Except it doesn't feel much like liberty when your freedom translates into a licence to worry where your next meal is coming from.

But no one said capitalism and its markets offered an easy ride. Taking responsibility for your own life, perhaps the most precious gift of democracy, is definitely hard work, very hard work. A lot of the time it translates into meanness, work-obsessive, type-A behaviour. It can be tough on the weak. It is tough on the idle (but, then, who cares?). But the central point is that the presence of the lunatic has a galvanizing effect on us. The Market offers us the potential to do things, to take just a little bit of control of our own lives. It is a tough animal to live with, but just as democracy is the least bad form of government, so a liberal market lunatic is the least bad form of economic system. Put it this way: for all its intellectual appeal, Communism wasn't exactly a hit.

So in the absence of anything better, the lunatic stays. But if we aren't going to follow him, what are we going to do with him?

It seems to me that unless you absolutely, pathologically hate giving money to government, there is a limited role for central planning in market economies. I say this, again, on the basis of seeing nothing better. Going the hard-line American route looks increasingly mad.

What, for example, is the best way to deal with large and dangerous craters in the road? To a European the answer is self-evident. The government – probably local government – takes money from the citizens and pays someone to fill the hole. The debate about market forces here is whether the hole-filler should be a local government employee or an independent contractor. To an American the question and the solution are different. The answer US-style may well be not to pay taxes on principle but to go out and buy one of those ludicrous-looking trailers with tyres the size of small houses. That way you don't notice the holes. Which is all very well, but rather short-term. Where would Southern California be without its publicly funded (and presently crumbling) irrigation infrastructure? In the desert, that's where.

Those who really embrace the lunatic, who think that the market should determine everything, do so in the most self-destructive way. In a way, in fact, that does not best serve the interests of the great god of The Market itself. Look at comparative transport policy in France and Britain, specifically Paris and London.

In London, there is a long-term plan to privatize the Underground. The Underground is going to be 'floated'. If that sounds bizarre, it's no coincidence. The central tenet of the policy is to make the company running the train services profitable. That means ensuring that every time a ticket is sold the company makes a turn, a profit, on that journey. This has created a transport system that is extremely expensive while remaining inefficient and lacking in the capital resources to replace the ageing Victorian infrastructure. A further consequence is that more people use the roads, making London even smellier than it already was. And if you're the caring type, you can toss in the fact that the extra traffic contributes substantially to road accident rates. Poor travel systems are an important factor in corporate planning. Few corporations consider that the expense, the dirt, and the interminable commuting times make London an attractive option. If you don't believe me, take a long trip on the Underground. It is *depressing*. So the city loses out, and fails to attract jobs. Hardly inspiring or good for London's economy, is it? And all for the sake of a short-term profit.

In Paris, on the other hand, huge government subsidy has created a clean and extremely efficient transport system. People use it (although the RATP, which runs the Métro, estimates that it loses some $90 million a year in fare-dodging) and corporations see the transport system as a definite plus point for the city. Mind you, they don't like the severity of the taxes (of which transport takes up only a tiny part). France is one of the most expensive countries in the world for employers.

But whatever the unpleasant realities of the French socialist bureaucracy, the larger point is that taking a view above and beyond short-term profit can and should work financially.

That, however, has clearly not been understood by some of those who claim to be the biggest fans of market economics. Take, for example, the attitude of the British Conservative government in privatizing its state-owned monopolies and trimming back public expenditure on industries it still owned. A constant theme in the running down of industries such as steel and coal production was that the market would not bear it, that the industries were not profitable. So they had to go.

Well, I can sympathize with the expense side of the argument. Subsidies are an iniquity, and should go. But business should be allowed to make a loss if there is a prospect of a return to profit. Even fund managers – people who invest in shares not to provide capital for industry, but solely for profit – even *they* accept that sectors of their portfolios may lose money for them over the short term. The clever ones often use a downturn to buy more shares and lower the average cost per share. Even as seekers after pure profit they will invest during the downturn of the market cycle. But UK government policymakers, who purport to be adherents of The Market, seem to think that they know better than The Market itself. If they close down an industry because it isn't profitable, they are effectively saying that it will not return to profit – that the caperings of the lunatic will never favour steel or coal again. So three possibilities present themselves. Either they know something the rest of the financial world doesn't, or they haven't really thought it through, or they are using non-profitability as a smoke-screen for other policy objectives.

So it seems to me that The Market is an OK thing, provided you recognize its tendency toward pure profit seeking and – according to your politics – temper that with a little central planning.

One of the ironies of the market revolution of the 1980s and 1990s is that in the US and the UK – the countries at the heart of it – there appears to be an impetus for change towards some sort of planned system. The US voted in Bill Clinton, even if it subsequently thought better of it, and the UK's populace is clearly sick of Thatcherism without Thatcher.

Regulation and control

Control on a practical, financial level means how the authorities try to stop investors, especially small investors, getting badly hurt. Here we touch upon important issues such as the role of paternalism in government, and the right of the individual to do perilous, stupid, enjoyable things like take large quantities of extremely strong drugs, make improper sexual advances to unsuitable high-health-risk people, and buy shares.

It seems clear that if individuals want to do these things, they will do so (and absolutely should be allowed to). Trying to stop them would be a complete waste of time. Even the regulate-or-die Galbraith agrees with this proposition.

'Regulation outlawing financial credulity or mass euphoria is not a practical possibility. If applied generally to such human condition, the result would be an impressive, perhaps oppressive, and certainly ineffective body of law,' he writes.

My view is that just as individuals should be encouraged to take responsibility for their own actions, so should the markets – or more particularly the companies and individuals trading in them. I would do away with most of the regulatory controls in place right now. They are clearly ineffective, anyway. The ideal would be to stick with clear financial reporting for companies – big investors would want to see the books before committing capital anyway. Beyond that, let the market take care of itself and weed out its own charlatans. To be a player would require payment of a major fee, of course. This would go toward a compensation scheme for the inevitable scams and nonsenses that, whether we like it or not, the market engenders.

So broadly speaking, my method of dealing with the lunatic would be to take his wallet and lock him in a padded cell with a bottle of whiskey. And then, no matter how hard he hammered on the door, not to let him out.

You see, although the lunatic is harmful and dangerous, he is also great fun. He is the spirit of mischief and creativity. He stimulates people and can galvanize them to take charge of their own lives. The market is a free spirit, and you have to be careful of trying to plan or regulate too much.

The Market – our final choice

A similar idea was expounded in a non-financial context by Albert Camus in *The Myth of Sisyphus*. Necessarily, rationality can take us only so far. To believe in God or to believe that God is dead is to make a leap of faith or non-faith – to abandon the intellect. What Camus counsels us to do is to adopt absurdism, to caper along the edge of the abyss where rationality meets faith, and to enjoy the fact that we can never know what lies in the abyss – the meaning of life, the cipher of certainty which is The Market.

The Camus plan offers little, but it is as much as we who have opted for this market system, and who have let it loose on the rest of the world, can hope for. We are the ones who have to deal with it. We have to be eternally vigilant, always on guard against fake investment schemes and – equally dangerously – believing that we are genius enough to outsmart the lunatic, that we really know how to make money. Camus liked to imagine that as Sisyphus had rolled his rock to the top of the mountain and was just at the point where it would thunder down again to the bottom, there was a smile on his face. Bound as he was to the limits of rationality, life was painful, difficult, repetitive and absurd – and yet enjoyably, redeemingly human.

We, in the market economies that we have created for ourselves at the end of the second millennium of Christian time, should accept that we have unleashed forces more powerful than ourselves. We too should smile in contemplation of a system that is painful, difficult, frequently unjust and often palpably absurd. Because this is the price we have to pay for the dynamism and the creativity that come with The Market. Above all, we in developed capitalist economies must remember this: however much we attempt to control our capital, however determined we are not to be parted from our money, it is we who are the fools.

Select Bibliography

John Carey, *The Faber Book of Reportage*, Faber and Faber, London 1987.

Albert Camus, *The Myth of Sisyphus*, Penguin, London 1990.

Joseph Conrad, *Heart of Darkness*, Hodder & Stoughton, London 1990.

R. Glenn Donaldson, *Psychological Barriers in Asset Barriers and the Efficient Market Hypothesis*, Princeton University Financial Research Centre Memorandum 114, Princeton, May 1990.

John Kenneth Galbraith, *A Short History of Financial Euphoria*, Whittle Direct Books, Knoxville 1990.

Carlo Ginzburg, *Myths, Emblems, Clues*, Hutchinson Radius, London 1990.

Stephen Glover, *Paper Dreams*, Jonathan Cape, London 1993.

William Golding, *Lord of the Flies*, Faber and Faber, London 1954.

Dominic Hobson, *The Pride of Lucifer*, Hamish Hamilton, London 1990.

Aldous Huxley, *Brave New World*, Chatto & Windus, London 1984.

Herbert Hart, *The Concept of Law*, Oxford University Press, Oxford 1961.

Roger Jones, *Physics as Metaphor*, Sphere Books, London 1983.

James Joyce, *Ulysses*, Penguin, London 1969.

Jean-Noel Kapferer, *Rumeurs – Le Plus Vieux Média du Monde*, Editions Seuil, Paris 1987.

Michael Lewis, *Liar's Poker*, Hodder and Stoughton, London 1989.

Hamish McRae, *The World in 2020*, HarperCollins, London 1994.

Joseph Nocera, *A Piece of the Action*, Simon & Schuster, New York 1994.

Paul Ormerod, *The Death of Economics*, Faber and Faber, London 1994.

Simon Schama, *Citizens*, Viking, London 1989.

Georg Simmel, *The Philosophy of Money*, edited by David Frisby, Routledge, London 1990.

James B. Stewart, *Den of Thieves*, Simon & Schuster, London 1991.

Ingo Walter, *Battle of the Systems – Control of Enterprise and the Global Economy*, Institut für Weltwirtschaft an der Universität Kiel, Kiel 1993.

Oscar Wilde, *De Profundis and Other Writings*, Penguin, London 1975.

Tom Wolfe, *The Right Stuff*, Jonathan Cape, London 1979.

Tom Wolfe, *Bonfire of the Vanities*, Jonathan Cape, London 1988.